After

The research discussed in this book was supported by NORFACE (New Opportunities for Research Funding Agency Co-operation in Europe) under grant 462-14-050 and the European Commission (ERA-Net Plus funding, grant agreement number 618106) for the project 'Our Children's Europe' as part of the *Welfare State Futures* programme.

Welfare State Futures: Our Children's Europe

WelfSOC examines the aspirations, assumptions, and priorities that govern the ideas of ordinary people about the future development of welfare in Europe. It relies on innovative deliberative forums and focus groups in order to investigate attitudes towards the future of the welfare state.

Five deliberative forums were conducted by the research teams in Denmark, Germany, Norway, Slovenia, and the United Kingdom between October and November 2015. These two-day events, organized with the help of national research agencies, gave the opportunity for participants to reflect on the future of the welfare state and address the following question: 'What should the priorities of the government in [country] be for benefits and services in 2040?' Early findings suggest that the discussion at such events generates attitude changes among participants, in relation to their ideas about government responsibility, welfare chauvinism, and the part to be played by the individual. It also indicates that the justifications for different policies differ between countries and this can be related to national welfare state traditions and regime types.

The first major publication related to this project is the current volume: *After Austerity: Welfare State Transformation in Europe after the Great Recession*, published by Oxford University Press in 2017. This book, co-edited by the coordinating team (Peter Taylor-Gooby, Benjamin Leruth, and Heejung Chung), conceptualizes policy responses to the Great Recession across Europe and includes a wide range of empirical chapters written by WelfSOC members and external contributors.

The next stage of the WelfSOC project uses focus groups conducted in October and November 2016 in the five countries in order to investigate the issues of solidarity, responsibility, and deservingness. The data is currently being coded and shared between the research teams. The material from the deliberative forums and the focus groups will be analysed further during 2017 and the findings published in comparative research papers and a further book.

More information about the project as well as working papers can be found on the website http://welfsoc.eu, or follow us on Twitter @WelfSOC.

WELFARE STATE FUTURES

After Austerity

Welfare State Transformation in Europe
after the Great Recession

Edited by
Peter Taylor-Gooby, Benjamin Leruth,
and Heejung Chung

OXFORD
UNIVERSITY PRESS

OXFORD
UNIVERSITY PRESS

Great Clarendon Street, Oxford, OX2 6DP,
United Kingdom

Oxford University Press is a department of the University of Oxford.
It furthers the University's objective of excellence in research, scholarship,
and education by publishing worldwide. Oxford is a registered trade mark of
Oxford University Press in the UK and in certain other countries

First Edition published in 2017
Impression: 1

Published in the United States of America by Oxford University Press
198 Madison Avenue, New York, NY 10016, United States of America

British Library Cataloguing in Publication Data
Data available

Library of Congress Control Number: 2017930571

ISBN 978–0–19–879026–6 (hbk.)
978–0–19–879027–3 (pbk.)

Printed and bound by
CPI Group (UK) Ltd, Croydon, CR0 4YY

Contents

List of Figures   vii
List of Tables   ix
Acronyms   xi
Notes on Contributors   xiii

1. The Context: How European Welfare States Have Responded
   to Post-Industrialism, Ageing Populations, and Populist
   Nationalism   1
   Peter Taylor-Gooby, Benjamin Leruth, and Heejung Chung

2. Stretching the Limits of Solidarity: The German Case   27
   Jan-Ocko Heuer and Steffen Mau

3. Where Next for the UK Welfare State?   48
   Peter Taylor-Gooby, Benjamin Leruth, and Heejung Chung

4. France at a Crossroads: Societal Challenges to the Welfare
   State during Nicolas Sarkozy's and François Hollande's
   Presidential Terms   67
   Benjamin Leruth

5. Changing Scandinavian Welfare States: Which Way Forward?   89
   Jørgen Goul Andersen, Mi Ah Schoyen, and Bjørn Hvinden

6. The Future of the Slovenian Welfare State and Challenges
   to Solidarity   115
   Maša Filipovič Hrast and Tatjana Rakar

7. Spain and Italy: Regaining the Confidence and Legitimacy
   to Advance Social Policy   136
   Ana M. Guillén and Emmanuele Pavolini

8. Welfare Reform in Greece: A Major Crisis, Crippling
   Debt Conditions and Stark Challenges Ahead   155
   Maria Petmesidou

Contents

9. The Europeanization of the Welfare State: The Case for
    a 'Differentiated European Social Model'   180
    Benjamin Leruth

10. Liberalism, Social Investment, Protectionism, and Chauvinism:
    New Directions for the European Welfare State   201
    Peter Taylor-Gooby, Benjamin Leruth, and Heejung Chung

Index   221

List of Figures

1.1. Average annual rates of change in earnings (selected countries: OECD). 4

1.2. Income inequality in OECD countries 1985–2013. 5

1.3. Percentage of foreign-born population, 2001–12 (selected countries: OECD 2016). 5

1.4. Spending on the core traditional welfare state (pensions, healthcare, sickness and disability) per head of population as percentage of total welfare state spending (Eurostat). 6

1.5. Percentage of people at risk of poverty or social exclusion, 2005–13. 10

3.1. Percentage of people in low-income households in the United Kingdom (below 60% median household income, before housing costs). 51

4.1. Social expenditure in France, 1985–2014 (as percentage of GDP). 69

4.2. Unemployment rate, old-age dependency ratio, and foreign-born population in France, 2000–15. 71

4.3. Government deficits and gross debt in France, 1978–2009 (% GDP). 74

4.4. Tensions between social groups in France. 81

4.5. Percentage of people at risk of poverty or social exclusion by age in France, 2004–14. 84

5.1. Social investment expenditures in OECD countries, 1997 and 2009 (% GDP). 91

5.2. Projected old-age dependency ratios 2050: Population 65+ as percentage of population 15–64. 93

5.3. GDP in Sweden, Denmark, and Norway, relative to the USA and EU15. 93

5.4. Employment rates (percentage) among women, 2000 (grey) and 2015 (black). 94

5.5. Employment rates (percentage) among 55–64 years old, 2000 (grey) and 2015 (black). 94

6.1. Slovenia's real GDP growth rate (percentage change on previous year). 116

6.2. The Slovenian government's consolidated gross national debt (as a percentage of GDP). 116

6.3. Total general government expenditure on social protection (as a percentage of GDP), 1999–2012. 120

6.4. At-risk-of-poverty rates for select groups, 2005–13.   125

6.5. Attitudes to income inequality and the Gini coefficient.   128

7.1. Control of corruption by governments.   148

7.2. Evolution of trust in national government (2003–14).   148

8.1. In-work poverty and poverty among households with children
     and among the unemployed in Greece (poverty line: 60% of the median
     equivalized income).   166

8.2. At-risk-of-poverty rate (2008, 60% poverty line).   167

8.3. People living in households with very low work intensity by income
     quintile (population aged 0 to 59 years).   168

8.4. Households above 60% poverty line experiencing hardship.   169

8.5. Households below 60% poverty line experiencing hardship.   169

9.1. Percentage of the population at risk of poverty or social exclusion
     in the European Union.   185

10.1. Social protection spending 2005 and 2012 (Esspros via Eurostat).   205

10.2. Percentage of children aged three to compulsory school age in formal
      childcare for 30 or more hours each week (Eurostat).   206

10.3. Research and Development spending, public and private
      (% of GDP, Eurostat).   207

List of Tables

1.1. Structural change   8

1.2. Policy responses associated with the crisis and their impact on cleavages and solidarities   13

4.1. Major policy responses associated with the crisis in François Hollande's and Nicolas Sarkozy's 2012 election manifestos   78

5.1. Gross and net public social expenditure, and total social expenditure (public plus private: % GDP)   92

5.2. Cumulative growth in public consumption, 2002–10 and 2011–15 (%)   103

9.1. Aspects of the European crisis, the EU's response, and future scenarios   192

10.1. Policy developments after the Great Recession: European, national, and EU levels   208

Acronyms

AfD	Alternative for Germany (Germany: populist right)
ALMP	Active Labour Market Policy
ANEL	Independent Greeks (Greece: Conservative–nationalist)
BSA	British Social Attitudes Survey
CEE	Central and Eastern European countries
EC	European Commission
ECB	European Central Bank
EOPYY	Greek National Health Service Organization
ESS	European Social Survey
EU	European Union
EU15	First 15 members of the European Union
EU28	Members of the EU between 2013 and the departure of the UK
FN	Front National (France: populist right)
GDP	Gross Domestic Product
GDR	German Democratic Republic (former East Germany)
GMI	Minimum income guarantee
ILO	International Labour Office
IMF	International Monetary Fund
ISSP	International Social Survey Project
ND	New Democracy (Greece: centre-right)
NPM	New Public Management
OECD	Organization for Economic Cooperation and Development
OMC	Open Method of Coordination
PASOK	Panhellenic Socialist Party (Greece: centre-left)
SAP	Social Action Programme
SYRIZA	Coalition of the Radical Left (Greece: left anti-EU, anti-austerity)
UK	United Kingdom
UMP	Union pour un Mouvement Populaire (France: former centre-right party)
UNHCR	United Nations High Commissioner for Refugees
VAT	Value Added Tax

Notes on Contributors

Jørgen Goul Andersen is Professor of Political Science and Director of the Centre for Comparative Welfare Studies at the Department of Political Science, Aalborg University, Denmark. His research centres on welfare policy, political behaviour (election studies, political parties, political attitudes, and political participation), political economy, and policy analysis.

Heejung Chung is a Reader in Social Policy at the University of Kent, England. Her research deals with cross-national comparison of labour markets, working conditions, and work/life balance issues, focusing on the role institutions and socio-economic factors play therein.

Ana M. Guillén is Professor of Sociology at the University of Oviedo, Spain. Her research interests include comparative social and labour policies, Europeanization, and European integration.

Jan-Ocko Heuer is a postdoctoral researcher at the Humboldt University of Berlin, Germany. His current research focuses on welfare state change, financialization, and social inequality.

Maša Filipovič Hrast is Associate Professor at the University of Ljubljana, Faculty of Social Sciences, and a member of the Research Centre for Welfare Studies. Her research interests focus on social policy, housing policy and social exclusion.

Bjørn Hvinden is Professor in Sociology and Head of Research at Norwegian Social Research (NOVA) at Oslo and Akershus University College of Applied Sciences, Norway. His main research interests are comparative and European social policies, social citizenship, climate change and welfare, disability, and solidarity.

Benjamin Leruth is an Assistant Professor in Public Administration at the Institute for Governance and Policy Analysis, University of Canberra. His research focuses on comparative European politics, Euroscepticism, differentiated integration in the European Union, and public attitudes towards immigration and the European welfare state.

Steffen Mau is Professor of Sociology at the Humboldt University of Berlin. His research focuses on social policy, social inequality, migration, and Europeanization.

Emmanuele Pavolini is Associate Professor in Economic Sociology and Social Policy at the University of Macerata in Italy. His research interests are comparative welfare state studies and in particular Southern European welfare states, family policies, healthcare, occupational welfare, and non-profit organisations.

Notes on Contributors

Maria Petmesidou is Professor of Social Policy at Democritus University (Greece) and Fellow of CROP/ISSC (Comparative Research on Poverty/International Social Science Council). Her current research focuses on policy learning and comparative frameworks with regard to the social inclusion of young people (EU funded project).

Tatjana Rakar is a Researcher and Assistant Professor at the University of Ljubljana, Faculty of Social Sciences, Centre for Welfare Studies. Her fields of research involve studies in social policy, family policy and civil society organisations.

Mi Ah Schoyen is a Senior Researcher at the Centre for Welfare and Labour Research (Oslo, Norway) and Akershus University College of Applied Sciences. Her interests lie in political science and comparative political economy and her research covers comparative welfare state/social policy, the welfare mix, and public pension systems.

Peter Taylor-Gooby is Research Professor of Social Policy at the University of Kent. He researches comparative social policy and social policy theory and writes novels with social policy themes.

1

The Context

How European Welfare States Have Responded to Post-Industrialism, Ageing Populations, and Populist Nationalism

Peter Taylor-Gooby, Benjamin Leruth, and Heejung Chung

European welfare states are undergoing profound change. This book examines welfare state transformations in Europe and considers likely new directions in social policy. The process of change is driven by complex interacting economic, political, and social pressures, operating at different speeds in different national, historical, and institutional contexts. We argue that the post-war welfare state settlement in Western Europe was based on broad class-coalitions supportive of a high standard of social provision across middle- and working-class groups (Baldwin 1990; Korpi 1983; Esping-Andersen 1990). These solidarities are now being eroded and new political parties and movements are emerging, driving new directions in policy. Post-Soviet welfare states in Eastern and Central Europe have made radical policy changes to accommodate the transition to market society. The Great Recession of 2007–8 has in many cases consolidated and accelerated change and imposed particular financial pressures in Southern Europe.

In this chapter we discuss the long-term trends that have undermined traditional welfare state settlements and the emerging cleavages that will influence how welfare states develop in the future. Mainstream definitions of social cleavage refer to divisions between groups with a strong basis for identity that are prepared to act on that division, and which form organizations such as political parties or trade unions to defend their interests and confront opposing organizations: identity, consciousness, and action (Lipset and Rokkan 1967). Here we use a looser definition, based on the work of

Svallfors (2007), which sees cleavages in terms of divisions between social categories of various kinds, giving rise to different interests and norms and leading to social action. The advantages of this approach are that we can identify cleavages as such without requiring the formation of organizations to promote common interests. We can do justice to the complexity and intersection of the various attitude cleavages that have emerged around class, age, gender, ethnicity/immigration, and nationalism. We see solidarity in similar terms as the recognition of common interests or identities which support political action, regardless of whether it involves collective institutions such as trade unions.

1.1 Longer-term Shifts in the Economic, Social, and Political Context of the European Welfare State

Much ink has been spilt in examining the slow break-up of the European welfare state settlement (for example Pierson 1994; Kuhnle 2000; Taylor-Gooby 2004; Starke 2006; Palier 2010). We will review the main points briefly in relation to economic, social, and political change during the past four decades.

1.1.1 *Economic Changes*

At the economic level, the main factors are globalization and technological change (Pierson 2001: 83–5; Swank 2010: 318, 328–9). The main drivers of economic globalization were the entry of developing and newly developed countries in Asia and South America into the world market, the emergence of China as a major exporting nation, the break-up of the Soviet empire, and the negotiation of international treaties to extend trade freedoms via the World Trade Organization (WTO) and other bodies.

Manufacturing employment has declined in developed countries and the more heterogeneous service sector has become the most important provider of jobs. This change results from the widespread use of new technologies leading to higher productivity at home, industrialization elsewhere, the expansion of international trade, and greater mobility of capital. The pace of change differed between countries. Manufacturing employment reached its highest point in Western Europe in the late 1970s and trade union membership peaked in the late 1950s in the US at about 35 per cent, in the late 1970s in the UK (50 per cent), in 1991 in West Germany (35 per cent), in the mid-1990s in Scandinavian countries (more than 70 per cent), and in the late 1990s in Southern European countries (just under 40 per cent: OECD 2015). Neo-liberal pressures have also led to greater dualization of the labour market

(Emmenegger et al. 2012), entrenching a division between higher value-added, higher-skilled, and unionized core workers and lower-skilled low-paid workers. This is reflected in greater inequality in income and in job security.

A further economic issue concerns the growth in importance of international agencies to promote the market against the nation-state (Deacon 2007). The most strikingly successful have been the single market and monetary union policies of the European Union (EU). One outcome has been severe tensions between economies at different stages of development that are no longer able to compensate national economic weakness by adjusting exchange rates in the aftermath of the Recession. The impact of international trade agreements in allowing market forces to destabilize national welfare state settlements is at present limited, but may become much stronger. The referendum vote in the UK in 2016 to leave the EU (Brexit) has created severe tensions and strengthened exit movements elsewhere, notably in France, Italy, and Denmark. The longer-term implications of this decision for European politics, economic development, and social solidarities are at the time of writing unclear. In the short term Brexit has led to an economic downturn in the UK and in trading partners.

1.1.2 Social Changes

At the social level, demographic changes, shifts in family patterns and gender roles, growing income and wealth inequalities, and the impact of immigration are important for welfare state politics. Population ageing has boosted demand for pensions and for health and social care, and has enlarged the proportion of non-workers depending on the labour of a relatively smaller workforce. This has implications for the future cost of welfare provision (estimated to increase by about four per cent of overall gross domestic product across the EU during the next half-century, with considerable cross-national variation) and for the size of the future workforce (European Commission 2015). How far population shifts can be compensated by productivity increases and immigration is at present unclear.

Gender roles and family patterns are also changing. Women play a much greater role in paid work and have overtaken men in educational achievement but still earn less. These shifts enable increased production, partially compensating population ageing, but intensify pressures on childcare and other services and reinforce demands for greater gender equality in pay and career opportunities (Esping-Andersen 2009). The rise in women's labour market participation as well as the greater diversity in family forms (with a higher proportion of single-parent and lone-adult households) challenge the male-breadwinner assumptions of the traditional welfare state.

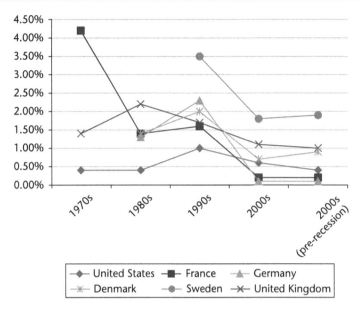

Figure 1.1. Average annual rates of change in earnings (selected countries: OECD).

Long-term trends to greater inequality in income and wealth (Atkinson 2007; Piketty 2014) and to greater precarity among those at the bottom have been intensified by the impact of the recession on wage-levels and employment (Häusermann and Schwander 2012). In the period since the 1960s the share of growth available for wages has steadily fallen, at different rates in different countries (Bailey et al. 2011), and the pace of increase in earnings has slowed (Figure 1.1). Hourly earnings lagged behind price inflation by some ten per cent over the period from 2007 to 2015 in the UK and Greece but rose by 22 per cent in Poland, 14 per cent in Germany, and ten per cent in France and Sweden (Touchstone 2016). Over the same period inequalities in income have increased markedly (Figure 1.2). Social provision has responded more effectively to greater inequality in some countries than in others.

Economic opportunities in Europe and the pressures of war and disorder in the Balkans, the Middle East, and North Africa have led to high levels of immigration, especially for Scandinavia, France, Germany, and the UK, where the foreign-born percentage of the population now exceeds ten per cent (see Figure 1.3). This has fuelled an anti-immigration backlash among those who see themselves as losers in competition for jobs, houses, and schooling (McLaren and Johnson 2004; O'Rourke and Sinnott 2006) and is a strong underlying factor driving populist anti-EU movements. All European welfare states impose restrictions on non-EU immigrants' access to welfare benefits, and, in most cases, some restrictions on EU immigrants (Sainsbury 2012). Populations in some European regions are becoming increasingly

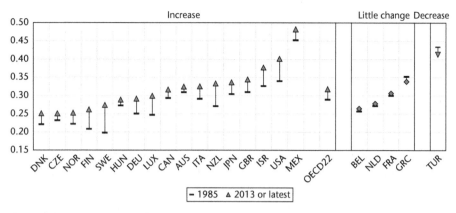

Figure 1.2. Income inequality in OECD countries 1985–2013.
Source: OECD (2015)

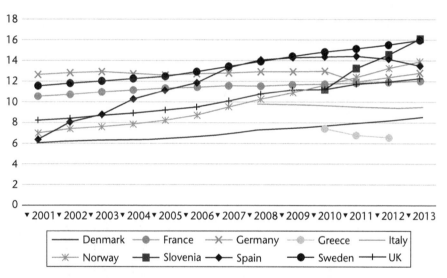

Figure 1.3. Percentage of foreign-born population, 2001–12 (selected countries: OECD 2016).

diverse as a result of rising immigration. This enriches society, but has also stimulated chauvinist responses (Freeman 2009; Mewes and Mau 2012).

1.1.3 *Political Changes*

These economic and social changes have led to two intertwined trends in welfare state politics. First, new needs are emerging, sometimes described as new social risks (Taylor-Gooby 2004), among young entrants to the labour market, lower-skilled workers, female workers, immigrants, and those in need

5

of social care. These groups are diverse and do not typically feel a common interest or exert a solidaristic political pressure for better provision. They are more likely to support particular components in party programmes than provide a stable foundation for a new politics of welfare. However, despite the additional impact of the Great Recession which has hit younger people and women hardest, there has been no great change in the proportion of social welfare spending going to the traditional 'old risk' welfare state. Figure 1.4 shows spending on traditional areas of welfare (pensions, healthcare, and sickness and disability) as a percentage of welfare state spending per head.

Spending on the old risk welfare state varies but in each country it amounts to more than 70 per cent of the welfare state. Only in Italy, Spain, and the UK was there a fall in the proportion of total spending on these risks before the recession, though there were slight falls afterwards, as spending on younger age groups rose to meet rising unemployment and poverty. The overall pattern is one of continuity.

Figure 1.4 shows that new social risks fail to make noticeable inroads on welfare state spending even at a time of exceptional need, when the political clout of those affected might be thought to be strongest. This reinforces the evidence that new risks, while real, do not necessarily cohere into a political force sufficiently powerful to produce major shifts in policy. Nonetheless, such risks command attention in debate and form elements in political bargaining, especially in consensus democracies. Bonoli and Natali (2012) suggest that they often enter the agenda in ways that do not require

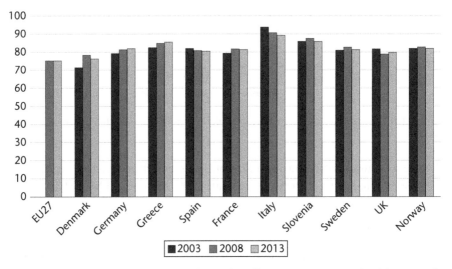

Figure 1.4. Spending on the core traditional welfare state (pensions, healthcare, sickness and disability) per head of population as percentage of total welfare state spending (Eurostat).

large increases in social spending. Thus new social risk policies have often been pursued by a variety of means, including regulation, which requires employers to bear part of the cost (as in many parental leave schemes), and activation, which rests on the restructuring of welfare benefit entitlements into carrot-or-stick incentives to mobilize unemployed people into paid work.

Second, the political forces that were traditionally seen to sustain both good wages for the mass of the working class and support for state welfare have grown weaker. The 'power resources' of the trade union and labour movement (Korpi 1989; Esping-Andersen 1990) have been undermined by the decline of industrial employment accompanied by a trend to relax labour market regulation in the face of more intense global competition (Palier and Thelen 2010). The opportunities for alliances between working- and middle-class groups (Mau 2015; Goodin and Le Grand 1987; Mau and Sachweh 2014) are under pressure as labour markets become more dualized, insecurities are unequally distributed (Emmenegger et al. 2012; OECD 2015), market incomes 'fan out' (Atkinson 2007), and class interests become more clearly distinct. The speed and significance of these processes varies between countries depending on economic and labour market conditions, family patterns, demographic shifts, and welfare state traditions.

Under these circumstances welfare state politics can move in a number of directions (see Table 1.1). Traditional redistributive welfare may be undermined but coalitions may form between risk groups favouring policies which benefit working parents, as well as old risk groups such as retirement pensioners. Equally, a perceived threat to living standards from immigration may promote a political alliance sufficiently powerful to generate anti-immigrant policies. Pressures from advantaged groups may reinforce trends to inequality and undermine support for traditional mass state services. Conversely, state welfare provision may be reconceptualized as social investment and may gain sufficient support to command substantial public spending. One important area of development is policies to enable women and parents to engage in paid work, including childcare, parental leave, and other workplace rights.

All accounts of the long-term shifts that have disrupted the welfare state settlement point to a complex of factors. All agree that the explanation must include structural economic changes (more intense global competition, rapid technological change, and the higher relative return for those with higher levels of skill), social changes (high immigration, demographic pressures, changes in the family, emergence of new social risks), and political changes (the decline in the strength of the political organization of the working class, the emergence of neo-liberal individualism and of new and less stable divisions around group interests and welfare chauvinism).

Table 1.1. Structural change

Field	Development	Change	Impact on welfare state	New policy objectives	Policy response
Economic	Globalization and technological shifts	More intense competition	Pressures on non-productive spending	Austerity	Education; training; workforce mobilization; cut-backs
	Labour market change	Decline in manufacturing sector/growth of service sector; greater premium on skill	Weakening of working class; dualization; expansion of female labour force	More skilled workers	Stress on skill: social investment; stress on mobilization: active labour market policies, flexibilisation; family-friendly work
	Baumol cost-disease	Falling productivity in human services	Real cost of health, social care and education rises	Drive for cost-efficiency	Privatization; use of voluntary sector; cuts
Social	Population ageing	Increased dependency	Extra costs for pensions, health and social care; intergenerational pressures	Cost-efficiency in these services	Efficiency savings; privatization; use of voluntary sector; cuts
	More women in full-time work	Larger labour force; less informal child and elder care	Demand for new social risk services	More childcare; more parental rights	Private vs state vs voluntary provision
	Fanning-out of market incomes; accelerating returns to wealth (Piketty)	Greater inequality; increased political influence of rich	Tax revolt; pressures on welfare for the poor; intensification of deserving/ undeserving split	Spending and tax cuts	Shift to more targeted services; privatization
	Wars and insecurity in Balkans, Middle East, Africa	Immigration into Europe	Immediate pressure on provision; long-term increase in labour force	Excluding/ controlling immigrants	Restricting benefits to established nationals

The outcome is a move away from the old politics of welfare (Pierson 2001), which rested centrally on social class divisions and posited a major role for the state in redistribution from better to worse off and over the family life-cycle. The structures that previously sustained the various welfare systems identified by writers like Esping-Andersen (1990) are being dismantled. There is considerable uncertainty as to the form of welfare state that will emerge, or whether a transition to a different political economy with weaker provision for the most vulnerable groups is under way. It is clear that demands for services for older people (pensions, and health and social care) are growing stronger just as these services grow more expensive, leading to intense pressures for cost-efficiency.

Similarly, demands for childcare and parental rights in the workplace become more marked. These services are rather cheaper and in some cases can be addressed through regulation rather than spending. Everywhere they have expanded. On the other hand the decline of social class and particularly traditional working-class pressures and growing inequality, coupled with the greater political influence of the rich, have led to demands for tax cuts, imposed pressures on spending and on cost-efficiency, and undermined the working-class/middle-class coalition that sustained traditional welfare states. The outcome is a move towards welfare states that sustain services for older people and expand provision for working families but do so under conditions of increasing financial pressure on services. Provision for the poor and especially the non-working population of working age is more stringently targeted and cut back. Welfare chauvinism becomes increasingly important especially in the countries where immigrant pressures are strongest and where the gap between the low-paid and workless and the better off is growing most obviously. This conflicts with recognition by policy-makers that immigration offers a way of addressing the issue of population ageing.

As a result of all these changes, new directions in welfare are proceeding at different speeds and with varied outcomes in different welfare states. In 2007–8 the Great Recession cut across 'business as usual' in European welfare states with very different impacts in different countries. The overall outcome has been to accelerate and embed the processes of change outlined above.

1.2 The Great Recession and the Politics of Austerity

Pressures on European welfare states intensified after the Great Recession 2007–9, when the slowdown in economic activity following the major banking crisis and government bailout of banks caused the combined EU GDP to fall by more than five per cent. Recovery from the slump was sluggish, with a further dip into recession in 2011–12 and a failure to attain previous GDP levels across the EU as a whole until 2013 (International Monetary Fund 2015). The economic collapse impacted most severely on the EU members least able to compete effectively (Ireland, Greece, Italy, Portugal, and Spain) and is more profound than any slump in the post-war period. The recession led to an immediate response from 'automatic' regulators in increased spending on cash benefits for unemployed people. In most countries spending programmes were established to protect jobs, support low wages, and promote training, investment, and research and development (Chung and Thewissen, 2011; Gough 2011). Nonetheless poverty increased from 21 per cent of the working-age population (25–54) across EU27 countries

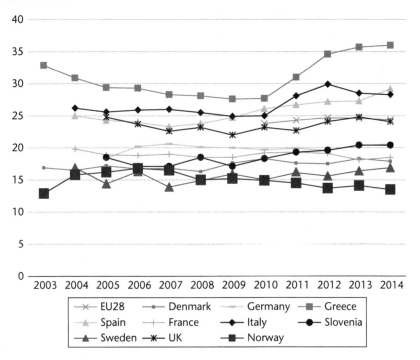

Figure 1.5. Percentage of people at risk of poverty or social exclusion, 2005–13.

Persons at risk of poverty are defined by the European Commission as 'a process whereby certain individuals are pushed to the edge of society and prevented from participating fully by virtue of their poverty, or lack of basic competencies and life-long learning opportunities, or as a result of discrimination' (Eurostat 2015).

Source: Eurostat

in 2008 to 24 per cent by 2013, with particularly high levels in Greece, Spain, the UK, and Italy (see Figure 1.5).

Governments across Europe faced the biggest recession for at least half a century and experienced an unprecedentedly sluggish recovery. This generated concern at the size of budgetary deficits and the impact on currency stability. In most cases austerity packages were introduced to achieve balanced budgets without increasing taxes. Eurozone members faced additional pressures because they were unable to devalue on a national basis. Many were confronted by a collapse of exports while the strongest economy, Germany, was favoured with an artificially low exchange rate. The outcome was additional pressure for spending cutbacks, especially on state welfare, structural reforms, and measures to promote greater flexibility in labour markets, endorsed by the European Central Bank. These changes in some cases reinforced policy shifts that had been in train for some time (for example the new more active labour-market policies associated in Germany with the Hartz IV reforms from 2003, in France with the expansion of RMI from 1988 onwards, and in the UK with the rundown of working-age insurance welfare after the introduction of Jobseeker's Allowance in 1996). The crisis accelerated existing policy shifts and provided a further justification for the new policy directions.

Austerity has been pursued with particular enthusiasm in the UK, Ireland, and Germany and with less vigour in France, Spain, Italy, and elsewhere. Two countries (France in 2012 and Greece in 2015) elected governments opposed to the new neo-liberal logic. Both have been forced to implement welfare and public sector cuts as a result of external economic pressures, reinforced by rising unemployment in the case of France (see Chapters 4 and 8). The outcome across Europe has been stringent cutbacks and higher levels of poverty (see Figure 1.5).

The current context of policy-making is one in which the neo-liberal logic of austerity provides the most influential approach to policy making (van Kersbergen, Vis and Hemerijck 2014). Neo-liberalism is strictly speaking a policy paradigm which calls for the reduction of state intervention and a pre-eminent role for the free market, so that taxation, regulation, and state provision should be kept to a minimum and welfare state services privatized wherever possible.

In practice, austerity and welfare state retrenchment have been closely linked to the emergence of a politics of individualism. This approach combines a morality of individual responsibility with diminished support for collective provision. It undermines the solidarities on which collective welfare is based. Mau (2015) argues that the middle class are increasingly able to meet needs in areas like education, housing, and (to a growing extent) pensions through private resources, generating tax-refusal and undermining the alliance between middle and working class, the political bedrock of the traditional welfare state. At the same time the state reduces welfare spending.

Neo-liberal austerity marks a retreat from welfare state interventionism grounded in neo-Keynesian political economy. However, some political parties in EU countries promote interventionist responses to the Great Recession. These rest on new cleavages and solidarities and include:

- Counter-cyclical state investment and spending on benefits to promote economic activity, since the poor are least likely to save any money they have.

- Social investment, which includes interventions (including expenditure) in areas such as education and training, research and development, social infrastructure such as housing and transport, provision to help women take paid jobs, and better opportunities especially for low-skilled workers, immigrants, labour market entrants, and other groups. Such expenditure is understood as investment because it will mobilize labour and improve productivity, enhancing the prospect of future economic growth. Social

11

investment may interact with generational and other divisions and lead to policy conflicts. In practice there is little indication of such cleavages emerging as major features of welfare politics.

- Predistribution, a welfare state response to austerity which shifts the emphasis from spending to regulation. Governments can achieve welfare goals by imposing high minimum wages, rent and utility price controls, and labour market regulations which help the weakest groups. In practice some of these policy directions have been pursued in a number of countries, but overall policies are dominated by commitment to budgetary balance (Hacker 2011).

- Fightback programmes, which directly contradict austerity and the neoliberal assumptions which underlie it. They demand higher tax-financed spending in all areas of social provision, extensive redistribution, and much greater opportunities for the poor. This approach has been politically significant, especially in Mediterranean countries. The experience of precarious employment and of more obvious social inequalities has generated resistance from the left by traditional parties or the new anti-austerity movements such the Indignados and Podemos in Spain, some elements in Green and Pirate parties, minority protest groups such as 'Occupy Wall Street' or 'We Are The 99%', and, from the right, UKIP in the UK, AfD in Germany, or Golden Dawn in Greece. Such parties have the potential to combine different social groups, including low-waged workers and unemployed people and those dependent on pensions and other state benefits (see Chapter 8 on Greece and Chapter 7 on Spain and Italy).

A further development which rests on state intervention but is not immediately a response to the recession is the rise of welfare chauvinism, particularly in countries where immigration is high (or is perceived to be high), such as Germany, the UK, and Greece, and often on the part of lower-income groups previously keen to support universal provision (Mewes and Mau 2012). This often (but not always) combines two themes: rejection of EU legislation granting the same rights to EU citizens as to nationals; and outright opposition to immigration from EU member states and elsewhere, with competition from immigrants seen as causing the economic difficulties that citizens experience. It is typically linked to support for sustaining national welfare provision for citizens only.

Welfare chauvinism had developed rapidly during the past two decades and been influential in countries such as Denmark, France, and the UK. It recently received further impetus from the recession, propelling chauvinism to the forefront of welfare politics. Some political parties such as UKIP in the UK and France's National Front have adopted a 'hard' chauvinism, which requires the exclusion of would-be immigrants. Others have pursued a softer approach, calling for temporary restrictions on access to welfare provision for immigrants, for example in Scandinavian countries (Chapter 5). The most dramatic outcome of such concerns is the British referendum vote in 2016 to leave the EU, despite opposition by the vast majority of government, business, and lobby group leaders (Jensen and Snaith 2016). The UK government has not so far triggered the procedure to leave the EU although it plans to do so in 2017. Brexit is likely to damage the UK economy (Giles 2016). Whether it has wider implications for other secessions from the EU or for a reform of the EU monetary system and of the Euro (Stiglitz 2016) is unclear.

These seven approaches are analytically distinct. The logic of austerity contradicts that of the new forms of interventionism, but the other approaches can be and are often combined. Table 1.2 outlines the link

Table 1.2. Policy responses associated with the crisis and their impact on cleavages and solidarities

Overall response	Policies	Cleavages	Solidarities
Retreat from interventionist state			
Cuts/austerity	Cutbacks; privatization	Advantaged groups vs disadvantaged	None
	Prioritize pensions, health care, not working-age benefits	Intergenerational	None
	Prioritize wage supplements and low income tax; cut benefits	Worker vs non-worker	None
	Prioritize social insurance	Secure vs precarious	None
Individual responsibility	Privatization; means-testing; some forms of social investment	Middle-class vs vulnerable	None
New forms of interventionism			
Interventionism	State-led investment to create jobs; welfare spending to maintain demand from the poor		Class alliance between working-class and middle-class groups
Social investment	Prioritize training and family support	Groups whose engagement in work or skill level can be enhanced vs others	Groups marginal to the labour market
Predistribution	High minimum wage, rent and utility price control; better job opportunities	Low-waged vs high-waged	Across lower-wage groups
Fightback	Anti-austerity measures; higher benefits; corporate tax		Solidarity of disadvantaged
Welfare chauvinism (may be combined with other policies)	Residence and citizenship tests; immigration control; national protectionism	Denizens vs immigrants	Nationalism

between policy responses to the crisis and welfare state cleavages and solidarities.

These policy responses have undermined previous class alliances, contributing to the erosion of well-established solidarities and to the emergence of new cleavages within European societies. These changes and the resulting political divisions are reflected in an increasing mistrust of politicians and of the existing political establishment and the fragmentation of EU politics (Eurobarometer 2016). In many countries the traditional parties of centre-left (Social Democrat) and centre-right (Christian Democrat) are losing supporters to new centrists and, more recently, more extreme parties. 'New left' parties have emerged in Greece (SYRIZA), Spain (Podemos), and Germany (Die Linke). Populist right anti-immigration and/or Eurosceptic parties, which started to appear in the early 1990s, are becoming more important in countries such as France (Front National), Poland (Law and Justice), Denmark (the Danish People's Party), and the United Kingdom (UK Independence Party or UKIP). Moving away from an anti-establishment rhetoric, some of these populist right parties have successfully established themselves as government coalition partners, such as the Norwegian Progress Party, Law and Justice in Poland, and the Finns Party. These moves have strong implications for the range and direction of European welfare states.

1.3 Theorizing the Way in which Welfare States Manage the New Policy Directions

A substantial literature examines the outcomes for welfare states in Europe. Following Streeck and Thelen (2005) but with some modification, we group together—under the three headings they provide—the various accounts of how the differences in European welfare states are to be understood and how the politics of welfare is likely to develop. These headings are *convergence* theories, which suggest that the similarities in context and structure between European welfare states will lead them to develop towards a common model, perhaps neo-liberal austerity or social investment; theories of *structured diversity*, which argue that real differences will be sustained over time, enabling us to group welfare states as in regime theory or varieties of capitalism, and what are termed *beyond continuity* approaches, which suggest that national policy directions may diverge as policy reforms cumulate in different ways in different contexts and as resistance to and support for changes develops. An important point is that, as mentioned earlier, the old solidarities across major population groups that previously sustained welfare states seem to be breaking down into more individualist and sectoral concerns, so that it is difficult to predict how alliances and coalitions of interest will emerge to drive welfare state change or to suggest a simple overall framework for the politics of welfare.

1.3.1 *Convergence*

These approaches understand the trajectory of welfare state development as shaped by an overriding external force, so that they move in the same direction and become more similar. The most obvious candidate is economic globalization. Rodrik's logic (1998) suggests a 'race to the bottom' as welfare states compete to offer the most attractive environment for business with low taxes and minimal regulation (see also Schwartz 2001). Other scholars point to upward pressures on social provision, particularly to improve the quality of labour as human capital strategies seek to attract knowledge-based industry in international competition.

The first Lisbon treaty with its goal of a dynamic knowledge-based economy sought to promote such a strategy. It emerges in the Europe 2020 programme and in other aspects of EU policy and is often understood as 'social investment'. Welfare provision, appropriately directed, may lead to a real economic return since it improves skill levels and motivation and helps to give workers access to jobs. In practice it has proved difficult to demonstrate a real return from social spending, except in tightly defined areas of education and training and in the provision of childcare that mobilizes extra women workers. Advocates of social investment typically use the term more broadly to include improvements in quality of life as an important return.

The widely held dualization approach to welfare state labour markets is also an example of convergence in the claim that the pressures of globalization and increased liberalization lead business to protect highly skilled core workers while working conditions for low-skilled, disadvantaged workers deteriorate, and unions are forced to accept these conditions (Emmenegger et al. 2012). This division then permeates the structure of benefits and services for the two groups, producing a two-tier welfare state.

A further modern convergence approach is the neo-liberal politics of individualism. This approach emphasizes the growth of a morality of individual responsibility and the decline of support for collective provision. According to this approach, and as we have seen, middle-class people are increasingly able to meet their needs and are less willing to pay taxes to finance services which they see as benefiting others. Accordingly, it becomes more difficult to construct the alliances between middle and working class on which the traditional welfare state was based (Mau 2015). This approach is reinforced by the shift towards austerity which transfers responsibility from state to individual.

1.3.2 *Structured Diversity*

A second group of analyses stresses the different institutional frameworks of different welfare states and argues that responses to current pressures can be understood as shaped by political, social, and economic context. Esping-Andersen's regime theory (1990; 1999), variously modified to include Mediterranean, Central, and Eastern Europe (CEE) and workerist welfare states (see Arts and Gelissen 2002), stresses stratification, the extent of decommodification, and feedback from existing institutions as primary factors in path dependency.

Hall and Soskice (2001) in a seminal work on 'varieties of capitalism' focus on the way in which corporatism between employers, unions, and states shapes markets and institutions. They distinguish coordinated and liberal market economies. Growth and competitiveness in the former rest on investment by employers and on state policies that enhance the skill profiles of workers, with the result that firms develop long-term interests in their employees. In this context, governments support firms through expansive research and development, education, and training programmes, but more importantly through stringent protection regulations for the core workers, with generous unemployment benefits typically delivered through social insurance programmes that discriminate in favour of those with established work records. Such economies are typically associated with more consensual polities and stronger negotiating rights for established workers. The divisions that arise may be between core and more marginal workers.

In liberal market economies firms rely on relatively low wages rather than higher levels of skill and investment to achieve competitiveness in the global market. Governments, typically majoritarian, promote competitiveness in this context by limiting regulation, taxation, and state welfare. Workers have little protection in their employment or income after losing a job. Here the central division is between labour and capital.

An approach from political science as opposed to political economy ranges democracies along a dimension from consensus to majoritarian (Lijphart 1999). A more consensual democracy combines a range of institutions (for example, proportional representation voting, bicameral parliaments, a federal level of government, a strong role for a supreme court in overseeing political decision-making, corporate representation of employers and trade union groups) that allow various interests to achieve representation and to participate in government and in policy making. The majoritarian democracies tend to have strong central government, first-past-the-post voting and strong party discipline, a powerful president or prime minister, and little opportunity for involvement by a second chamber, local government, the judiciary, or social partners. In this setting the party in government may be more interested in the response of the mass public to its policies and the impact on the next election than the views of other interests whose support must be obtained to allow a decision to be implemented (Schmidt 2002).

Consensus institutions provide much greater opportunities for class alliances. Where these alliances take place in the context of strong left politics, as in Nordic countries, a welfare state on the social democratic regime model emerges. Where it takes place in a climate of Christian Democrat politics a corporatist outcome as in Germany, France, and much of the remainder of Europe is most likely (Gingrich and Häusermann 2015).

1.3.3 *Beyond Continuity*

Streeck and Thelen (2005) claim that neither a convergence nor a structured diversity approach captures the changes in welfare states that are now underway. This third model argues that current pressures are broadly similar between countries, but that these must be seen in the context of the real differences in the way that they are managed, so that it is not possible to identify one pattern of response. In addition, the direction of transformation is not dominated by regime, variety of capitalism, or other category. For example, in Esping-Andersen's taxonomy France, Germany, and Italy are coordinated market economies and are corporatist regimes, but have developed in rather different directions in response to current pressures, rejecting austerity, committing to deficit-elimination, and seeking to evade the requirements of ECB growth and stability policies.

Streeck and Thelen suggest that contemporary political economies are developing through incremental but cumulatively transformative processes. Institutional change is determined primarily by factors interacting at national level. An important point is that the operation of the various long- and short-term pressures in the national context is mediated by political factors. These differ substantially, and can only be understood in context. For this reason any approach to the development and likely future direction of state welfare must not only take into account the economic and social changes that are extensively analysed in discussion of European welfare states, the declining power and influence of the labour movement, and the role of chauvinism and neo-liberalism, it must also give a central role to the current politics of welfare in the national context. That is what we do in this book.

In principle these and other developments might form the basis for a new, restructured politics of welfare, either converging on one form or displaying a structured diversity. We have reviewed the range of approaches that are now emerging in Table 1.1 and have analysed their political implications in Table 1.2. In practice many of the approaches can be combined. Developments tend to vary so much in the national context that we cannot simply read off trends in welfare politics from economic or social shifts. In short, while social change generates new interests, the articulation of social interests in national contexts does not structure these into a coherent politics. Hence the approach of this book, which examines the emerging new politics of welfare across different European countries covering the main regime types and countries whose distinctive programmes have attracted attention, such as France, Greece, and the UK, and includes the most important European economies.

1.4 National Contexts

In the remaining chapters of this book we discuss the process of welfare state development and transformation, taking into account responses to the Great Recession, and examine possible future developments in a range of European countries and at European level. The countries are chosen to provide coverage of the full range of categories of welfare state and the various responses to the recession and to austerity. They include major representatives of Esping-Andersen's regime types (corporatist Germany and France, liberal UK, social democratic Scandinavia, and Mediterranean Spain, Greece, and Italy, as well as post-socialist Slovenia). They provide contrasting varieties of capitalism—liberal (UK) and corporatist (Germany, France)—and majoritarian (UK) and consensus democracies (Germany). The countries featured are at the forefront of current debates: Greece, compelled to accept stringent austerity; Germany, foremost advocate of budgetary balance; France, seeking to pursue elements of a traditional post-war state investment neo-Keynesian programme; the UK, singled out for praise by the IMF Managing Director for leading the way in neo-liberal fiscal policies 'that have actually worked' (Lagarde 2015); and the Scandinavian countries, where social democracy is facing major challenges. An additional chapter will consider the role of the EU and how it is likely to develop.

Most work on European welfare states is based on the analysis of developments and necessarily considers the recent past. A key feature of this book is that, in addition, it discusses possible future policy scenarios. It does this on the basis of the analysis of background context and of current policy. The background enables us to understand the specific features of policy approach and of the issues and problems that have been recognized as important in the country. Current policy directions indicate the issues that are on the agenda and the extent to which they form the basis of political cleavages and solidarities. Our analysis of current politics and directions in public opinion shows the directions that are likely to be taken. Our understanding of the issues that are emerging in relation to such factors as demographic and family change, immigration, and the impact of austerity points to likely future outcomes.

Chapter 2 focuses on the largest and most developed European nation, Germany. It has a consensus-based corporatist polity, a substantial manufacturing sector with major exports, and relatively constrained social spending. It has had a long-term commitment to social insurance provision for the main needs of the majority of the population. The viability of this system has increasingly been challenged by an expansion in the proportion of the labour force employed in temporary, short-term, or part-time jobs and by the pressures of a growing older population on social insurance. The main issues were traditionally the role of the government in redistribution and the place of immigrant workers. In recent years, new social risks have arisen in response to pressures from globalization, the decline of nation-state authority, demographic shifts, and new immigration patterns. These changes led to new policies in the late 1990s and early 2000s to contain pension spending, expand provision for working women and childcare, increase activation for unemployed people, and make the labour market more flexible. Whether these changes will lead to a more inclusive welfare system or to a retreat is unclear.

Chapter 3 discusses the situation in the United Kingdom. The UK is distinctive among the larger and more developed European states in three ways: it has a majoritarian first-past-the-post governmental system, with a high degree of centralization of political authority, and a liberal-leaning economy with a substantial financial sector, a high degree of inequality, relatively low and targeted social spending, and limited labour market regulation. It is also the only major EU member country so far to vote for exit from the EU, potentially destabilizing the union and certainly inflicting economic damage on itself and on European trading partners. There is a measure of consensus on the main policy issues: austerity (all main parties are committed to eliminating the budget deficit, but over rather different time periods); restricting immigration (endorsed both by former left voters in deindustrialized areas and by the right); and sustained spending on mass needs and deserving groups (health and social care, pensions, education) with more meagre provision for poor minorities of working age (wage supplements, stronger workplace rights, unemployment benefits). However, this settlement is under pressure from increasing inequality in wealth and income, welfare chauvinism, the economic pressures from Brexit, and growing resistance to neo-liberal policies from disadvantaged groups.

Real wages (taking account of living costs) actually fell in real terms by about ten per cent in the UK between 2007 and 2015 (Touchstone 2016). In relation to future cleavages and solidarities the key issues are whether a clear political division develops between groups damaged by the emerging settlement (lower-income, lower-skilled, unemployed and young, the majority women) and those advantaged (higher income and older people), and whether this is able to gain a purchase within the current political institutions.

Chapter 4 examines the 'generous' welfare state in France, the second largest economy of the European Union. It has a semi-presidential system of governance with a high degree of decentralization. The French welfare state has faced considerable pressures from the cost of pensions and social insurance provision and has moved slowly towards more targeted provision for those of working age and controls on pension spending in recent years. The impact of the Great Recession of 2007–8 confronted French social policy with major challenges. Among these, the rise of unemployment and inequalities combined with major pension reforms led to high levels of dissatisfaction across the country. The socialist Ayrault and Valls governments, elected under Hollande's 2012 presidency, have struggled to introduce a package of welfare improvements and state-led investment to stimulate demand, and have been forced to retreat towards austerity. Besides unemployment, issues such as immigration, Euroscepticism, and security have attracted considerable media attention and suggest new directions in welfare state reform. The evidence of substantial commitment to neo-liberal attitudes reinforces the possibility of a shift in this direction.

In Chapter 5 the three main Scandinavian countries (Denmark, Norway, and Sweden) are compared. These three nations are the main European representatives of the social democratic model of welfare. They are all small to medium-sized, rich, and highly open economies. Policy-making generally benefits from a stable political climate and pragmatic rather than ideologically driven decision-making. Cabinets, even those formed by minority governments, tend to stay in office for the full term. In Scandinavia, the state plays a stronger role than elsewhere as the key provider, and increasingly also as a funder and regulator of services provided by others. It seeks to protect its citizens against social risks across the whole life course, alleviating some of the demands put on family solidarity in other countries. There is a long tradition of publicly provided care services for children and the elderly along with public healthcare and education. Tax-financed basic income security programmes are combined with contribution-based income-replacing benefits linked to previous work status. Overall, this means that social spending is high. The Scandinavian countries still enjoy relatively low levels of inequality and poverty as well as high employment rates for both women and men. However, differences are opening out between Sweden, which has developed more targeted welfare for those of working age and cut back noticeably on overall spending, moving in a more corporatist, less inclusive direction, and the other countries. The key question for the future is whether the social settlement can be sustained and whether the future will be dominated by welfare chauvinism, or austerity, or greater targeting of welfare. The weakening of attitudinal support for the traditional Scandinavian model supports this possibility.

Chapter 6 considers Slovenia. Following the collapse of Yugoslavia this country avoided amalgamation with Serbia and enjoyed a period of independence. It joined the EU in 2004. Social provision in Slovenia pursued a more gradual path of development, avoiding the sharp increases in inequality that occurred in the more liberal-oriented post-socialist countries. The country faced a pronounced recession after the 2008 economic crisis, followed by a second recession in 2012 (along with Greece and Italy). This was further exacerbated by political instability with a restructuring of left and right political coalitions. These pressures, coupled with an emphasis on austerity, led to structural reforms of the welfare system which resulted in a step change in the reform process. The demands for change also generated conflicts and tensions between different groups, imposing strain on the previous pattern of solidarities. These tensions are also reflected in public unrest and opposition to the reforms. Support for basic welfare provision for the mass of the population seems likely to remain strong, but the persisting tensions suggest that further modifications and possible retrenchments of welfare are likely.

Chapter 7 focuses on Spain and Italy, which experienced major crises in both political and socio-economic institutions in the early 1990s. Spain and Italy are the fourth- and fifth-largest economies in the EU, the latter also a member of the G8. Both are mixed-market economies and typically classified as Mediterranean welfare states with social insurance pensions, more universal tax-financed health and education systems, and limited and means-tested social assistance and social care. Both have faced large immigration flows across the Mediterranean.

The 2007–8 crisis led to deep and prolonged recessions in both countries. The main issues in relation to welfare state politics have been the difficulty of introducing an austerity programme in the context of a sluggish recovery from the recession, and exceptionally high levels of immigration which add welfare chauvinism to the existing regional cleavages in politics. Government in Italy has suffered from chronic instability, leading to constitutional reforms, while in Spain it is only very recently that ruling parties have found it difficult to sustain support. In both countries levels of political mistrust are high. Current patterns of attitudes imply weak neo-liberalism and chauvinism (more marked in Italy), with links to a welfare state fightback. One possibility is a shift towards a more coherent and far-reaching neo-liberal austerity, another is much greater resistance to austerity, with the context for both likely to be coloured by national identity politics.

Chapter 8 analyses the situation in one of the most unstable countries in the European Union: Greece. Greece had an established middle-class occupational welfare system which was substantially expanded after the country joined the EU in 1981. Spending increased rapidly on healthcare and on a system of benefits for unemployed people. Among the countries of the European periphery, Greece has been hit hardest and longest by the sovereign debt crisis following the Great Recession. In 2010 Greece entered into a 'rescue-deal' with the so-called troika (the three international lenders—the EC, the IMF, and the ECB) conditional on implementing austerity-driven structural adjustment. The collapse of demand led the economy into deep and chronic recession. The rise to power of a previously marginal radical left-wing party (SYRIZA) in the snapshot election of late January 2015 highlights many of the failures of structural adjustment.

Greece led the attempt to promote alternatives to neo-liberal austerity. The failure in mid-2015 of Greek resistance to a package of profound cuts, privatization, and major tax rises imposed from outside underlines the dominance of neo-liberal austerity programmes in Europe. The question of whether the resulting falls in living standards (some ten per cent between 2007 and 2015) can be made acceptable to those who lose out will be at the centre of developments in Greek welfare state politics. There is little indication in the attitudinal evidence of endorsement of spending constraint and privatization.

Chapter 9 discusses the potential for a Common European Social Policy, advocated by many scholars and economists as a response to the crisis at the European Union level (see for example Habermas 2012) and thrown into sharp relief by the UK's 2016 exit referendum decision. Since the ratification of the Treaty of Rome in 1957, the European integration project has been formally committed to reduce socio-economic inequalities between member states. Today, the European Union provides cooperation between member states in a wide range of policy areas, from a Common Security and Defence Policy to a Common Agricultural Policy. However, social inequalities remain high, the response of European institutions to the Great Recession combines neo-liberalism and austerity with little capacity to protect living standards, and public attitudes towards the welfare state vary considerably from one member state to another. Europe has failed to display solidarity among its members in key social policy areas such as managing mass immigration from less developed countries (especially from Syria and Libya) which bears most heavily on the Mediterranean member states. The commitment to the single market, and to the single currency for the core European countries, imposes additional pressures, opening up the possibility of a 'two-speed Europe' or of a move away from social solidarity in the interests of economic cohesion. This has been exacerbated by the insistence of the ECB on the Stability and Growth Pact (strengthened by the 'Six Pack' and 'Two Pack'), which requires Eurozone members to constrain national debt and budgetary deficits stringently. This was tightened in 2005 and then in 2011. Whether Brexit will trigger exit referendums in other countries to leave the EU remains to be seen.

In the concluding chapter we sum up the various developments across Europe and draw together accounts of how the different welfare states are likely to develop in the short and longer term in a discussion of likely patterns of European welfare futures. Solidarities everywhere are under strain and it is unclear how far new cleavages are opening up and how they influence welfare state politics. Our examination of past, present, and possible future developments in these countries will support discussion of the way in which political debates about state welfare will develop in Europe. In particular we will examine how far welfare politics is pursuing converging, parallel, or diverging paths in different national contexts and how the pattern of debate is likely to develop in the future. Globalization, technological developments, demographic and family shifts, the fanning-out of inequality, the decline of traditional working-class solidarities, and the pressures of immigration all place demands on European welfare states. These have led to realignments of the class coalitions on which the traditional welfare state was founded and to new developments supporting greater productivism, deepening intergenerational and deserving/undeserving divisions, and constraining spending everywhere. Of particular importance is the decline in trust in the political establishment, including the main parties, resulting in the rise of welfare chauvinist parties and fightback movements across Europe. The Great Recession and the turn towards neo-liberal austerity have dealt a hammer blow in Southern Europe and consolidated the shift towards neo-liberalism elsewhere. Analysis of welfare state politics across a range of countries will show whether welfare states capable of meeting the needs of the most vulnerable groups can survive in the new Europe.

References

Arts, W. and Gelissen, J. (2002) 'Three Worlds of Welfare Capitalism or More?', *Journal of European Social Policy* 12(2): 137–58.

Atkinson, A. (2007) 'The Distribution of Earnings in OECD Countries', *International Labour Review* 146(2): 41–60.

Bailey, J., Coward, R., and Whittaker, M. (2011) *Painful Separation*, London: Resolution Foundation, http://www.resolutionfoundation.org/publications/painful-separation/, accessed 12 Aug. 2016.

Baldwin, P. (1990) *The Politics of Social Solidarity, 1875–1975*, Cambridge: Cambridge University Press.

Bonoli, G. and Natali, D. (2012) *The Politics of the New Welfare State*, Oxford: Oxford University Press.

Chung, H., Thewissen, S. (2011) 'Falling Back on Old Habits? A Comparison of the Social and Unemployment Crisis Reactive Policy Strategies in Germany, the UK and Sweden', *Social Policy & Administration* 45(4): 354–70.

Deacon, B. (2007) *Global Social Policy and Governance*, London: Sage.

Emmenegger, P., Häusermann, S., Palier, B., and Seeleib-Kaiser, M. (eds.) (2012) *The Age of Dualization: The Changing Face of Inequality in Deindustrializing Societies*, Oxford: Oxford University Press.

Esping-Andersen, G. (1990) *The Three Worlds of Welfare Capitalism*, Princeton, NJ: Princeton University Press.

Esping-Andersen, G. (1999) *Social Foundations of Post-Industrial Economies*, Oxford: Oxford University Press.

Esping-Andersen, G. (2009) *The Incomplete Revolution*, Cambridge: Polity Press.

Eurobarometer (2016) *Standard Eurobarometer 85*, Spring 2016, https://data.europa.eu/euodp/en/data/dataset/S2130_85_2_STD85_ENG, accessed 30 Jan. 2017.

European Commission (2015) *The 2015 Ageing Report (2013-60)*, Brussels: European Commission, http://ec.europa.eu/economy_finance/publications/european_economy/2015/pdf/ee3_en.pdf, accessed 30 Jan. 2017.

Freeman, G. P. (2009) 'Immigration, Diversity, and Welfare Chauvinism', *The Forum* 7(3), article 7, 1–16.

Giles, C. (2016) 'Brexit in Seven Charts—the Economic Impact', *Financial Times*, http://www.ft.com/cms/s/2/0260242c-370b-11e6-9a05-82a9b15a8ee7.html#axzz4GkVCMY8k, accessed 8 Aug. 2016.

Gingrich, J. and Häusermann, S. (2015) 'The Decline of the Working-Class Vote, the Reconfiguration of the Welfare Support Coalition and Consequences for the Welfare State', *Journal of European Social Policy* 25(1): 50–75.

Goodin, R. E. and Le Grand, J. (1987) *Not Only the Poor*, London: Allen & Unwin.

Gough, I. (2011) 'From Financial Crisis to Fiscal Crisis', in K. Farnsworth and Z. Irving (eds.), *Social Policy in Challenging Times*, Bristol: Policy Press, 49–64.

Habermas, J. (2012) *The Crisis of the European Union: A Response*, Cambridge: Polity Press.

Hacker, J. (2011) 'The Institutional Foundations of Middle-Class Democracy', *Policy Network*, http://www.policy-network.net/content.aspx?CategoryID=354&ArticleID=3491&fp=1, accessed 12 Aug. 2016.

Hall, P. A. and Soskice, D. (eds.) (2001) *Varieties of Capitalism*, Oxford: Oxford University Press.

International Monetary Fund (2015) *World Economic Outlook*, Washington, DC: International Monetary Fund.

Jensen, M. and Snaith, H. (2016) 'When Politics Prevails: The Political Economy of a Brexit', *Journal of European Public Policy*. doi: 10.1080/13501763.2016.1174531, accessed 8 Aug. 2016.

Korpi, W. (1983) *The Democratic Class Struggle*, London: Routledge and Kegan Paul.

Kuhnle, S. (ed.) (2000) *Survival of the European Welfare State*, London/New York: Routledge.

Lagarde, C. (2015) *Press Conference Statement*, 17 April 2015, http://www.theguardian.com/politics/2015/apr/17/imf-chief-praises-british-governments-handling-of-economy, accessed 12 Aug. 2016.

Lijphart, A. (1999) *Patterns of Democracy*, New Haven, CT: Yale University Press.

Lipset, S. M. and Rokkan, S. (eds.) (1967) *Party Systems and Voter Alignments*, New York: Free Press.

McLaren, L. M. and Johnson, M. (2004) 'Understanding the Rising Tide of Anti-Immigrant Sentiment', in A. Park, J. Curtice, K. Thomson, C. Bromley, and M. Phillips (eds.), *British Social Attitudes*, 21st Report, London: Sage Publications, 169–200.

Mau, S. (2015) *Inequality, Marketization and the Majority Class*, Basingstoke: Palgrave Macmillan.

Mau, S. and Sachweh, P. (2014) 'The Middle-Class in the German Welfare State', *Social Policy & Administration* 48(5): 537–55.

Mewes, J. and Mau, S. (2012) 'Unravelling Working-Class Welfare Chauvinism', in S. Svallfors (ed.) *Contested Welfare States*, Stanford, CA: Stanford University Press.

OECD (2015) *In It Together: Why Less Inequality Benefits All*, Paris: OECD, http://www.oecd.org/social/in-it-together-why-less-inequality-benefits-all-9789264235120-en.htm, accessed 30 Jan. 2017.

O'Rourke, K. H. and Sinnott, R. (2006) 'The Determinants of Individual Attitudes towards Immigration', *European Journal of Political Economy* 22(4): 838–61.

Palier, B. (ed.) (2010) *A Long Goodbye to Bismarck?*, Amsterdam: Free Press.

Palier, B. and Thelen, K. (2010) 'Institutionalizing Dualism', *Politics & Society* 38(1): 119–48.

Pierson, P. (ed.) (2001) *The New Politics of the Welfare State*, Oxford: Oxford University Press.

Pierson, P. (1994) *Dismantling the Welfare State? Reagan, Thatcher, and the Politics of Retrenchment*, Cambridge: Cambridge University Press.

Piketty, T. (2014) *Capital in the 21st Century*, Cambridge, MA: Harvard University Press.

Rodrik, D. (1998) 'Globalisation, Social Conflict and Economic Growth', *The World Economy* 21(2): 143–58.

Sainsbury, D. (2012) *Welfare States and Immigrant Rights*, Oxford: Oxford University Press.

Schmidt, V. (2002) 'Does Discourse Matter in the Politics of Welfare State Adjustment?', *Comparative Political Studies* 35(2): 168–93.

Schwartz, H. (2001) 'Round Up the Usual Suspects!', in P. Pierson (ed.) (2001) *The New Politics of the Welfare State*, Oxford: Oxford University Press, 17–44.

Starke, P., Kaasch, A., and van Hooren, F. (2013) *The Welfare State as Crisis Manager: Explaining the Diversity of Policy Responses to Economic Crisis*, Basingstoke: Palgrave Macmillan.

Stiglitz, J. (2016) *The Euro*, Harmondsworth: Penguin Books.

Streeck, W. and Thelen, K. (eds.) (2005) *Beyond Continuity*, Oxford: Oxford University Press.

Svallfors, S. (2007) *The Political Sociology of the Welfare State*, Stanford, CA: Stanford University Press.

Swank, D. (2010) 'Globalisation', in F. Castles et al. *The Oxford Handbook of the Welfare State*, Oxford: Oxford University Press.

Taylor-Gooby, P. (2004) *New Risks, New Welfare*, Oxford: Oxford University Press.

Touchstone (2016) *UK Real Wages Decline of over 10% Is the Most Severe in the OECD (Equal to Greece)*, London: Touchstone, http://touchstoneblog.org.uk/2016/07/uk-real-wages-decline-10-severe-oecd-equal-greece/, accessed 12 Aug. 2016.

Van Kersbergen, K., Vis, B., and Hemerijck, A. (2014) 'The Great Recession and Welfare State Reform', *Social Policy & Administration* 48(7): 883–904.

2

Stretching the Limits of Solidarity

The German Case

Jan-Ocko Heuer and Steffen Mau

2.1 Introduction

Germany is the largest national economy in Europe—and the fourth-largest worldwide—and has considerable influence on the economic and political development of the European Union and the Eurozone. Germany has also shaped European policy responses to the latest crises. In the financial, economic, and sovereign debt crisis that hit Europe after 2007 (the Great Recession) it pressed for austerity measures in EU member states in exchange for bailout funds from the EU and other international organizations to counter budget deficits and rising sovereign debts. In the more recent European immigration and refugee crisis Germany has advocated an 'open arms' policy and accepted more than one million refugees and immigrants in 2015 alone (The Wall Street Journal 2015; Bundesamt für Migration und Flüchtlinge 2016). Both policies have received much domestic and international criticism and created new cleavages at national, EU, and international levels. In the light of Germany's economic model and political culture, the responses of the German government seem reasonable, but given wide cross-national differences in economic strength and institutions, it has been questioned if 'making Europe more German' is a suitable policy response for other nations.

The German case features a heavily export-driven economic model, with Germany being the leading export nation in Europe and the largest net exporter globally. The main export products—motor vehicles, machinery, electronic equipment, and chemicals—stem from a substantial manufacturing sector whose production is characterized by differentiation, incremental innovations, and a highly skilled and specialized labour force. The export-oriented high-skills economy was grounded in neo-corporatist capital/labour arrangements with a high degree of involvement of trade unions and work councils in economic decision-making in exchange for wage restraint by the labour force and its representatives. Germany has also been viewed as prototypical example of a 'coordinated market economy', characterized by dense and long-term networks among firms and social partners, collaborative education and training schemes, and high levels of employment protection (Hall and Soskice 2001). This consensual style of economic governance has been mirrored in the political system, as Germany is usually seen as a 'consensus democracy' (Lijphart 1999) with consensus-promoting political institutions, a stable system of political parties, and stable federal governments led by either the centre-right Christian Democrats (CDU/CSU) or the centre-left Social Democrats (SPD). More recently, as we will show, this political economy has partly eroded and given way to new economic and political institutions, actors, and ideas (e.g. Streeck 2009).

This economic and political system provides the background for the prime example of a 'conservative' welfare state, with status-preserving social policies institutionalized in compulsory social insurance schemes and promoting a 'male breadwinner/female homemaker' family model (Esping-Andersen 1990; Lewis 1992). However, Germany, like other conservative welfare states, seemed initially ill-equipped to respond to the economic and social challenges of increasing globalization, technological change, a growing service sector, population ageing, immigration, new family patterns and gender roles, growing social inequalities, and new social risks. In this chapter we will outline the transformations of the German welfare state since the 1980s by answering three questions. First, how did the German welfare state respond to these long-term economic and social challenges and which were the main directions of social policy? Second, did the more recent challenges of the 'Great Recession' and the immigration and refugee crisis alter the course of the German welfare state and, if so, in which policy directions? And third, what do these long-term and short-term developments imply for the future of social policy in Germany, and which new issues and cleavages might emerge and shape the future trajectory of the German welfare state?

In answering these questions we will put forward three arguments. First, after a prolonged period of institutional inertia, the German welfare state has undergone profound reforms in many policy areas since the early 2000s. These reforms have fundamentally reoriented the normative and institutional structure of German social policy in three main directions: towards welfare cuts and budget austerity; towards more individual responsibility for social security; and towards a 'social investment' paradigm (see section 2.2). Second, due to the timing of welfare state reforms—with structural changes being made shortly before the Great Recession—the recent crises have not been seen as structural challenges in Germany but merely as a shortfall in demand

and a fiscal problem; thus, except for a short period of neo-Keynesian responses to the Great Recession to counter declining exports, the course of German social policy did not change much during the latest crises (section 2.3). And third, while these social policy reforms in the directions of austerity, individual responsibility, and social investment have mitigated some of the structural problems of the German welfare state and have mostly received approval from the German population, they have also intensified existing structural problems that linger below the surface of a well-performing economy and created new ones. In this respect we expect that four challenges will shape the future of the German welfare regime: 1) growing inequalities of income and wealth; 2) continuing dualization of the labour market with divisions between insiders and outsiders and securely and precariously employed workers; 3) the turn of the middle class towards individual instead of collective responses to growing instabilities and inequalities; and 4) the rise of welfare chauvinism fuelled by growing immigration and resulting in divisions between parts of the established and the incoming population (section 2.4). We conclude with a short summary and outlook (section 2.5).

2.2 Challenges for the Conservative German Welfare State and New Directions in Social Policy

The German welfare state has traditionally been seen as the archetype of a conservative welfare state, deeply rooted in authoritarian and paternalist strategies of modernization and bearing the legacy of compulsory organization of artisans and craftsmen in guilds, thereby emphasizing occupational differentiation and status privileges (Esping-Andersen 1990). Since its formation, from the 1880s to the 1920s, the core of the German welfare state has consisted of major social insurance schemes built around labour market positions and providing wage replacement for the typical risks of wage labour: sickness, invalidity, old age, and unemployment; this was supplemented by tax-financed and means-tested social assistance benefits for those without sufficient entitlements to social insurance. Membership in social insurance schemes was compulsory for most employees, and—with the exception of sickness insurance—benefit levels were related to prior contributions, which, in turn, were related to income levels; thus, status differences in the labour market were reflected in the social security system and ensured individual status maintenance in times of unemployment (Stolleis 2013).

This status-preserving social insurance model had two important effects on societal arrangements of production and reproduction: first, the social security system was directly linked to the labour market and implicitly based on a 'standard employment relationship' (Mückenberger 1985) of stable and continuous full-time employment enshrined in strict labour market regulations and far-reaching collective agreements and ensuring a 'family wage' sufficient to pay for the needs of a nuclear family (Hinrichs 2010: 47–8); second, this arrangement—complemented by corresponding education, care, family, and tax policies—encouraged a division of work within the family between a 'male breadwinner' earning income and rights to social security benefits on the labour market, and a 'female homemaker' responsible for domestic work, care and child-rearing, and dependent on the partner's income and social security entitlements (Lewis 1992).

However, the long-term economic and social changes since the 1970s proved to be a massive challenge for conservative welfare states in general and the German one in particular. The encouragement of a 'female homemaker' family model resulted in low (and mainly atypical) female employment and left the financing of the core welfare institutions to the male half of the population. This model was not only challenged by new family patterns and gender roles, but also by rising numbers of single-woman households and single mothers lacking social security entitlements and therefore at high risk of poverty (Bundesministerium für Arbeit und Soziales 2013: 461–2). Also, population ageing shifted the ratio between contributors and beneficiaries in social insurance schemes towards the latter, resulting in an increasing imbalance between revenues and expenses. A particular challenge for the German welfare state was the collapse of the German Democratic Republic (GDR) in 1989 and the unification of West and East Germany in 1990. In the former GDR the economy crashed and about one third of jobs disappeared, while the eastward expansion of the West German welfare system meant that 16 million people received welfare entitlements based on fictitious contribution histories from their employment careers, which required large financial transfers from West Germany. Moreover, while unemployment exploded in East Germany, it had been on the rise in West Germany since the mid-1970s as well. After the end of a short-lived economic boom and in the light of increasing globalization, higher social insurance contributions were seen as a threat to the international competitiveness of the export-oriented German economy, and employers complained about the level of non-wage labour costs and inflexibilities in the labour market. Thus, in the late 1990s, Germany was generally considered 'the sick man . . . of Europe' (The Economist 1999).

Yet, after a long period of institutional inertia, the German welfare state was fundamentally reformed. The reform trajectory can be divided into several phases, with the critical juncture being the early 2000s. Before this period, reforms were minor and in line with traditional social policy paradigms. Since the late 1970s the main response to cost increases in healthcare, unemployment, and pension schemes had been raises in contribution rates. Even though in 1982 the incoming Christian–Liberal coalition government under

Helmut Kohl (CDU) had announced a 'mental and moral turn' including welfare reforms, the 1980s were dominated by continuity in welfare policies with selective but modest cost-saving measures. The collapse of the GDR in 1989 was seen as confirmation of the West German 'social market economy' (*Soziale Marktwirtschaft*), and thus the West German welfare regime was extended to the East. Massive unemployment in East Germany was countered by public job creation schemes and an extension of early retirement, while the ensuing costs were counterbalanced by further increases in social insurance contributions and the introduction of a 'solidarity surcharge' (*Solidaritätszuschlag*) on income tax and other taxes.

In the mid-1990s the direction of welfare policies began to change. This was not yet a departure from the core norms and institutions of a conservative welfare state regime, but the basic orientation of social policy reforms shifted towards cost-cutting, benefit reductions, contribution rate stability, privatization, and marketization. A telling example is the establishment of long-term care insurance in 1995 as a new fifth pillar of the social insurance system: while this seems to signify an affirmation and reinforcement of the traditional German social insurance model, this new insurance scheme did not follow the model of 'full' insurance but provided only partial coverage against the risk of care dependency and was supposed to encourage additional private provision. Beyond that, an ideational split and deadlock in the political system emerged during this period: previously both Christian Democrats and Social Democrats had been committed to preserving the basic principles of the German welfare state, but now the governing Christian Democrats (CDU/CSU) and the liberal Free Democratic Party (FDP) supported employers' demands for far-reaching reforms, including benefit cuts, more flexible labour market arrangements, and lower non-wage costs for employers. By contrast, the Social Democrats (SPD) and the Green Party (*Bündnis 90/Die Grünen*) opposed most reform proposals and used their veto powers to block some of them. In hindsight, this period has been called a 'transitional period' (Hinrichs 2010: 46) or 'latency period' (Nullmeier 2014: 185) for the following reforms.[1]

The most important period of social policy change in Germany was the early 2000s when the most fundamental restructuring of the welfare regime since the end of World War II took place. The foundation had been laid in 1998, when a new federal government formed by the SPD and the Green Party (the first Red–Green alliance on the federal level) under the Social Democrat Gerhard Schröder superseded the sixteen-year chancellorship of Helmut Kohl and pledged—partly inspired by 'New Labour' in the UK (see Chapter 3)—to create a sustainable welfare state and to tackle mass unemployment by increasing the productivity and competitiveness of the German economy.[2] In the following years the Red–Green government implemented major reforms in all areas of social policy. In *old-age pensions*, an ongoing trend towards cost-cutting, benefit reductions, and private provision was intensified by means of a considerable decrease in the level of public pensions, the creation of a voluntary but state-subsidized private pension scheme ('*Riester-Rente*'), and the introduction of a needs-based basic pension for those without sufficient entitlements; this trend was fortified in 2007 by a gradual increase in the regular retirement age from age 65 in the year 2012 to age 67 in 2029 (Hinrichs 2005; Bonin 2009). In *healthcare*, the creation of quasi-markets, reductions in services covered by the social insurance system, co-payments for additional services, and allowances for prevention measures established different levels of healthcare services for different groups of the population and aimed at 'activation' and 'responsibilisation' of healthcare recipients (Ullrich et al. 2012).

The most controversial reforms were made in the area of *labour market policies* with the so-called 'Hartz-reforms' (Seeleib-Kaiser and Fleckenstein 2007: 431–5).[3] These reforms were implemented in several steps between 2003 and 2005 and included a restructuring of labour market services, funding for further vocational training, and the facilitation of new types of employment. The promotion of these types of non-standard, unsecured and often low-paid employment has been argued to strengthen precarization and labour market dualization (Eichhorst and Marx 2011). Especially contested was the last reform (Hartz IV) in 2005, which merged long-term unemployment benefits and social assistance benefits into a new benefit at the level of social assistance benefits and thus meant that even individuals with long insurance contribution histories would end up at the social assistance level after twelve months of unemployment (or, following a reform in 2008, after up to 24 months for persons aged 50 and over). If they refused a job offer, such people would receive a further 30 per cent benefit cut. The recipient's savings and spouse's salary are taken into account in benefit calculations. Moreover, 'one-euro-jobs' were created, meaning a combination of job creation scheme and community work in which the state employs people for one euro an hour with the aim of improving their chances on the regular labour market.

While these reforms were mostly backed by the CDU/CSU and the FDP, they received strong criticism from trade unions and left-leaning Social Democrats and led to the establishment of a new left-wing party—called 'Labour and Social Justice: The Electoral Alternative' (*Arbeit und Soziale Gerechtigkeit: Die Wahlalternative*)—which merged in 2007 with the Party of Democratic Socialism (*Partei des demokratischen Sozialismus*; the successor to the governing party of the GDR) to form a new party called 'The Left' (*Die Linke*). This was another step in a growing dissolution of the traditional political party system, even though the electoral base of *Die Linke* remains primarily in East Germany.

Not least due to strong opposition to the welfare reforms, the Red–Green alliance could not defend its parliamentary majority in the federal election of 2005, and a 'Grand Coalition' government between the CDU/CSU and SPD under Christian Democrat Angela Merkel was formed. In the following years the reform fervour abated. Policy-making concerned itself with amendments and minor revisions, and the German welfare state returned to previous levels of reform activity (Nullmeier 2014: 191). The most important changes were in family policy, as the Grand Coalition expanded its predecessor's initiatives and introduced a relatively generous tax-financed parental leave scheme. This replaced 67 per cent of income for up to 14 months (*Elterngeld*), including two months earmarked for the partner and thus supposed to encourage shared parental responsibilities between mothers and fathers. The state also invested in public childcare facilities and improved tax deductions for child costs. In combination with the reorientation of labour market policies, this represented a shift from the conservative 'female homemaker' family model towards universal labour market participation and an accompanying 'adult worker' or 'dual breadwinner' model (Lewis et al. 2008; Boling 2015).[4]

Following the establishment of a Grand Coalition, the political system also returned to its consensual style, even though occasional quarrels about social policy occurred. For example, to placate the conservative clientele of the CDU's sister party—the Bavarian CSU—and against opposition even from within the governing coalition parties, the Grand Coalition introduced a childcare subsidy for home-based care by parents in 2012. However, in 2015 this *Betreuungsgeld* was declared unconstitutional by the German Federal Constitutional Court on the grounds that the federal government lacked the legislative powers; thus, this subsidy is being discontinued. Also against resistance from the coalition partners, the SPD pushed through a full pension at age 63 for those with a contribution history of 45 years in 2014, and in 2015 the introduction of a minimum wage (8.50 euros per hour; adapted in 2017 to 8.84 euros) in response to the considerable rise of temporary, unsecured, and low-paid forms of employment.

This variety of reforms in the German welfare state since the 1980s covers a few basic directions of policy change, although reforms over several decades and in various social policy fields obviously do not always follow clear and unified paradigms and can be overlapping and contradictory.[5] The first and arguably most persistent change in German social policy has been a shift towards benefit cuts and budget austerity. This reorientation of social policy began in the 1980s and was intensified in the mid-1990s, but its most obvious outcome was the redirection of unemployment and pension schemes in the 2000s from their traditional aim of status maintenance towards basic protection for pensioners and the long-term unemployed. These reorientations are particularly noteworthy, as they do not only represent a reduction in benefits but a departure from the core principle of status preservation in the conservative German regime. Yet, even in fields where no paradigmatic change occurred—such as in healthcare—the general tendency since the 1990s has been towards cost-cutting and benefit reductions.

A second major change in social policy has been a shift towards increased individual responsibility for social security. This has become especially manifest in the area of old-age provision—with the shift from a one-pillar (public) pension system to a multi-pillar system requiring private provision to ensure an adequate pension level—and in labour market policies with the shift towards an 'activation' paradigm based on the assumption that there are sufficient job opportunities for unemployed persons and that the state has to 'nudge' people to take more individual responsibility for finding work. The various Hartz reforms promoted a new balance between rights and obligations, made the receipt of benefits conditional upon individual efforts and cooperation, and cut the link between benefits and prior contributions for the long-term unemployed. Finally, in healthcare this development is signified by allowances for prevention measures and the introduction of individual health services whose costs must be borne by the patients themselves.

The third—and most recent—major change in German social policy is the growing importance of a 'social investment' paradigm based on the idea that it is better to invest in human capital, skills, and lifetime learning in order to foster employability and employment than to pay for unemployment and passive transfers (Morel et al. 2012). This development includes 'activation' measures in labour market policy as well as the reorientation of family policy towards publically funded childcare and education programmes intended to help integrate women into the labour market by improving opportunities for combining labour and domestic work and to improve education and qualification levels of children, not least of those from lower-class families. The adoption of a 'social investment' paradigm required the adjustment of two core values of the German welfare state—the preservation of the previous labour market status in social security, and the 'female homemaker' family model (van Kersbergen and Hemerijck 2012: 487)—and thus it has been argued that conservative welfare states such as Germany 'probably have undergone the most dramatic and path-breaking reforms in their adoption of the social investment paradigm' (van Kersbergen and Hemerijck 2012: 485).

Put more generally, we find benefit cuts and paradigmatic change in traditional areas of social policy, although some expansionary measures buck this general trend. By contrast, in other areas—such as education, family policy, and activating labour market policies—spending has increased, often justified as 'social investment' policy. This also explains how the aggregate level of total social spending in relation to GDP has remained rather constant in Germany since the 1990s.[6]

2.3 Social Policy Responses to the Great Recession between Old Habits and New Directions

The financial and economic crises that hit Europe in 2008 developed into the deepest recession since the 1930s. The trajectory of the German economy during the Great Recession was unusual compared with other European economies: initially it slipped deeper into recession than other economies, with a decline in GDP by 5.6 per cent in 2009 and below the EU28 average of minus 4.4 per cent (OECD 2016a). It also recovered more quickly and returned to growth already in early 2010. Moreover, the unemployment rate remained relatively unaffected by the recession and rose only from 7.4 per cent in 2008 to 7.6 per cent in 2009 and declined afterwards (OECD 2016b). This led economists to praise 'Germany's jobs miracle' (Krugman 2009), although one has to bear in mind that the employment rate had been relatively high before the crisis and that since the mid-2000s the jobs created have partly been precarious.

The limited impact of the Great Recession on the labour market and the speedy economic recovery have been ascribed to three main causes. First, the German government responded quickly to the crisis in the financial sector by adopting several 'express laws' with the aim of supporting troubled financial institutions and maintaining confidence in the financial sector to prevent a 'credit crunch'.[7] Second, the 'automatic stabilizers' of developed economies that dampen fluctuations in GDP, such as income taxes and welfare spending, played a particular role in Germany, as the economy not only benefited from its own stabilizing mechanisms but, as a major exporter, also imported the effects of automatic stabilizers in other economies (Streeck 2010; Dolls et al. 2012). More generally, membership in the Eurozone and the resulting fixed exchange rate allowed the German economy to benefit from its strong competitive position within the Eurozone. And third, in contrast to earlier crises, the German government deliberately and actively used demand management, social policy, and labour market measures to counter the effects of the recession (e.g. Chung and Thewissen 2011; Vis et al. 2011; van Kersbergen et al. 2014).

The most important social policy measure to dampen the effects of the recession on the labour market was the extension and financial modification of a short-term work scheme (*Kurzarbeitergeld*). This measure allowed companies to respond to declining demand by reducing the working time of their employees instead of laying them off, and the employees received 60–67 per cent of the difference between their net pay and their reduced pay from the public purse. During the crisis the funding of this measure was shifted from social security contributions to general taxes, and its maximum duration was extended from six months to 18 and later to 24 months. It is estimated that about 1.5 million employees—or 5.1 per cent of the labour force—were temporarily on this short-term work scheme during the recession (Starke 2015: 22–4). The massive use of this measure can be explained by the core characteristics of the German economy, as it was mainly used to protect the core industrial workforce in the export-oriented sectors and thus served to maintain the firm- or sectoral-specific skill profiles of qualified workers for their companies (Chung and Thewissen 2011: 364). This shows that despite its partial departure from status-preserving social policies, the German welfare state 'fell back on old habits' during the crisis and displayed its conservative legacy by focusing on protection and status maintenance of labour market insiders (Chung and Thewissen 2011: 366).

The German government also used several other social policy measures to counter the effects of the recession on the labour market and to stimulate consumer spending and economic growth, including a temporary cut in unemployment insurance contributions, increases in child benefits, tax allowances for children, improved tax deductibility of healthcare and nursing care contributions, and lower health insurance contributions (for overviews see Vis et al. 2011: 346–7; Starke 2015: 18). It has been noted that 'the main part of the German package affected the revenue side, i.e., the German package included a large element of tax cuts' (Zohlnhöfer 2011: 234), which is noteworthy not only because the OECD estimates that the multiplier effects of tax cuts are only around half as large as the multiplier effects of increased expenditures but also because tax cuts are potentially permanent and thus decrease the future scope of action for the welfare state (Zohlnhöfer 2011: 234).

Most of these measures were part of four fiscal stimulus packages adopted between October 2008 and May 2009 with an overall financial volume of 90 billion euros that included public investments and increases in public expenditures. The largest package was adopted in January 2009 and amounted to 50 billion euros and thus 2.1 per cent of GDP (Armingeon 2012: 550–1). It included a 'wrecking premium'—a government subsidy of 2,500 euros if consumers bought a new car while scrapping their old one older than nine years of age—resulting in 1.7 million applications and thus reaching its goal of increasing private consumption during the crisis (Zohlnhöfer 2011: 235).

Due to this demand management by means of fiscal stimulus packages, Germany has been viewed as 'a special case because . . . a Keynesian type of response seems to have been most systematically formulated' (Vis et al. 2011: 347). It has also been noted that 'this was the first time in more than 25 years that a German federal government adopted counter-cyclical packages at all' (Zohlnhöfer 2011: 233). However, two qualifications are necessary: first, the financial size of these packages should not be overestimated, and some have called them 'notable, but by no means extraordinary' (Zohlnhöfer 2011: 233) or even 'largely symbolic' (Armingeon 2012: 559). And second, it is important to note that 'the main actors saw the fiscal packages as a necessity in times of a dramatic recession, but they also made clear that they wanted to return to a policy of budget consolidation as soon as the crisis was over' (Zohlnhöfer 2011: 234). In other words, neo-Keynesian demand management was conceived from the outset as a purely temporary measure to counter the immediate effects of the Great Recession on the export-led Germany economy.

More generally, in Germany the Great Recession was not seen as a structural challenge, but merely as a demand shock and a fiscal problem (Clasen et al. 2012: 16–17). This was not least due to the timing of social policy reforms, which in hindsight turned out to be advantageous, because 'the main reforms of the German welfare system were implemented right *before* the crisis and partly explain the comparatively successful developments of the economy and labour market' (Blum and Kuhlmann 2016: 134).

Therefore, after neo-Keynesian demand management and the temporary social policy measures had expired in 2010, the German welfare state returned to its overall social policy course of austerity and benefit cuts in some areas, increasing 'self-responsibilisation' via marketization and privatization, and expenditure shifts towards social investment policies (see 2.2). In fact, in 2010 the Christian–Liberal government that had come into office in 2009 announced the most extensive programme of spending cuts in post-war history for the years 2011–14, which included—aside from cuts in the public sector—social policy cuts including reductions in housing benefits, parental allowances, and subsidies for statutory health insurance; this was complemented in the same year by reductions in benefits for the long-term unemployed and high-earning parents (van Kersbergen et al. 2014: 898). However, even during this return to, or continuation of, budget austerity, the government also continued to pursue its social investment policies, which consisted of a higher ceiling for all child-related tax allowances, tax deductions for childcare, investments in education and research, higher student allowances and extra stipends, and a 'Skilled Workers Initiative' ('*Fachkräftekonzept*') with activation measures, plus measures to attract high-skilled workers from abroad (van Kersbergen et al. 2014: 898). This indicates that the turn towards social investment was intended to become permanent and was not abandoned in times of limited fiscal space for manoeuvre.

The financial future of social policy will presumably be shaped by two main developments. In 2009 the German constitution (*Grundgesetz*) was amended to include a balanced budget provision—a so-called 'debt brake' (*Schuldenbremse*)—which requires that from 2016 onwards the federal government may not run a structural deficit of more than 0.35 per cent of GDP, and from 2020 onwards the federal states (*Länder*) may not run any structural deficit at all. Second, the recent immigration and refugee crisis, which resulted in the admission of an estimated one million refugees and immigrants to Germany in 2015, will, at least initially, create considerable costs in social policy and integration measures and thus strain the budgetary limits. However, in March 2016 the Grand Coalition announced plans to keep the federal budget of 2017 within these limits, despite expenditures of ten billion euros to tackle the refugee crisis and—as demanded by the SPD as 'compensatory' measures for the 'domestic population'—increases in spending for social housing and labour market measures (Die Zeit 2016).

2.4 What Future for German Social Policy? Four Possible Challenges and Cleavages

Traditionally the moral economy of its core institutions had generated broad popular support for the German welfare state. The earnings-related social insurance system protected and reproduced 'the existing pecking order of society' (Goodin et al. 1999: 33) and is easy to legitimize, because it instils a sense of individually earned rights and is morally undemanding: 'no one needs to believe in lofty principles of solidarity, justice, or equality to become—and remain—a rational supporter of the system (...). Its modest goal is the guarantee of income—and of relative income status!—for employees and their dependants' (Offe 1992: 129). Due to the principle of status maintenance, cross-class redistribution was relatively low and the middle class was an important beneficiary of the system; therefore, middle-class persons—skilled workers, white-collar employees, and civil servants—were strong defenders of the core welfare institutions in Germany (Mau 2003; Mau and Sachweh 2014).

Given the fundamental departure from core norms and principles of the German welfare state, it might be expected that the population in Germany would reject the new policy directions, yet studies and survey data indicate that most, but not all, policy changes and their normative underpinnings are accepted (Nüchter et al. 2010). For example, there is very high acceptance of, and support for, female labour market participation and the shift towards a 'dual breadwinner' family model as well as for social investment policies in education and childcare.[8] The reorientation of pension and labour market policy towards increased individual responsibility is also accepted by large parts of the population. The greatest scepticism exists regarding welfare cuts and the shift from status preservation towards basic protection in unemployment and public pension schemes (e.g. Sachweh et al. 2009; Nüchter et al. 2010).

The acceptance of most social policy changes by the population and the strong economic performance of the German economy following the Great Recession do not mean, however, that the German welfare state has left all structural problems behind; in fact, some problems have not been tackled by recent reforms or have even been aggravated, and the reforms have created some new problems and pressures. In this respect, we expect that four challenges and cleavages will shape the future of the German welfare state regime.

One issue which has moved up the public agenda is the issue of growing inequality. In the 1990s and early 2000s Germany experienced marked increases in the unequal distribution of income and wealth (Grabka 2014; Fratzscher 2016). As in most OECD countries, the rift between top incomes and lower incomes widened, partly linked to the growing wage inequality between high- and low-skill occupations. The changes in the labour market, particularly the expansion of a low-income sector and the emergence of a new 'service proletariat' (Bahl and Staab 2010), the restructuring of the welfare state (in its lowering of unemployment protection), and the adjustments to the tax system, particularly the lowering of the top income tax, the introduction of a flat-rate capital income tax, and relatively low taxes on inheritances and gifts, paved the way to a more unequal distribution of earnings and assets (OECD 2015). Although this trend was accompanied by some public criticism, it did not trigger a political backlash towards more government redistribution. Attitudes towards inequality remained relatively stable despite growing inequality (Kenworthy and McCall 2008). Although 82 per cent of the population claim that inequality is too high (Mau and Heuer 2016: 4), there is less support for a stronger welfare system or more redistribution. Roughly one fifth of the German population seems to accept higher levels of inequality, and a considerably larger share seems sceptical that the state can or should actively decrease inequalities (Sachweh et al. 2009: 613; Mau and Heuer 2016: 6). Alongside all inequality critique, there is an implicit 'consent to inequality' (Rosanvallon 2013), making political actors rather unwilling to push this theme more emphatically. The topic is often couched less in redistributive terms than in the language of life chances, social mobility, education, and social investment.

A second critical feature of the German welfare state is the divide between well-protected insiders and precarious outsiders (Palier and Thelen 2010; Emmenegger et al. 2012). This feature had already been highlighted by Esping-Andersen (1996) when characterizing the continental welfare regime. However, while in the past the insider–outsider division was highly dependent upon labour market participation, with the number of working poor being negligible (Goodin et al. 1999), this has changed. Since the Hartz reforms in the mid-2000s, the unemployment rate has decreased and labour market participation has increased, but the labour market has become more heterogeneous or even divided. Labour market flexibilization, the creation of a low-income sector, a stronger emphasis on in-work benefits, and the growth of the service sector have all led to a larger segment of low-wage and low-protection employment.

Germany saw a growing group of non-standard workers—fixed-term contracts, part-time work, marginal employment (institutionalized via 'mini jobs'), contract work and flexible low-pay jobs—but only partly at the expense of standard employment (Eichhorst and Marx 2011). As far as opportunities for people in atypical employment for a mid-term transition into regular employment are concerned, recent evidence suggests that certain segments are trapped into non-standard employment (Brülle 2013; Böhnke et al. 2015). Thus, there are signs of a dualization of the labour market between a core labour force in 'standard employment' with high employment protection and a rising share of people in atypical, low-paid, and less protected employment. In fact, the German production and welfare regime with its focus on high-skilled labour and status maintenance in social security has arguably fostered this tendency towards dualization.

The combination of labour market restructuring, welfare state calibration, and growing inequality has also influenced the social structure and self-perceptions of German society. The notion of a 'middle-class society' with high levels of social protection, compressed inequality, and a permeable social structure allowing lower class people to join the ranks of the middle class through education and work has been eroded with the experience of new insecurities, a shrinking middle class, a weakening of upward mobility, and a stagnation of incomes of the lower 40 per cent (Mau 2012; Fratzscher 2016). While it would be an exaggeration to talk about a decline of the middle class, the lower middle class in particular faces new social risks and has difficulties in making ends meet (Burkhardt et al. 2013; Schimank et al. 2014). Status fear has become more widespread—including fears of deprivation and concerns about long-term security, and the costs of housing and education (Schöneck-Voß et al. 2011; Burkhardt et al. 2013)—as well as efforts and investments to maintain status. We also see that particularly the middle classes have embraced increased individual responsibility and social investment policies, and one can even say that the middle classes were partly receptive to the neo-liberal agenda: while the state transfer programmes, public education, and regulation protecting workers are still cornerstones of status protection of the better-off middle class, for certain fractions, particularly the upper middle class, asset accumulation, private education, and private provision have gained in importance (Mau 2015). Thus, there is a rift not only between the middle class and the lower classes but also within the middle class, linked to distinct ideas about what the welfare state should do.

A fourth important challenge for German social policy lies in dealing with immigration. While the inclusion of migrants and refugees into the welfare system was relatively uncontested for some time, this has changed. One starting point was the debate in 2013 about intra-European migrants coming from Bulgaria and Romania and claiming welfare benefits. Conservative political actors regarded 'entry' into the benefit system, particularly social assistance, as too liberal. They believed that welfare transfers could attract immigrants. Over time this debate has intensified, leading to fierce conflicts. In particular, the recent refugee crisis with an influx of over one million people in 2015 has triggered serious concerns about the degree of openness of society. While during the initial phase the so-called welcome culture was embraced by a large majority, with the ongoing and uncontrolled movement of refugees and asylum seekers the public mood has shifted towards more sceptical views. While a large majority of Germans remain committed to the right to asylum and the political responsibility to accept people in need, many people feel also they are paying too much (ARD DeutschlandTrend 2016). This has also brought about new opportunities for right-wing populist and xenophobic political movements to promote their political agenda. The regional elections in the aftermath of the refugee crises have boosted the right-wing party *Alternative für Deutschland* (AfD)—founded in 2013 as platform for opposition to the euro currency—and put enormous pressure on the German political system; for instance, in 2016 the AfD entered parliaments in several federal states with up to one quarter of the votes cast. Apart from outright anti-immigrant arguments, the party and related movements articulate resentment to the inclusion of refugees into the welfare system. Issues of affordability and costs as well as conflicts of resource allocation between natives and new-comers feature quite prominently together with the claim that Germany cannot and should not be the 'welfare agency of the world'. To some extent, the support for these political actors is fuelled by the status fear and welfare chauvinism of the lower classes and the lower middle classes, which were most affected by the restructuring of the labour market and the welfare system as well as by the increasing social inequality (Mau 2014; Hensel et al. 2016). Setting refugees and the native population against each other has triggered fundamental social cleavages related to questions of openness and closure, which are likely to reshape the landscape of German politics.

2.5 Conclusion

This chapter has outlined major social policy changes in Germany since the 1980s in the light of both long-term economic and social challenges as well as more recent developments such as the Great Recession and the immigration and refugee crisis. We have argued that the fundamental restructuring of the German welfare regime especially in the early 2000s, representing a departure from status-preserving social policies and from the 'female homemaker' family model, has mitigated some of the structural problems of the conservative German welfare state regime. Moreover, due to the timing of welfare reforms, the Great Recession had a limited impact on the German welfare state and thus—after a short period of neo-Keynesian demand management and social policy measures protecting labour market insiders—the overall directions of social policy did not change much in recent years. However, we have also argued that some of these social policy reforms have evaded existing problems or created new ones and that they might result in the emergence of new cleavages and polarizations.

Future redistributive and political conflicts seem especially likely over labour market issues, growing social inequalities, and immigration. The centrality of the labour market for social security remains a core characteristic of the German welfare state, but it has taken another form due to the promotion of female employment on the one hand, and the introduction of means-tested basic security benefits on the other. While before the reforms the social security system had mirrored the status order on the labour market, it now partly amplifies status differences and creates strong cleavages between labour market insiders and outsiders and securely versus precariously employed workers. How these cleavages will develop seems to depend not least on the international competitiveness of the German economy as well as on the integration of the new immigrants into the German economy and society.

Notes

1. While the political system experienced a deadlock, the industrial relations system turned out to be adaptable under competitive pressure: a considerable decentralization of wage-setting institutions combined with wage restraint by the trade unions increased Germany's economic competitiveness and has, according to some scholars, had more impact on economic performance before and during the Great Recession than the higher-profile labour market reforms (Dustmann et al. 2014).
2. The main reforms in 2003–5 were implemented under the heading 'Agenda 2010', which alluded to the 'Lisbon strategy' of the European Union and was supposed to promote economic growth and reduce unemployment by means of changes in labour market regulations, vocational training, education policies, healthcare policies, pension policies, labour market policies, and family policies.
3. The reforms are named after Peter Hartz, the chief human resources manager of Volkswagen and head of a commission established in 2002 to develop recommendations for labour market reforms.
4. This policy change is reflected in female employment rates, which rose in West Germany from 64.7 (in 1994–9) to 71.8 per cent between 1994–9 and 2005–9, and in East Germany—which already had high rates due to the legacy of the GDR—remained at the high level of 81.6 per cent in 2005–9 (Deutsches Institut für Wirtschaftsforschung n.d.). Female employment in Germany at 73.1 per cent considerably exceeded the EU28 average of 63.5 per cent in 2014 (Eurostat n.d.).

5. We focus on changes that are likely to affect future cleavages and solidarities in the German welfare state and thus largely ignore administrative and organizational changes that, for example, were aimed at creating a more managerial structure in public organizations and also affected the para-public social insurance schemes.

6. The lowest share was 25.0 per cent in the year 1992, and the highest 29.8 per cent in 2003. The share rose to 30.8 per cent in 2009, but this was partly due to the inclusion of basic private health insurance into the statistics; statistics before and after 2009 are not directly comparable. In 2014 total social spending was 849.2 billion euros and thus 29.2 per cent of GDP (Bundesministerium für Arbeit und Soziales 2015).

7. The most important support and bailout package for the financial sector in December 2008 had a total volume of up to 480 billion euros (about 20 per cent of GDP) and included liquidity guarantees of up to 400 billion euros, capital injections of up to 10 billion euros per financial institution, and purchases of toxic assets of up to 5 billion euros per bank (Zohlnhöfer 2011: 231–3).

8. Data from the German General Social Survey (ALLBUS) show that agreement to the statement 'it is much better for everyone concerned if the man goes out to work and the woman stays at home and looks after the house and children' fell from 70.3 to 27.3 per cent between 1982 and 2012 (West Germany only). Moreover, data from the International Social Survey Programme show that support for more government spending on education in Germany more than doubled between 1985 and 2006 and with 82.4 per cent in 2006 even surpassed support for increased spending on healthcare (65.7 per cent) or old-age pensions (51.5 per cent).

References

ARD DeutschlandTrend (2016) 'Skepsis in der Flüchtlingsfrage wächst', *ARD DeutschlandTrend*, 15 Jan. 2016, https://www.tagesschau.de/inland/deutschlandtrend-471.html, accessed 10 June 2016.

Armingeon, K. (2012) 'The Politics of Fiscal Responses to the Crisis of 2008–2009', *Governance* 25(4): 543–65.

Bahl, F. and Staab, P. (2010) 'Das Dienstleistungsproletariat: Theorie auf kaltem Entzug', *Mittelweg 36* 19(6): 66–93.

Blum, S. and Kuhlmann, J. (2016) 'Crisis? What Crisis? Restructuring the German Welfare System in Times of Unexpected Prosperity', in K. Schubert, P. de Villota, and J. Kuhlmann (eds.) *Challenges to European Welfare Systems*, Berlin: Springer, 133–58.

Böhnke, P., Zeh, J., and Link, S. (2015) 'Atypische Beschäftigung im Erwerbsverlauf: Verlaufstypen als Ausdruck sozialer Spaltung?', *Zeitschrift für Soziologie* 44(4): 234–52.

Boling, P. (2015) *The Politics of Work-Family Policies: Comparing Japan, France, Germany, and the United States*, Cambridge: Cambridge University Press.

Bonin, H. (2009) '15 Years of Pension Reform in Germany: Old Successes and New Threats', *Geneva Papers on Risk and Insurance Issues and Practice* 34(4): 548–60.

Brülle, J. (2013) 'Unterschiede in den Arbeitsmarktchancen von atypisch Beschäftigten: Effekte von Beschäftigungsformen oder Erwerbspräferenzen?', *Zeitschrift für Soziologie* 42(2): 157–79.

Bundesamt für Migration und Flüchtlinge (2016) '476.649 Asylanträge im Jahr 2015', 6 Jan. 2016, Nuremberg: Bundesamt für Migration und Flüchtlinge (BAMF), https://www.bamf.de/SharedDocs/Meldungen/DE/2016/201610106-asylgeschaeftsstatistik-dezember.html, accessed 10 June 2016.

Bundesministerium für Arbeit und Soziales (2013) *Lebenslagen in Deutschland: Der Vierte Armuts- und Reichtumsbericht der Bundesregierung*, Bonn: Bundesministerium für Arbeit und Soziales (BMAS), http://www.bmas.de/SharedDocs/Downloads/DE/PDF-Publikationen-DinA4/a334-4-armuts-reichtumsbericht-2013.pdf;jsessionid=2AA0E46A53AB37DDDA7CAD9451B101A7?__blob=publicationFile&v=2, accessed 10 June 2016.

Bundesministerium für Arbeit und Soziales (2015) *Sozialbudget 2014*, Bonn: Bundesministerium für Arbeit und Soziales (BMAS), http://www.bmas.de/SharedDocs/Downloads/DE/PDF-Publikationen/a230-14-sozialbudget-2014.pdf?__blob=publicationFile&v=2, accessed 10 June 2016.

Burkhardt, C., Grabka, M. M., Groh-Samberg, O., Lott, Y., and Mau, S. (2013) *Mittelschicht unter Druck?*, Gütersloh: Verlag Bertelsmann Stiftung.

Chung, H. and Thewissen, S. (2011) 'Falling Back on Old Habits? A Comparison of the Social and Unemployment Crisis Reactive Policy Strategies in Germany, the UK and Sweden', *Social Policy & Administration* 45(4): 354–70.

Clasen, J., Clegg, D., and Kvist, J. (2012) *European Labour Market Policies in (the) Crisis*, Working Paper 2012.12, Brussels: European Trade Union Institute (ETUI), http://www.etui.org/content/download/7692/73372/file/WP+2012.12+Web+version+BBA.pdf, accessed 10 June 2016.

Deutsches Institut für Wirtschaftsforschung (n.d.) *Durchschnittliche Frauenerwerbsquote in West- und Ostdeutschland von 1990 bis 1994 und von 2005 bis 2009*, Hamburg: Statista GmbH, http://de.statista.com/statistik/daten/studie/13541/umfrage/frauenerwerbsquote—entwicklung-der-erwerbstaetigkeit-von-frauen/, accessed 10 June 2016.

Die Zeit (2016) 'Bundeshaushalt 2017: Regierung hält an Haushalt ohne neue Schulden fest', *Die Zeit*, 23 Mar. 2016, http://www.zeit.de/politik/deutschland/2016-03/bundeshaushalt-2017-bundesregierung-wolfgang-schaeuble, accessed 10 June 2016.

Dolls, M., Fuest, C., and Peichl, A. (2012) 'Automatic Stabilizers and Economic Crisis: US vs. Europe', *Journal of Public Economics* 96(3–4): 279–94.

Dustmann, C., Fitzenberger, B., Schönberg, U., and Spitz-Oener, A. (2014) 'From Sick Man of Europe to Economic Superstar: Germany's Resurgent Economy', *Journal of Economic Perspectives* 28(1): 167–88.

Eichhorst, W. and Marx, P. (2011) 'Reforming German Labour Market Institutions: A Dual Path to Flexibility', *Journal of European Social Policy* 21(1): 73–87.

Emmenegger, P., Häusermann, S., Palier, B., and Seeleib-Kaiser, M. (eds.) (2012) *The Age of Dualization: The Changing Face of Inequality in Deindustrializing Societies*, Oxford: Oxford University Press.

Esping-Andersen, G. (1990) *The Three Worlds of Welfare Capitalism*, Princeton, NJ: Princeton University Press.

Esping-Andersen, G. (1996) 'Welfare States without Work: The Impasse of Labor Shedding and Familialism in Continental Europe', in Esping-Andersen (ed.) *Welfare States in Transition: National Adaptations in Global Economies*, London: SAGE Publications, 66–87.

Eurostat (n.d.) *Employment Rate by Sex, Age group 20–64—% [t2020_10]*, Luxembourg: Eurostat, http://ec.europa.eu/eurostat/tgm/refreshTableAction.do?tab=table&plugin=1&pcode=t2020_10&language=en, accessed 10 June 2016.

Fratzscher, M. (2016) *Verteilungskampf: Warum Deutschland immer ungleicher wird*, Munich: Carl Hanser Verlag.

Goodin, R. E., Headey, B., Muffels, R., and Dirven, H.-J. (1999) *The Real Worlds of Welfare Capitalism*, Cambridge: Cambridge University Press.

Grabka, M. M. (2014) 'Ungleichheit in Deutschland—Langfristige Trends, Wendepunkte', *Sozialer Fortschritt* 63(12): 301–7.

Hall, P. A. and Soskice, D. (2001) 'An Introduction to Varieties of Capitalism', in Hall and Soskice (eds.) *Varieties of Capitalism: The Institutional Foundations of Comparative Advantage*, Oxford: Oxford University Press, 1–68.

Hensel, A., Geiges, L., Pausch, R., and Förster, J. (2016) *Die AfD vor den Landtagswahlen 2016: Programme, Profile und Potenziale*, OSB-Arbeitspapier Nr. 20, Frankfurt am Main: Otto Brenner Stiftung (OSB), https://www.otto-brenner-shop.de/uploads/tx_mplightshop/AP20_AFD.pdf, accessed 10 June 2016.

Hinrichs, K. (2005) 'New Century—New Paradigm: Pension Reform in Germany', in G. Bonoli and T. Shinkawa (eds.) *Ageing and Pension Reform around the World: Evidence from Eleven Countries*, Cheltenham: Edward Elgar Publishing, 47–73.

Hinrichs, K. (2010) 'A Social Insurance State Withers Away: Welfare State Reforms in Germany—or: Attempts to Turn Around in a Cul-De-Sac', in B. Palier (ed.) *A Long Goodbye to Bismarck? The Politics of Welfare Reforms in Continental Europe*, Amsterdam: Amsterdam University Press, 45–72.

Kenworthy, L. and McCall, L. (2008) 'Inequality, Public Opinion and Redistribution', *Socio-Economic Review* 6(1): 35–68.

Krugman, P. R. (2009) 'Free to Lose', *New York Times*, 12 Nov. 2009, http://www.nytimes.com/2009/11/13/opinion/13krugman.html, accessed 10 June 2016.

Lewis, J. (1992) 'Gender and the Development of Welfare Regimes', *Journal of European Social Policy* 2(3): 159–73.

Lewis, J., Knijn, T., Martin, C., and Ostner, I. (2008) 'Patterns of Development in Work/Family Reconciliation Policies for Parents in France, Germany, the Netherlands, and the UK in the 2000s', *Social Politics* 15(3): 261–86.

Lijphart, A. (1999) *Patterns of Democracy: Government Forms and Performance in Thirty-Six Countries*, New Haven, CT: Yale University Press.

Mau, S. (2003) *The Moral Economy of Welfare States: Britain and Germany Compared*, London: Routledge.

Mau, S. (2012) *Lebenschancen: Wohin driftet die Mittelschicht?*, Berlin: Suhrkamp Verlag.

Mau, S. (2014) 'Die tiefe Sehnsucht nach dem nationalen Schutzraum', *Berliner Republik* 2014(2): 29–31.

Mau, S. (2015) *Inequality, Marketization and the Majority Class: Why Did the European Middle Classes Accept Neo-Liberalism?*, Basingstoke: Palgrave Macmillan.

Mau, S. and Heuer, J.-O. (2016) *Wachsende Ungleichheit als Gefahr für nachhaltiges Wachstum: Wie die Bevölkerung über soziale Unterschiede denkt*, Bonn: Friedrich-Ebert-Stiftung (FES).

Mau, S. and Sachweh, P. (2014) 'The Middle-Class in the German Welfare State: Beneficial Involvement at Stake?', *Social Policy & Administration* 48(5): 537–55.

Morel, N., Palier, B., and Palme, J. (eds.) (2012) *Towards a Social Investment Welfare State? Ideas, Policies and Challenges*, Bristol: Policy Press.

Mückenberger, U. (1985) 'Die Krise des Normalarbeitsverhältnisses: Hat das Arbeitsrecht noch Zukunft?', *Zeitschrift für Sozialreform* 31(7 and 8): 415–35; 457–75.

Nüchter, O., Bieräugel, R., Glatzer, W., and Schmid, A. (2010) *Der Sozialstaat im Urteil der Bevölkerung*, Opladen: Verlag Barbara Budrich.

Nullmeier, F. (2014) 'Die Sozialstaatsentwicklung im vereinten Deutschland: Sozialpolitik der Jahre 1990 bis 2014', in P. Masuch, W. Spellbrink, U. Becker, and S. Leibfried (eds.) *Grundlagen und Herausforderungen des Sozialstaats: Denkschrift 60 Jahre Bundessozialgericht*, Berlin: Erich Schmidt Verlag, i, 181–99.

OECD (2015) *In It Together: Why Less Inequality Benefits All*, Paris: OECD Publishing, http://www.oecd-ilibrary.org/deliver/8115091e.pdf?itemId=/content/book/9789264235120-en&mimeType=application/pdf, accessed 10 June 2016.

OECD (2016a) *Gross Domestic Product (GDP): GDP, Volume—Annual Growth Rates in Percentage*, Paris: OECD, https://stats.oecd.org/index.aspx?queryid=60702, accessed 10 June 2016.

OECD (2016b) *Short-Term Labour Market Statistics: Harmonised Unemployment Rates (HURs)*, Paris: OECD, http://stats.oecd.org/index.aspx?queryid=36324, accessed 10 June 2016.

Offe, C. (1992) 'Smooth Consolidation in the West German Welfare State: Structural Change, Fiscal Policies, and Populist Politics', in F. F. Piven (ed.) *Labor Parties in Post-Industrial Societies*, New York: Oxford University Press, 124–46.

Palier, B. and Thelen, K. A. (2010) 'Institutionalizing Dualism: Complementarities and Change in France and Germany', *Politics & Society* 38(1): 119–48.

Rosanvallon, P. (2013) *The Society of Equals*, Cambridge, MA: Harvard University Press.

Sachweh, P., Burkhardt, C., and Mau, S. (2009) 'Wandel und Reform des deutschen Sozialstaats aus Sicht der Bevölkerung', *WSI-Mitteilungen* 62(11): 612–18.

Schimank, U., Groh-Samberg, O., and Mau, S. (2014) *Statusarbeit unter Druck? Zur Lebensführung der Mittelschicht*, Weinheim: Beltz Juventa Verlag.

Schöneck-Voß, N. M., Mau, S., and Schupp, J. (2011) *Gefühlte Unsicherheit: Deprivationsängste und Abstiegssorgen der Bevölkerung in Deutschland*, SOEPpapers on Multidisciplinary Panel Data Research 428, Berlin: Deutsches Institut für Wirtschaftsforschung (DIW), https://www.diw.de/documents/publikationen/73/diw_01.c.392115.de/diw_sp0428.pdf, accessed 10 June 2016.

Seeleib-Kaiser, M. and Fleckenstein, T. (2007) 'Discourse, Learning and Welfare State Change: The Case of German Labour Market Reforms', *Social Policy & Administration* 41(5): 427–48.

Starke, P. (2015) *Krisen und Krisenbewältigung im deutschen Sozialstaat: Von der Ölkrise zur Finanzkrise von 2008*, ZeS-Arbeitspapier 02/2015, Bremen: Universität Bremen, Zentrum für Sozialpolitik (ZeS), http://www.socium.uni-bremen.de/uploads/News/2015/ZeS-AP_2015_02.pdf, accessed 10 June 2016.

Stolleis, M. (2013) *Origins of the German Welfare State: Social Policy in Germany to 1945*, Berlin: Springer.

Streeck, W. (2009) *Re-Forming Capitalism: Institutional Change in the German Political Economy*, Oxford: Oxford University Press.

Streeck, W. (2010) 'The Fiscal Crisis Continues: From Liberalization to Consolidation', *Comparative European Politics* 8(4): 505–14.

The Economist (1999) 'The Sick Man of the Euro', *The Economist*, 3 June 1999, http://www.economist.com/node/209559, accessed 10 June 2016.

The Wall Street Journal (2015) 'Germany's Merkel Sticking to Open-Arms Migrant Policy', *The Wall Street Journal*, 13 Nov. 2015, http://www.wsj.com/articles/germanys-merkel-sticks-to-open-arms-migrant-policy-1447437314, accessed 10 June 2016.

Ullrich, P., Kausch, S., and Holze, S. (2012) 'The Making of the Healthcare Self: State Metamorphoses, Activation, Responsibilisation and Red-Green Alliance's Healthcare Reforms in Germany', *Hamburg Review of Social Sciences* 7(1): 52–72.

Van Kersbergen, K. and Hemerijck, A. (2012) 'Two Decades of Change in Europe: The Emergence of the Social Investment State', *Journal of Social Policy* 41(3): 475–92.

Van Kersbergen, K., Vis, B., and Hemerijck, A. (2014) 'The Great Recession and Welfare State Reform: Is Retrenchment Really the Only Game Left in Town?', *Social Policy & Administration* 48(7): 883–904.

Vis, B., van Kersbergen, K., and Hylands, T. (2011) 'To What Extent Did the Financial Crisis Intensify the Pressure to Reform the Welfare State?', *Social Policy & Administration* 45(4): 338–53.

Zohlnhöfer, R. (2011) 'Between a Rock and a Hard Place: The Grand Coalition's Response to the Economic Crisis', *German Politics* 20(2): 227–42.

3

Where Next for the UK Welfare State?

Peter Taylor-Gooby, Benjamin Leruth, and Heejung Chung

3.1 Introduction

The UK has often been categorized as a liberal market-centred welfare state (Esping-Andersen 1990). In comparison with other large European welfare states it has moderate levels of welfare state spending, substantial reliance on private provision, a large means-tested sector, and rather greater income inequality. Developments during the past fifteen years have moved the country's welfare system further in a liberal direction, and current policies are set to continue the trend. However, new approaches to welfare provision, particularly under the New Labour government from 1997 to 2010, sought to develop predistribution, social investment, and elements of fightback alongside the continuing trend to increasing privatization, greater individual responsibility, more strident chauvinism, and deeper cuts. Neo-liberalism dominates, but not entirely.

In 2016 the UK voted by 52 to 48 per cent on a 72 per cent turnout in a simple majority referendum to leave the EU. At the time of writing (September 2016) it is unclear when Brexit negotiations will start, and when the United Kingdom will effectively leave the European club. The narrowness of the majority coupled with the fact that virtually all economic and business commentators and most politicians within mainstream political parties spoke in favour of remaining in the EU illustrates the low level of political trust in the country and the extent of political divisions. The nationalist movement in Scotland (with less than a twelfth of the UK population) is pursuing independence vigorously.

The United Kingdom is distinctive among the larger and more developed European states in two ways: it has a majoritarian first-past-the-post electoral system in which political authority tends to be centralized, and a liberal-leaning economy. London is by far and away the largest city in Europe, providing one of the three major world financial trading markets and with a powerful and lightly regulated finance sector. The manufacturing sector is relatively small. Corporate taxes are among the lowest in Europe. The electoral system makes coalition exceptional and the party of government is able to pursue its programme with relatively few constraints. The centre-left Labour and centre-right Conservative parties predominate.

Social spending has been relatively low by European standards (see Introduction, Figure 1.4), and targeted, in keeping with the liberal welfare state regime. The main areas of social provision (health care and all cash benefits and pensions) are directly controlled by central government. Local government is responsible for social care and social housing and much of pre-18 schooling. In recent years central government has extended its power in these areas and local autonomy is strictly limited.

This chapter shows how the liberal-leaning political and economic legacy, combined with a first-past-the post political system, has promoted a neo-liberal response to austerity and how this has promoted individualism which weakens fightback. This is reflected in an overriding commitment to deficit reduction and low taxation on the part of both main parties—in the language of Table 1.2 in Chapter 1, to cuts and austerity and individual responsibility. This is not the whole story. Party divisions are widening on a range of issues: the level of state spending, the importance of welfare for working-age people; the extent to which social aims should be pursued through predistribution; the value of social investment such as free childcare; and the desirability of welfare interventions through regulation of rents, prices, and working conditions. There is also a growing popular welfare chauvinism and a mistrust of the political establishment which has, particularly on the right, fuelled disenchantment with the EU and set the scene for the exit vote in the 2016 referendum.

It seems likely that future policy divisions will lie between further austerity, continuing privatization, increased emphasis on individualized welfare solutions, growing inequality, and further weakening of the labour movement on the one hand, and attempts to maintain provision, using the more market-friendly strategies of predistribution and social investment rather than traditional redistributive intervention, on the other. It is unclear whether or not the country will in fact leave the EU in the way that the current government plans, opting for a 'hard Brexit' without access to the single market, and what the impact on economic development and immigration will be. So far most indicators suggest that there will be a sharp downturn.

The UK welfare state has moved away from the bipartisan consensus on a basic adequate level of provision which endured from 1945 up to the later 1970s. Whichever direction is followed, restrictions on immigration seem set to tighten. We will examine these issues in more detail starting from the shifts in welfare state politics in recent years. Then we move on to consider current policy directions and to examine possible future trends, followed by a conclusion.

3.2 The Shift towards Neo-Liberalism

From the 1970s onwards the UK welfare state has experienced a general shift towards neo-liberalism which has been led by both the centre-right and the centre-left parties. The main long-standing issues forming the background to UK welfare state politics concern the pressures of population ageing, the trend towards inequality and declining social mobility, tax resistance, and an underlying market-centredness. These set the context for continuing debates about the priority of health, social care, and pension provision as against services for working-age people, the expansion of means-testing, the balance of taxes between better and worse off, ethnic minority, gender, and workplace rights and family support, the role of the private sector, value for money in state services, and managerial reform. The political context includes recognition by most experts of the need for immigration to fulfil a need for workers conflicting with fears that immigrants undercut wages and compete for housing and schooling (Dustmann and Glitz 2005; Spencer 2011).

The self-consciously right-wing Conservative government from 1979–97, initially under the leadership of Margaret Thatcher, summed up its approach in the first sentence of its spending plan: 'Public expenditure is at the heart of Britain's present economic difficulties' (PEWP 1979: 1). The Conservatives pursued a vigorous programme of spending cuts, privatization (most notably in selling a third of social housing to sitting tenants and much of public services), and attacks on trade union rights after the bitterly fought 1984–5 miners' strike against privatization of the industry. In this period the UK made a decisive shift towards a more liberal approach to welfare, and low-tax market-centred presumptions have framed policy-making since. The shift towards neo-liberalism reinforced individualism and weakened the labour movement, undermining the welfare institutions that promote solidarity.

'New Labour', which succeeded the Conservatives and was led by Tony Blair until 2008, initially pursued a 'Third Way' programme (for details see Hills and Stewart 2005). This included the cautious expansion of state provision through social investment, particularly the promotion of more equal opportunities through educational investment, and expansion of means-tested welfare and the introduction of a minimum wage, supplemented by means-tested tax credits for those on low incomes, a programme sometimes termed 'progressive universalism' with elements of predistribution. One of the most important reforms involved the 'New Deal' for unemployed people, with greater training opportunities but stronger requirements to pursue and take jobs. A new state contributory pension was introduced for low to middle earners. Social investment policies were also introduced, including Sure Start day nurseries targeted at lower-income families, a 15 hours free childcare programme for three and four year olds, extension of maternity and paternity leave, education spending targeted on low-performing areas, and reformed industrial training. The national insurance rate was increased by one per cent in 2002 to finance higher National Health Service (NHS) spending. New Labour however, did not reinstate trade union rights, pursue more progressive taxation, renationalize major industries, or expand universal benefits and services. The objective was to welcome the dynamism of a neo-liberal economy, but direct some of the proceeds to social spending.

A right-wing coalition led by the Conservatives and including Liberal Democrats replaced the Labour government in 2010 and pursued a neo-liberal austerity agenda. In 2015 the Conservatives won the election on an austerity and balanced budget platform and are now implementing a programme of far-reaching cuts in public provision (particularly in benefits for those of working age), privatization, and further attacks on trade unions. We examine the policies in more detail in section 3.3.

Poverty among pensioners started to fall from 1989 as a result of pension increases (Figure 3.1). This trend continued under the 1997 Labour and 2010 coalition governments, although rises in the pension age restrict the numbers affected by these changes. Labour's introduction of the national minimum

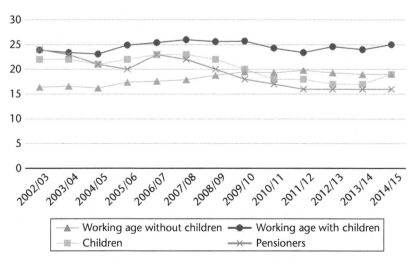

Figure 3.1. Percentage of people in low-income households in the United Kingdom (below 60% median household income, before housing costs).
Source: JRF (2015)

wage and of tax credits reduced poverty among children and working families to a moderate extent; however, the failure to uprate adequately saw some of the improvement lost after 2007. Wage restraint and benefit cuts from 2010 onwards have led to rising poverty among all working-age people and children.

In addition, immigration became an increasingly important political issue from the early 2000s as more EU citizens particularly from Eastern and Central Europe entered the UK after the 'big bang' enlargement of the EU in 2004. These groups were attracted by the buoyant, flexible, and relatively unregulated labour market. They joined a flow of immigrants from elsewhere and particularly from the UK's former colonial nations in the Indian subcontinent, Caribbean, and Africa. Unrest and war in Afghanistan, former Yugoslavia, and the Middle East also generated flows of migrants.

Immigration is essential to maintain the age structure of the population and a young and flexible workforce. Currently more than 11 per cent of the UK population are foreign-born, comparable to other major European countries such as France and Germany (see Chapter 1, Figure 1.3). There is persistent strong anti-immigration sentiment on the right and among some working-class former left voters, especially in deindustrialized areas. In an opinion poll in 2014, 38 per cent of those who put themselves on the political left and 80 per cent of those on the right agreed that immigration should be reduced (Britsocat 2015). Anti-immigration parties gained a small but increasing share of the vote throughout the period, despite the difficulties in securing enough support to elect an MP in the first-past-the-post system. Their popularity influenced larger parties and promoted welfare chauvinist policies. Non-EU immigrants are now regulated by skill, income, country of origin, and personal relationships to citizens. These restrictions stem from the 1981 Nationality Act and were tightened in the managed migration policy which grew increasingly restrictive from 2006 onwards, with a cap in 2010 and further restrictions on immigrant rights since.

The UK negotiated a rebate on payments to the European Community in 1984. In 1992 it signed the Maastricht Treaty but retained an opt-out from the third stage of the Economic and Monetary Union (full membership of the Eurozone). The UK opts out of the Schengen Agreement on cross-border immigration control and policing and the Charter on Fundamental Rights. In addition, the country enjoys a flexible opt-out from policies falling in the scope of the EU's Area of Freedom, Security, and Justice. The current Conservative government led by Theresa May has accepted the Brexit referendum outcome and plans to start the negotiations to leave in 2017.

The background context of UK welfare policy is one of continuing concern about the rising costs of provision, greater use of the market and private sector, the increasing saliency of immigration as a political issue, and a division between rather more generous treatment of pensioners and increasing stringency and stronger incentives for those of working age. Conservative governments have been more vigorous in pursuing cuts, privatization, and austerity than Labour. Governments of both parties have moved in a neo-liberal direction, although some elements of the Labour programme such as the National Minimum Wage (NMW) indicate predistribution, while the Sure Start children's service coupled with some free childcare from 2008 onwards is a social investment programme. The 2010–15 coalition government allowed NMW rates to fall but retained the 15 hours free childcare for three and four year olds and expanded it to include some two year olds, and the 2015 Conservative government restored NMW to previous rates and is in the process of increasing childcare entitlement to 30 hours a week for working parents.

3.3 Current Issues: the Impact of the Great Recession and Responses to It

The world banking crisis in 2007–8 precipitated both an economic crisis as lending collapsed and a fiscal crisis as state revenues fell and demands on state budgets rose (Gough 2011: 50). The UK had achieved economic growth of between two and three per cent for most of the post-war period, slightly slower than other major European countries. The national economy contracted by about five per cent in 2009, roughly equivalent to the EU average contraction, and the country narrowly avoided a second recession in 2012–13. Subsequently the economy recovered to approach its previous growth rate, now rather faster than the Eurozone countries which were affected by the Greek crisis and the rigid balanced-budget policies of the European Central Bank (ECB) and Germany. The UK has become a European economic leader although the impact of Brexit is as yet unclear. Whether the country will also become a leader in new directions in welfare state policy is currently unclear.

The immediate response to the recession was an automatic increase in spending on unemployment and low pay benefits, and a number of measures to protect business and jobs (tax cuts, a car scrappage scheme, provision of training opportunities, bonuses for job creation) as well as an increase in tax-free personal allowances (Chung and Thewissen 2011). The management of the recession, led by Gordon Brown as Chancellor and then Labour Prime Minister, was initially successful, leading to a swift recovery on the pattern of the mid-1970s. Gordon Brown was also influential in initiating the move to government funding of failing banks and leading an international commitment to coordinated financial sector investment. However, the Labour Party lost power after an inept election campaign in 2010, to be succeeded by a

Conservative-led Conservative–Liberal Democrat coalition. The recession served to justify profound and far-reaching policy changes which have further entrenched the liberal regime.

The coalition government faced a relatively high deficit and continuing pressures from population ageing and from inequality. The government committed itself to reduce immigration 'from the hundreds to the tens of thousands', lending force to welfare chauvinism as a response to the crisis. Despite restrictions on visas and rigid enforcement of regulations, the government had little capacity to restrict immigrants from the EU. The numbers of non-EU immigrants fell from 350,000 to 290,000 while the numbers of EU immigrants rose from 175,000 to 230,000 between 2010 and 2015, the remainder being made up of British overseas citizens. The outcome was a slight increase in overall immigration during the life of the government (ONS 2015a). The issue of immigration remains high on the political agenda.

The coalition pursued a radical programme of structural reform in welfare. The decision to invest in substantial restructuring indicates a determination to achieve a major and permanent shift in UK state welfare, expanding the role of the private and non-state welfare, developing and entrenching new payment-by-results systems and requiring people to take much greater individual responsibility for outcomes. The objective was a decisive shift towards a smaller and more liberal social sector and an embedded individualism in welfare politics (Taylor-Gooby 2013). This follows the logic of austerity and individual responsibility (as described in Chapter 1, Table 1.2) and contains little in the way of interventionism, social investment, predistribution, and fightback.

The government also announced its intention to eliminate the deficit within five years, and finance four-fifths of the austerity programme from spending cuts and one-fifth from taxation. This was the greatest proportional cut in public spending per capita in the UK since at least 1964 and probably since 1949 (IFS 2015: 152). The programme included real increases in spending on pensions (the largest single programme) and on health care (the next largest). Spending on 4–18 schooling (the third-largest programme) and for the relatively minor programme of overseas aid was also to be held constant, so that all spending cuts were focused on other areas.

In practice, pension spending rose but spending on health care and education fell slightly, failing to match the population increase. Welfare benefits were cut sharply despite rising demand. The government also cut taxes on business, increased VAT, and raised tax thresholds, funnelling savings to higher earners and reducing income tax for middle to lower earners. The net effect of tax policies was to shift the burden of paying for deficit reduction more towards lower-income groups (Johnson 2015: 5). The formidable constraints on policy meant that the cuts in the unprotected areas were exceptionally severe and that structural reforms were not pursued as vigorously as they might have been.

The cuts to service spending fell most harshly on local government, which lost about a third of its resources between 2010 and 2015. Local government cuts reduced non-mandatory services enormously and had major impacts even on the statutory responsibilities of social care and children's services. The numbers of over 65s receiving local authority social care services fell by a third between 2009 and 2014 (Burchardt et al. 2015). There is considerable concern that the weakness of social care leads to bed-blocking in the NHS as hospitals are unable to discharge frail older people. The numbers on waiting lists for hospital treatment for more than 18 weeks rose sharply from 2.5 million to 3 million between 2010 and 2014 and is continuing to do so (The Guardian 2014).

The pressures on local government have resulted in major cuts in non-mandated services such as social housing, road repairs, public transport, libraries and cultural services, the transfer of some provision to voluntary groups, the merger of services among different local authority areas, and extensive privatization. While directly employed staff are mostly unionized, privately employed staff are not, so that wage costs fall. In addition, one of the most effective of the Labour reforms, the Sure Start programme of integrated children's services centred on day nurseries, has been radically curtailed and remaining centres mostly privatized. The Working Tax Credit childcare component was cut by one eighth, also affecting opportunities for parents of young children to pursue full-time employment. More importantly, the cost of childcare for under-fives rose by a third during the 2010–15 parliament, more than three times the rise in incomes, making childcare costs in the UK and OECD the highest in the OECD countries (OECD 2015a).

The new Work Programme was provided almost entirely by commercial contractors. Private provision under contract was extended across the NHS by a statutory requirement to commission from 'any qualified provider' with severe pressure to take the lowest bid, and (as already mentioned) across local government services, from refuse collection to childcare.

A number of benefit cuts and freezes were introduced. Short-term benefits were held at or below the level of the consumer price index, meaning that, over time, they lagged behind living standards. This hit unemployed people and low-wage workers without children hardest. Rent benefits were restricted to the bottom third of rents, with the result that spending was held down despite rising rents, and increasing housing stress particularly for those on low incomes. Other cuts to rent benefits were also introduced, including the so-called bedroom tax (limiting benefit for households who had a low room-occupancy rate). A benefit cap limiting the total amount that most people of working age can claim at average wage levels, regardless of need or family size or the fact that those in work would have access to additional means-tested support, was introduced in 2013 (Lupton et al. 2015, Table 3). The cap will be lowered by nearly ten per cent in 2016.

A new Universal Credit which will bring together the main means-tested non-pension benefits is being rolled out, despite severe delays and implementation problems. However, in most cases the new benefit will reinstate or reduce current levels of entitlement. The reforms to cash benefits entrench the division between pensions (uprated by the highest of 2.5 per cent, price, or earnings indices) and other benefits (to be uprated by the lowest of one per cent or the price index) and ensure that it will grow wider over time. Future pension costs are to be contained by raising the retirement age (now 65 for men and 63 for women) to 66 by 2020 and 67 by 2028, and by consolidating all pension entitlements into a flat-rate pension by 2016.

These changes are being introduced in the context of further cuts in entitlement and a threefold increase between 2009 and 2014 in the use of benefit denial as a penalty for failure to follow increasingly stringent rules (Oakley 2014). No real evidence exists on the experiences of those right at the bottom, although the Tressell Trust, which provides some two thirds of UK Food Banks, reports a tripling of applications, about half of them from sanctioned claimers, between 2012/13 and 2013/14 (Tressell Trust 2016). Homelessness is increasing rapidly in the context of rising housing stress (Lupton et al. 2015: 53).

The recession also weakened the bargaining position of employees. Unemployment rose from about five to seven per cent by 2014 and then fell slowly. Work became more insecure for many people, and zero-hour contracts (flexible contracts which do not commit the employer to offer a specified number of hours of work each week), involuntary part-time working, and low-income self-employment expanded. By 2014 the number of self-employed people (4.6 million) and their contribution to total employment (15 per cent) were at their highest for forty years or more. Young people were most severely affected. Unemployment among younger workers under the age of 24 increased from 10 per cent in 2006 to 20 per cent by 2013 (Lupton et al. 2015; ONS 2015b). The damage inflicted by unemployment and sub-employment at this stage will permanently 'scar' their careers (Knabe and Ratzel 2011).The government introduced high fees for employment tribunals, effectively denying industrial justice to low-income people. It also doubled to two years the period in a job required before employment protection rights were gained. Standards of employment protection in the UK had been relatively low in comparison to other EU countries but had risen under the previous government. They now fell back. Average wages fell in real terms up to mid-2014 and the UK continued to have one of the highest incidences of low pay among OECD countries (Lupton et al. 2015: 53).

A major labour market problem is the failure to achieve any real increase in productivity. The UK achieved relatively high levels of productivity (understood as output per hour worked) in the 1990s and early 2000s, exceeding Eurozone performance and matching the G7 average between 1990 and 2007. However, it failed to recover after the crisis, with a two per cent gain between 2007 and 2014 against four per cent in the Eurozone and slightly more in G7 (OECD 2015b). Hours worked by each worker have always been high compared to Western and Northern Europe but lower than in Mediterranean countries.

The change seems to be at the level of the individual worker. One aspect of this is the reduction of incentives for employers to invest as people become more willing to accept lower wages and as the taxes on business are reduced (Disney et al. 2013). All things being equal, this results in lower spending on training and on capital goods. Other factors, mainly exogenous and importantly the fall in global energy prices, and the continued weakness of European competitors also play a part. These changes further weaken the labour movement and promote individualism against solidarity.

The most far-reaching effect of the recession for the welfare state in the UK has been to provide a justification for policies to pursue deep cuts in spending, and to weaken the solidarity and bargaining position of the labour movement. Electoral politics has directed the cuts towards working-age people and away from older people, whose pensions and health care are protected although social care is cut. The outcome has been to accelerate changes that have been part of the Conservative programme since 1979. The party has made more progress in promoting its ideas in five years of coalition and in the period since 2015 than it had in its previous eighteen years in government from 1979 to 1997.

The Conservatives won the 2015 election outright and immediately introduced further cuts directed mainly at those of working age and at local government which will lose a further quarter of its budgets (Treasury 2015). As in 2010 they promised to maintain spending on the NHS, on 5–16 schooling, and on International Development at current levels and to impose stringent cuts on most other areas, with the exception of military spending which was protected in response to terrorist attacks in Paris and elsewhere in Europe. The cuts will halve transport subsidies, cut the central government workforce by a quarter, and involve a new sell-off of most of the remaining social housing. Whether cuts on this scale are deliverable without preventing departments from meeting their statutory obligations is unclear (LGA 2015). The NMW has been relabelled the National Living Wage and uprated to restore the cuts of the coalition period to highlight the division between workers and those dependent on welfare. The party also intends to cut benefit rights for EU and non-EU immigrants: this will be part of the negotiations between Brussels and London over the future UK–EU relationship post-Brexit.

To sum up, the period from the Great Recession to the present has been one of an initial response of cautious counter-cyclical investment and spending containment, overshadowed from 2010 by an overriding concern to balance the budget through a harsh austerity programme. This has been pursued by right-wing governments who have used the opportunity to undermine the labour movement, expand private provision, and entrench a shift towards a more limited and liberal welfare state with a strong emphasis on individual responsibility. A shift against immigration among the electorate has enhanced pressures for further controls on immigration and a welfare chauvinist response to the crisis, fuelling demand for Brexit.

The overall direction of recent reform is to promote individualism, neo-liberalism, and welfare chauvinism. The impact of the reforms is also to weaken the institutional bases of solidarity so that it is more difficult to resist further changes. An element of predistribution remains in the enhancement of the minimum wage and childcare provision. Political parties have become more polarized in their programmes. The chief opposition party, Labour, promotes rent, wage, and price controls, reinstatement of trade union rights, and a substantial programme of social investment. It is weakened by internal struggles between more centrist and more left-wing groups, has lost political support, and has little opportunity to influence policy. The UK has moved further towards the model of a liberal market-centred welfare state.

3.4 Future Scenarios: The UK Welfare State at a Crossroads?

We consider possible future policy directions by building on what has happened in the recent past and by examining evidence from public opinion polls.

It is significant that existing policies (and the policy proposals of the main opposition party, Labour) tend to favour older people, protecting the living standards of most pensioners, although setting in train a programme of future increases in pension ages that will help to contain the cost of population ageing. At the same time, expansion of free pre-school childcare and maintenance of paid parental leave entitlements direct some resources (but not as much) to younger groups. The divisions in policy between older and younger and working and non-working groups reflect trends in attitudes revealed by the main opinion surveys.

The British Social Attitudes survey (the most authoritative annual survey) shows that the greatest proportion of participants endorse retirement pensions (67 per cent) followed by benefits for disabled people (60 per cent) as their top priority for extra spending (Britsocat 2015). Child benefits come next at 40 per cent, while benefits for single parents receive only 17 per cent support and for unemployed people 12 per cent. Support for the first two groups has remained roughly constant since the survey series began in 1983. Support for child benefit has risen over time, initially at 20 per cent, while the priority of unemployed people has declined rapidly from over 30 per cent in 1993.

The survey also shows how attitudes to unemployed people have hardened. Although the proportion of workless households in poverty has changed little since the later 1990s at about 70 per cent (ONS 2015b), the proportion believing that 'benefits are too high and discourage work' has risen from under 30 to over 50 per cent during the same period (Baumberg et al. 2012).

Labour voters are more sympathetic to unemployed people than Conservatives but the differences are not marked: 16 per cent of the former put unemployed benefits as top or next priority as against eight per cent of the latter. When compared with previous rounds the survey shows an overall decline in social solidarity (Taylor-Gooby 2016). Sixty-nine per cent of Labour voters and 85 per cent of Conservatives support the high-profile benefit cap that limits total working-age household entitlement regardless of need.

Party differences are more striking on broader issues. As of 2014, Labour supporters are more concerned about inequality: 71 per cent against 39 per cent of Conservative identifiers think 'there is one law for the rich and one for the poor' and 72 against 41 believe that 'ordinary people do not get their fair share of the nation's wealth'. Party supporters are also split on whether the government should spend more on benefits for the poor, and whether unemployment benefits are too high. However, both Labour and Conservative supporters have similar high levels of support for the NHS. Attitude surveys also show strong and rising welfare chauvinism. For example, 60 per cent of British Social Attitudes 2014 respondents believe that EU immigrants should have benefit entitlement limited to six months maximum and 67 per cent believe that the same cap should apply to non-EU immigrants, anti-immigrant feeling being rather stronger among Conservative than among Labour voters (Britsocat 2015; see also Ipsos MORI 2015).

The patterns of public opinion indicate real party differences on the role of government and inequality issues but a considerable consensus on prioritizing the needs of older people and on curtailing benefits for those of working age and immigrants. In this context it is hardly surprising that austerity and deficit reduction, as well as control on immigration, remain central objectives for both major parties. Both proposed at the 2015 election to load most future cuts onto working-age welfare and to continue spending on older people, although Labour's commitment to predistribution would to some extent modify this. Attitudes and party politics suggest that age divisions and working/non-working divisions will form the parameters of social policy, together with commitment to spending restraint.

One way forward is a continued pursuit of the current neo-liberal individu-alist programme. In the UK context of a low-spending tradition, widespread acceptance of a need for continuing austerity, and extra demands from popu-lation ageing, there are real problems for any pro-welfare party in expanding or even maintaining social provision. To be seen as competent it must present a programme that addresses the deficit, to be electable it must respond to key themes in public opinion, and to be progressive it must develop policies that promote greater equality and help those at the bottom. These requirements can be formulated as a trilemma: the formidable obstacles to any increase in taxation or deficit make generous benefits impossible while public opinion stigmatizes working-age claimants and gives low priority to benefits for this, the largest group in poverty (Taylor-Gooby 2012).

The resolution of the problem requires policies that contain spending and do not involve direct transfers to the working-age poor. Programmes addressing the traditional left concerns of poverty and inequality must rest on regulation rather than spending, or on spending presented as investment. The two most prominent suggestions are 'predistribution', combining a generous minimum/living wage, price regulation for utilities and transport, and a limited form of rent control in major cities (Hacker 2011); and 'social investment', to improve the productivity and availability of labour through education, training/apprenticeships, childcare and parental policies, and activation, for example higher-quality apprenticeships and a jobs programme for young people on benefits (Hall 2015; Morel et al. 2012). A third possibility which receives less attention is the reforming of trade union law and of labour regulation to improve the bargaining power of labour. This is the platform of the current Labour leader, Jeremy Corbyn, and is highly popular with a left minority but unpopular with the mass of the electorate (see for example Casalicchio 2016).

The path currently taken by the Conservatives centres on austerity but includes elements of the first two: a slightly higher national living wage (which will in fact exceed somewhat the highest level of the early 2000s), and an increased budget for training and apprenticeships especially for the younger cohort. Hours of free childcare for those in work are also being increased although with severe cost constraints. However, at the same time the Conservative-led government has raised tax thresholds, increasing the income gap between those in and those out of work. The core of the policy consists of major cuts in working-age benefits and public services. It remains to be seen whether this will help realign electoral politics so that the Conser-vatives are seen as a party of low-income workers against welfare claimants. The path taken by Labour in recent years follows a less stringent programme of cutbacks and prioritizes the needs of older people, but also includes more spending on childcare, education, and training, a higher minimum wage, rent control, and more social housing.

This brief analysis suggests that UK welfare state policy will, in the short term, continue to display the clear division of recent years between benefits and services for the older population and those for working-age people (with the exception of cost of childcare). Whoever forms the government, it is unlikely that there will be a substantial increase in state spending, or any move closer to the European average. This implies that the trajectory of the recent past towards a neo-liberal austerity politics supported by a more forceful individualism will continue. Elements of welfare chauvinism also emerge in the stance of the major parties on immigration, most strongly among the Conservatives.

Two issues are of most importance: whether there will be a left attempt to expand the regulatory role of government to enhance the position of the less well-off and to extend workers' rights (as proposed by Labour leader Jeremy Corbyn), or whether regulation will focus on limiting the spending autonomy of local government and encouraging the private provision of state-funded services, as it has under the coalition; and how far policy feedback reinforces a particular trend in policy so that it becomes virtually impossible to shift to a new direction.

Two feedback loops appear possible. The first assumes increasing inequality, poor provision, and poor rights for workers at the bottom, with limited wage supplementation and strong compulsion on unemployed people to work. This will reduce incentives for employers to invest in capital goods or increase wages and do little to improve productivity, with the result that the UK continues on the path of recent years. The second possibility is that measures to strengthen rights, increase skill levels, and promote state-led investment under a different government will, over time, enhance productivity across the economy and help lower-paid people move towards higher wages. This approach might shift the pattern of UK inequality, productivity, and welfare provision back towards the Western European average, leading ultimately to a larger and a less divided welfare state.

Looking beyond current political directions, other factors come into play in the longer term. From an external perspective, developments in global competition are likely to reinforce the tendency to develop a more dualized economy in which the gap in rewards between highly and less highly skilled workers grows wider, and in which the capacity of workers' groups to resist this is weakened. The decision to leave the EU will expose the economy even more to the world market, with pressures on skill levels and training and also on workers' rights and pay, and it will in principle be possible to depart from EU directives on working conditions and health and safety at work.

A further external factor (responding also to internal developments) is immigration, conditioned by international factors and particularly by disorder and war elsewhere, to which the UK has contributed. Britain, with its imperial heritage, has maintained a relatively high level of immigration especially from the Indian subcontinent and the Caribbean. Immigration is seen by most policy-makers as a necessary response to population ageing, but depends on the attractiveness of the UK as a labour market. This may diminish if other EU countries resume traditional growth rates. As previously mentioned, strong anti-immigration sentiment on the right and among some groups of working-class former left voters, especially in deindustrialized areas, has led to demands for restrictions on entry and on benefit rights. These constraints were strengthened under the 2010 coalition, but had little impact on numbers of immigrants. Further restrictions including the ending of free movement of labour within the EU after Brexit might damage the UK's capacity to attract an adequate workforce, but would increase the incentives for employers to invest in higher value-added employment. Terrorism in Europe and further immigration pressures from Syrian war refugees have exacerbated the problem.

Popular concerns about immigration are now so strong that the 2015 Conservative government sought to renegotiate free movement of labour with the EU in the run-up to the Brexit referendum. Demands included denying benefits to EU immigrants for a period of four years, safeguarding the interests and independence of the City of London outside the Eurozone, allowing immigration restrictions, and permitting the national parliaments of EU members to block European legislation. Exit from the EU may well isolate the UK from the rest of Europe and damage growth but will also facilitate restrictions on EU immigration.

Internal developments include population ageing and the retrenchment of state welfare within the short-term scenarios sketched out above. The pressures on the UK from population ageing are lower than in most other European countries, due to a combination of lower spending commitments, rather higher birth rates, and rapid increases in the pension age. Some commentators argue that productivity in labour-intensive services in the public sector tends to be lower than in the private sector (Baumol and Bowen, 1966). Since 2007 the UK private sector has only achieved weak improvements compared with competitors in Europe. The public sector has matched these over the period (Gill and Kliesmentyte 2015: 1–2). However, population shifts will impose real pressures on spending, which may be addressed by tax increases, service dilution, or shifting responsibilities from state to citizen. Developments in all three areas are likely, with the right favouring more private provision and individual responsibility and the left a greater role for regulation and cautious tax increases. In practice the extent to which policy follows one or other of the short-term scenarios set out above and the extent to which feedback effects promote a shift towards a smaller or more substantial welfare state in the longer term are likely to play an important role.

This brief discussion of possible welfare state futures in the UK draws attention to the increasing differences between the various positions, the current weakness of those who seek to fight back and defend the welfare state against austerity, and the importance of policies which shift voters' ideas and interests towards individualism or alternatively towards solidarity and which encourage and promote those directions cumulatively.

3.5 Conclusion

In this chapter we have set out the context of welfare state development in the UK, analysed recent changes, and discussed possible future scenarios. The UK has always been market-centred in its approach to welfare and is becoming more so. Our analysis shows that population ageing, growing inequality, and more intense global competition have all tended to promote deeper divisions in policy objectives and outcomes, to sharpen the choice between contraction and continuity in the state sector, and to raise the question of how far redistribution and welfare ends can be pursued by regulation rather than direct provision. Future developments are uncertain due to the interplay of external and internal factors and the possibility of feedback effects that may set the politics of social policy in a particular direction.

From a political perspective, party positions on the welfare state seem more polarized than ever. The bipartisan consensus on welfare that prevailed until the late 1970s is finally at an end. Most mainstream politicians accept the central tenet of neo-liberal austerity politics, the overriding importance of reducing the deficit. They prioritize benefits and services for older people, who constitute an important electoral force. Chauvinist responses, mostly aiming to reduce migrants' access to welfare provisions and to introduce more stringent border control, are also widely accepted, but to varying degrees. The Conservative Party, currently in government, is pursuing even tougher policies.

Within the overall framework of austerity there is now a clear division between right and left on the size of the state, the role of the private sector, the extent to which government should seek to ensure that the living standards of families on benefits fall below those of the lowest-paid worker, and the extent of inequality. In addition, democracy in the UK seems to be developing towards a multi-party system, in which the groups defending the welfare state are becoming increasingly fragmented. Opinion surveys reinforce the evidence of voting behaviour that there is a decisive swing towards individualism and that solidaristic ideas have been substantially weakened.

We suggest that UK welfare futures will be located somewhere between two scenarios: firstly, a contracting welfare state in a more individualistic society, in which the political capacity to resist pressures towards greater inequality and declining provision for the working-age population is weakened by the politics of inequality and by the fact that low productivity reinforces low wages for less-skilled workers; and, secondly, a more broadly based equilibrium, in which predistributive price, rent, wage, and labour market regulation sustains living standards at the bottom and in which social, human, and physical capital investment reinforces higher skill and a more equal spread of productivity. This would strengthen the interests supporting the working-age welfare state and contain but not reverse pressures towards greater individualism and towards inequality. The risk for the first model is that welfare provision is caught in a downward spiral that eventually destroys solidarity and weakens even the capacity to provide for older groups. The risk for the second is that higher labour costs undermine competitiveness making the system unsustainable.

The first approach presents the UK as the New York of Europe without the productivity; the Hong Kong without the social housing and educational opportunities; the Shanghai without a dominant state sector; the Tokyo without the middle class. In the second it becomes a nation in which progress some way towards the currently dominant regional model of corporatism, whether conservative or Nordic in flavour, is self-reinforcing.

References

Baumberg, B., Bell, K., and Gaffney, E. (2012) *Benefits Stigma in Britain*, London: Elizabeth Finn Care.

Baumol, W. and Bowen, W. (1966) *Performing Arts, the Economic Dilemma*, New York: Twentieth Century Fund.

Britsocat (2015) *British Social Attitudes Survey Database*, developed by the Centre for Comparative European Survey Data, http://www.britsocat.com/, accessed 1 Sep. 2016.

Burchardt, T., Obolenskaya, P., and Vizard, P. (2015) *The Coalition's Record on Adult Social Care*, LSE, Report 17, http://sticerd.lse.ac.uk/dps/case/spcc/WP17.pdf, accessed 1 Sep. 2016.

Casalicchio, E. (2016) 'Theresa May holds massive popularity lead over Jeremy Corbyn, poll shows', *Politics Home*, 4 Sep. 2016, https://www.politicshome.com/news/uk/politics/opinion-polls/news/78626/theresa-may-holds-massive-popularity-lead-over-jeremy, accessed 26 Jan. 2017.

Chung, H. and Thewissen, S. (2011) 'Falling Back on Old Habits?', *Social Policy & Administration* 45(4): 354–70.

Disney, R., Wenchao, J., and Miller, H. (2013) 'The Productivity Puzzles', in C. Emmerson, P. Johnson, and H. Miller (eds.) *The IFS Green Budget, February 2013*, London: Institute for Fiscal Studies. doi: 10.1920/re.ifs.2013.0074, accessed 1 Sep. 2016.

Dustmann, C. and Glitz, A. (2005) *Immigration, Jobs and Wages: Theory, Evidence and Opinion*, London: Centre for Economic Policy Research / Centre for Research and Analysis of Migration.

Esping-Andersen, G. (1990) *The Three Worlds of Welfare Capitalism*, Princeton, NJ: Princeton University Press.

Gill, P. and Kliesmentyte, D. (2015) *Comparing Public Service Productivity Estimates with Other Productivity Estimates* (information note), London: Office for National Statistics.

Gough, I. (2011) 'From Financial Crisis to Fiscal Crisis', in K. Farnsworth and Z. Irving (eds.) *Social Policy in Challenging Times*, Bristol: Policy Press, 49–64.

Hacker, J. (2011) *The Institutional Foundations of Middle Class Democracy*, London: Policy Network.

Hall, P. (2015) 'The Future of the Welfare State', in C. Chwalisz and P. Diamond (eds.) *The Predistribution Agenda*, London: Policy Network, 255–65.

Hills, J. and Stewart, K. (2005) *A More Equal Society?*, Bristol: Policy Press.

IFS (2015) *Fiscal Facts: Taxes and Benefits*, Institute for Fiscal Studies, http://www.ifs.org.uk/tools_and_resources/fiscal_facts/, accessed 1 Sep. 2016.

Ipsos MORI (2015) *Political and Social Trends*, Ipsos MORI, https://www.ipsos-mori.com/researchspecialisms/socialresearch/specareas/politics/trends.aspx#keytrends, accessed 1 Sep. 2016.

Johnson, P. (2015) *Opening Remarks: IFS Budget Analysis*, Institute for Fiscal Studies, http://www.ifs.org.uk/uploads/budgets/budget2015/budget2015_pj.pdf, accessed 1 Sep. 2016.

JRF (2015) *JRF Data*, Joseph Rowntree Foundation, http://data.jrf.org.uk/, accessed 1 Sep. 2016.

Knabe, A. and Ratzel, S. (2011) 'Scarring or scaring?', *Economica* 78(310): 283–93.

LGA (2015) *LGA Responds to 2015 Spending Review*, Local Government Association, http://www.local.gov.uk/web/guest/spending-review/-/journal_content/56/10180/7586753/NEWS, accessed 1 Sep. 2016.

Lupton et al. (2015) *The Coalition's Social Policy Record: Policy, Spending and Outcomes 2010–2015*, LSE, Report 4, January, http://sticerd.lse.ac.uk/dps/case/spcc/RR04.pdf, accessed 1 Sep. 2016.

Morel, N., Palier, B., and Palme, J. (2012) *Towards a Social Investment Welfare State?*, Bristol: Policy Press.

Oakley, M. (2014) *Independent Review of the Operation of Jobseeker's Allowance Sanctions Validated by the Jobseekers Act 2013*, London: DWP, https://www.gov.uk/government/uploads/system/uploads/attachment_data/file/335144/jsa-sanctions-independent-review.pdf, acessed 1 Sep. 2016.

OECD (2015a) *OECD Family Database*, http://www.oecd.org/els/family/database.htm, accessed 27 July 2015.

OECD (2015b) *OECD Level of GDP per capita and Productivity Database*, OECD.Stat, http://stats.oecd.org/, accessed 27 July 2015.

ONS (2015a) *Migration Statistics Quarterly Report*, May 2015, Office for National Statistics, London: HMSO, https://www.ons.gov.uk/peoplepopulationandcommunity/populationandmigration/internationalmigration/bulletins/migrationstatisticsquarterlyreport/2015-05-21, accessed 1 Sep. 2016.

ONS (2015b) *Households Below Average Income: 1994/1995 to 2013/2014*, Office for National Statistics, London: HMSO, https://www.gov.uk/government/statistics/households-below-average-income-19941995-to-20132014, accessed 1 Sep. 2016.

PEWP (1979) *Public Expenditure White Paper*, House of Commons Debate 5 Dec. 1979, vol. 975, London: Hansard Society, 443–574.

Spencer, S. (2011) *The Migration Debate*, Bristol: Policy Press.

Taylor-Gooby, P. (2012) 'Root and Branch Restructuring to Achieve Major Cuts', *Social Policy & Administration*, 46(1): 61–82.

Taylor-Gooby, P. (2013) *The Double Crisis of the Welfare State and What We Can Do About It*, Basingstoke: Palgrave.

Taylor-Gooby, P. (2016) 'The Divisive Welfare State', *Social Policy and Administration*, 50(6), 712–33.

The Guardian (2014) 'NHS Waiting List Passes 3m for First Time in Six Years', *The Guardian*, 12 June 2014, http://www.theguardian.com/society/2014/jun/12/nhs-waiting-list-over-3-million, accessed 1 Sep. 2016.

Treasury (2015) *Spending Review and Autumn Statement 2015*, Cm 9162, https://www.gov.uk/government/publications/spending-review-and-autumn-statement-2015-documents, accessed 1 Sep. 2016.

Tressell Trust (2016) *Latest Foodbank Figures Top 900,000*, Tressell Trust, http://www.trusselltrust.org/foodbank-figures-top-900000, accessed 12 Jan. 2016.

4

France at a Crossroads

Societal Challenges to the Welfare State during Nicolas Sarkozy's and François Hollande's Presidential Terms

Benjamin Leruth

4.1 Introduction

France is the second-largest economy of the European Union, and the seventh-largest worldwide. It has a semi-presidential system of governance with a high degree of decentralization. The French welfare state survived strong societal and political changes during the 1960s and 1970s and established itself as one of the most 'generous' welfare states in the world, its social expenditure increasing from 13.4 per cent of GDP in 1960 to 29.5 per cent in 1981 (Ambler 1991; Kus 2006). Despite being severely hit by the oil shocks of 1973 and 1979, which put an end to the so-called thirty prosperous years (*trentes glorieuses*), the French authorities did not pursue welfare retrenchment until the mid-1990s, following Prime Ministers Édouard Balladur's and Alain Juppé's pension and healthcare reforms.

The Great Recession of 2007–8 confronted French social policy with major challenges. Among these, the rise of unemployment (especially among young people) combined with major pensions and labour market reforms led to strong dissatisfaction across the country. Besides the long-term problem of unemployment, issues such as immigration, Euroscepticism and security attracted considerable media attention. As a consequence of such public distrust the populist right Front National became the largest political party during the 2014 European election. Welfare chauvinist policies, combining exclusion, authoritarianism, and redistributive state-centred economics, are promoted by the Front National but also increasingly by the centre-right party Les Républicains (formerly known as Union pour un Mouvement Populaire, UMP) under the leadership of former French President Nicolas Sarkozy. This stance had the potential to create further cleavages within a strongly divided French society.

The chapter begins with a brief history of welfare state development in France, from the *dirigiste* era to the early 2000s (section 4.2). Section 4.3 analyses Nicolas Sarkozy's presidency (2007–12) and the series of policy responses implemented to tackle the Great Recession. Section 4.4 then focuses on the period from 2012 to 2016, constituting most of François Hollande's presidential term which is set to end in May 2017. It highlights some of the most recent deregulatory measures advocated by the socialist government, which have been strongly controversial and which led to major strikes across the country. The final section concludes the chapter and reflects on possible scenarios for the medium-term future, based on recent attitude surveys and key political developments.

The discussion of the development of the French welfare state in the third and fourth sections has a particular focus on the impact of the Great Recession in France under the presidencies of Nicolas Sarkozy and François Hollande. The two presidents offered contrasting conservative and socialist ideologies, but both suffered strong levels of public distrust. The highest profile challenges to the presidencies differ: recession and growing deficit under Sarkozy, and terrorism and the so-called migration 'crisis' under Hollande.

4.2 The French Welfare State Prior to the Great Recession

Unlike many European welfare states, in which the state plays a dominant role, the French social welfare system is mostly based on what is called *sécurité sociale*, self-managed non-state agencies which are the providers of social insurance for health care, pensions, and many other benefits. As emphasized by Palier (2000: 116), 'the system is supposed to be managed by those who pay for it and have an interest in it, subject to only limited control by the state, which is supposed to have only a supervisory role'. In comparative perspective, the French welfare model can be considered as conservative corporatist: most social rights are earned and financed by paying social contributions through work, and most benefits are managed within insurance funds involving social partners (Palier and Petrescu 2007). France was not a pioneer in terms of social security, as the country adopted general social insurance in 1966 more than forty years after Germany and twenty years after the UK (Ambler 1991).

In terms of economic development, France has a long-standing tradition of *dirigisme*, a statist approach aiming to achieve rapid modernization through

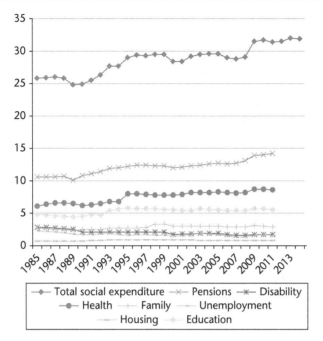

Figure 4.1. Social expenditure in France, 1985–2014 (as percentage of GDP).
Source: OECD, aggregated data

national planning, the nationalization of core industrial sectors, and protectionism (Kus 2006). Until 1983 *dirigisme* was the predominant policy framework advocated by French governments. A neo-liberal turn occurred under the Mitterrand presidency, but this U-turn did not affect the French welfare state. As Levy (2000: 309) argues, 'France's welfare state has emerged from the shadows of dirigisme.' Even the post-*dirigiste* era of associational liberalism[1] did not lead to welfare state retrenchment though it 'revolved around empowering non-state institutions to act as allies in the reconstruction of the French political economy' (Vail 1999: 314; see also Levy 1999). Despite the fact that France faced social security deficits in the early 1970s (much like the majority of European states), the French government mostly increased social expenditure until the mid-1990s. This was financed through annual increases in social contributions paid by employees while the level of direct income taxation decreased considerably (Palier 2000; Kus 2006).

Figure 4.1 shows the evolution of social expenditure in France between 1985 and 2013, demonstrating that welfare spending reached an all-time high in 2013 at 32 per cent of GDP. France is currently the biggest social spender among OECD countries, suggesting that the French welfare state still tends to be rather 'generous' in comparative perspective. The main area of social spending is pensions, which increased from 10.6 per cent of GDP in

1985 to 14.2 per cent in 2011. The country also has generous family policies compared to other countries and this area has continued to expand throughout the past decade. Such policies include a high degree of public investment in childcare services for children under three, relatively long parental leave schemes, combined with cash benefits for parents (Lewis et al. 2008). This, along with the 35-hour working week law, has contributed to higher fertility rates in France compared with other European countries such as Germany or the UK (Thévenon 2005). As far as elderly care policies are concerned, the French authorities developed a cash-for-care allowance for older dependent people which came into force in the late 1990s (Le Bihan and Martin 2010). However, spending on unemployment and disability benefits fell slightly over time.

As far as the French political landscape is concerned, its party system is dominated by two main political groupings: the Socialist Party on the left, and Les Républicains on the right. The former has historically promoted a strong *état providence* by emphasizing the role of the state in improving the workers' quality of life and the need for redistribution of wealth and equality of opportunity (Sloam 2005). The latter, however, favours a low-welfare society: one of the main objectives of the party is to put an end to state 'dependency' by improving employment opportunities and boosting economic growth by promoting a neo-liberal agenda. In contrast to the British party framework which is strongly influenced by the first-past-the-post electoral system, smaller political parties play an important role in supporting the formation of a government. In the past decades the French centrists exerted some considerable influence under the leadership of President Valéry Giscard d'Estaing (1974–81). On the left side of the political spectrum, the Green Party, the Left Front, the Radical Party of the Left, and the Communist Party are traditional allies of the Socialist Party, and formed a 'Plural Left' majority between 1997 and 2002 under UMP Jacques Chirac's first presidential term. The most significant legacy of this pro-welfare left alliance is the 35-hour working week policy. In more recent years the radical right, anti-immigration, and welfare chauvinist Front National (FN) became increasingly influential, after a breakthrough in the 2002 French presidential elections when former leader Jean-Marie Le Pen reached the second round. His daughter Marine Le Pen, leader since 2011, has pursued a successful campaign to 'de-demonize' the party. The increasing popularity of the FN also had an impact on the mainstream right agenda under the leadership of Nicolas Sarkozy, who advocated welfare chauvinist measures as part of his 2012 manifesto.

Much like other European countries, France faced a series of major socio-demographic changes during the past two decades, as captured in Figure 4.2. The unemployment rate, which is often used as the main indicator of the government's performance in France, has been consistently higher than the average OECD rate. In most recent years, youth unemployment has been an

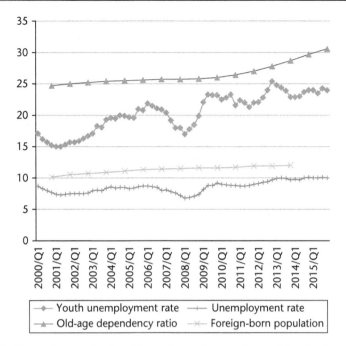

Figure 4.2. Unemployment rate, old-age dependency ratio, and foreign-born population in France, 2000–15.

Source: National Institute of Statistics and Economic Studies—France (unemployment rate, quarterly); World Bank (old-age dependency ratio, yearly); OECD (foreign-born population, yearly—data available until 2013)

increasingly problematic issue, as this rate increased from 17.1 per cent in 2000 to 24.0 per cent in late 2015.[2] France also has one of the highest levels of temporary employment in Europe (14 per cent in 2015). The old-age dependency ratio (i.e., the number of people aged 65 and over as a percentage of the labour force) was relatively stable at around 20 per cent until the early 1990s. It increased from 24.7 per cent in 2000 to 30.6 per cent in 2015, above the European Union average and putting a strain on old-age pensions and healthcare provision. Furthermore, the percentage of population who were born abroad slightly increased from 10.1 per cent in 2000 to 11.9 per cent in 2012, though this increase is much less than in the UK and the Scandinavian countries (see Chapter 1). These socio-demographic changes create significant challenges for the future of the French welfare state and reforms started in the early 1990s.

Three particular aspects of the French welfare state have been reformed in order to cope with these demographic changes: pensions, healthcare, and the labour market. While some of these welfare reforms aimed at reducing welfare costs and imposed austerity measures to comply with the Maastricht criteria, others were Keynesian policies intended to improve the workers' quality of life.

Firstly, old-age welfare provisions constitute the main source of welfare expenditure in France (as Figure 4.1) shows. Even though spending increased by 3.6 per cent between 1985 and 2011 mostly due to an ageing population, successive governments gradually led a series of reforms which included increases in retirement age from 60 to 67 by 2023 and cuts in the benefit levels of basic and complementary pensions. In 1993 the centre-right government managed to reform private-sector occupational basic and supplementary pensions and faced very little opposition from the general public, in 'a move designed to dampen resistance among the unions' overwhelmingly public-sector membership' (Vail 1999: 319) while the private sector tends to be largely non-unionized. This reform was subsequently followed by a controversial austerity programme in 1995 under a newly elected centre-right government led by Prime Minister Alain Juppé. Even though this so-called 'Juppé Plan' mostly focused on healthcare reforms, it also included controversial proposals to reform public-sector pensions, following the 1993 reform of private-sector pensions, and the creation of a 0.5 per cent tax on all personal incomes to reduce the social security deficit (*Contribution pour le Remboursement de la Dette Sociale*, or CRDS). Public-sector pensions are highly politicized. After a national paralysis and general strikes which lasted for nearly a month in response to the proposed measures and the lack of social dialogue between the government and the unions, the government eventually withdrew all public-sector pension reforms, although the CRDS tax was implemented.[3]

Secondly, healthcare reforms were also advocated by centre-right governments in the early 1990s. A series of new healthcare measures were successfully implemented in 1993, including trimming hospital expenditure, an increase in patient charges, and the reform of hospital administration. From 1995 to 1997 healthcare provisions from the Juppé Plan were implemented with little opposition from the general public and practitioners. Among these reforms was the introduction of spending limits decided by the French parliament on a yearly basis, thus replacing the previous system which consisted of negotiations between doctors and sickness funds to determine levels of healthcare expenditure and revenue. The system was further decentralized to reduce regional inequalities and improve coordination between private and public hospitals. Furthermore, the Juppé Plan switched finance from social insurance contributions to income tax. Accordingly, the general social contribution (*Contribution Sociale Généralisée*, CSG), which is an income-based tax used to finance non-contributory benefits, increased from 2.4 per cent in 1993 to 3.4 per cent in 1996, and even further to 7.5 per cent under the Plural Left government, while the employees' health insurance contribution was reduced from 5.6 per cent to 0.75 per cent. The CSG was perceived as a fairer tax than social contribution for employees as well as a tool to lower social charges for employers (Bouget 1998; Palier 2005).

Thirdly, labour market policies have been reformed considerably in the past two decades. The 35-hour working week policy, which was introduced under the left-wing Jospin government and which came into force between 2000 (for firms employing more than twenty workers) and 2002 (for all firms) is one of the biggest welfare reforms led by the Socialist Party.[4] The reform's main objectives were to create more jobs while employees would continue to earn roughly the same monthly income, to facilitate collective bargaining between employers and employees, and to improve the quality of life for employees, allowing for a better work–life balance.

Current studies indicate that the effects of these policies are mixed. The 35-hour working week policy increased social contribution exemptions for employers (Vail 2008), but the impact on proportional job creation is contested. Estevão and Sá (2006; 2008) estimated that the policy failed to create more jobs and increased job turnover,[5] and that employees in large firms became more dissatisfied with their hours of work compared to employees in smaller firms. In contrast, Hayden (2006: 530) assessed the policy positively—'perhaps a two-thirds success overall'—emphasizing quality-of-life improvements for the majority of employees and the fact that French firms' competitiveness was maintained or even enhanced. A further objective of the laws was to encourage investment by employers, faced with, effectively, higher labour costs. There is some indication of success in this.

In sum, there are two directions which the French welfare state reforms took. On the one hand there were mostly neo-liberalistic reforms in the shape of welfare cuts and austerity measures implemented in the early 1990s, in response to population ageing and rising unemployment and the accumulating public deficit in the 1970 and 1980s. These reforms mostly dealt with old-age spending through changing pension rules as well as healthcare provisions. On the other hand, the 35-hour working week was a Keynesian policy promulgated by the Plural Left government in the early 2000s and aimed at creating jobs as well as improving the workers' quality of life. The two following sections focus on some of the most recent events, by analysing France's experience of the Great Recession and the policy responses advocated under Nicolas Sarkozy's and Francois Hollande's presidencies.

4.3 2007–12: Sarkozy's Presidency, the Great Recession, and Neo-*Dirigisme*

On 6 May 2007 UMP (centre-right) leader Nicolas Sarkozy won the French presidential election with 53.1 per cent of votes, against socialist candidate Ségolène Royal. Sarkozy, whose campaign was mostly driven by the key radical right issues of immigration, crime, and violence, pledged to start a series of economic and social reforms to put an end to what he called 'state handouts' (Marthaler 2008). He also offered a neo-liberal programme that consisted of two main reforms. The first increased labour supply, by easing the regulation of overtime work and reducing taxation on earnings from it. The second promised 'that labour market flexibilization would be based on French-style flexicurity and not purely and simply "Anglo-Saxon" flexibility' (Amable et al. 2012: 1179).

In addition, in an attempt to convince the electorate that in terms of social policy improvements his presidency would break with Chirac's much-criticized era of maintaining the status quo, his manifesto pledged to cut the unemployment rate to five per cent by 2012. Finally, Sarkozy committed his government to reduce the level of public debt, which ran at 75 per cent of the GDP in 2007 (see Figure 4.3).

The centre-right government appointed in June 2007 initiated a series of reforms to reduce the level of public expenditure. Firstly, the government announced a reduction of 50 per cent in public-sector recruitment to replace retired employees. Secondly, it introduced a fiscal package entitled 'law in favour of labour, employment and purchasing power' (*loi en faveur du travail, de l'emploi et du pouvoir d'achat*), which reformed the taxation system and lowered labour costs for businesses through tax exemptions for overtime hours, without affecting the 35-hour working week laws. Thirdly and perhaps most importantly, the government launched a General Review of Public Policies (*Révision Générale des Politiques Publiques*), an initiative without similar precedent among OECD countries as it directly involved the French central government and sub-national public authorities in reforming public institutions through a process of administrative simplifications and in reducing the deficit from 75 per cent of the GDP to below 60 per cent by 2012 (OECD, 2012; see also Lafarge, 2010).

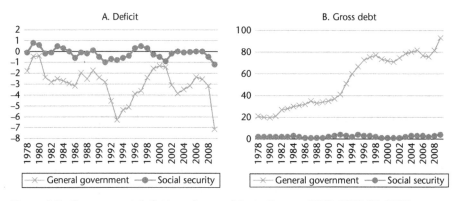

Figure 4.3. Government deficits and gross debt in France, 1978–2009 (% GDP).
Source: adapted from OECD (2012: 32)

The Great Recession hit France in the second quarter of 2008. The country's GDP growth rate fell to −0.53 per cent. Unemployment increased from 6.8 per cent in the first quarter of 2008 to 9.2 per cent by the end of 2009, with youth unemployment at an all-time high of 23.3 per cent by the second quarter of 2009 (see Figure 4.2).

To combat the financial and economic crisis, Sarkozy switched from a neo-liberal discourse to adopt a 'neo-*dirigiste*' response, often considered as a return to economic Gaullism for the French right-wing government (see Hoang-Ngoc 2009). In the context of France and in contrast to *dirigisme* which prevailed until the early 1980s, neo-*dirigisme* is a form of policy that does not involve nationalization or protectionism, but rather (temporary) re-regulation and state-led investment in order to boost and protect employment in times of crisis. Furthermore and in contrast to neo-Keynesianism as used in the context of this volume, neo-*dirigisme* does not rely on further welfare spending to maintain demand from low-income groups.

The Fillon government (2007–12) introduced a 26 billion euro rescue plan and unveiled a stimulus package in December 2008. This policy response to the crisis prioritized public infrastructure projects and investment in public companies. A new ministry in charge of the Implementation of the Recovery Plan was created. In response to this stimulus package, a general strike was called on 29 January 2009 and trade unions demanded more support for workers' purchasing power. In February 2009 the Fillon government further announced a series of neo-Keynesian social measures aimed at helping the unemployed as well as low-income workers, such as a €200 bonus for recipients of in-work benefits, lower income tax, and higher unemployment benefits. As Vail (2014: 72) posits, these two packages 'reflected statist liberalism's "statist" orientation (through direct spending and a macroeconomic strategy) and "liberal" footprints favouring means-tested income support and support for business'.

As part of the General Review of Public Policies and in order to cope with the increasing old-age dependency ratio, the French government further initiated a major pension reform. The proposal, which was approved by the National Assembly in 2010, included raising progressively the normal retirement age for full state pensions from 65 to 67 from 2016 onwards and early, reduced pensions from age 60 to 62, while the contribution period started to increase by around one quarter every three years until 2020. This led to a series of violent major protests across the country for more than a week, further harming social dialogue within French society.

Overall, despite a reassertion of a neo-Keynesianism *à la française*, Nicolas Sarkozy's management of the financial crisis combined with his controversial personality proved unpopular. From early 2010 onwards, opinion polls suggested that a majority of French voters wanted the left to win the 2012 presidential elections (Milner 2012). Mostly as a result of the Great Recession, the government failed to reduce the general government debt-to-GDP ratio, which instead rose from 75 to 110 per cent between 2007 and 2012. The unemployment rate increased from 8.1 in 2007 to 9.1 per cent at the end of Sarkozy's presidential term. Similarly the percentage of people at risk of poverty or social exclusion increased from 16.4 to 18.1 per cent. Milner (2012) highlighted some key inconsistencies and ambiguities in Sarkozy's labour market policies, as he failed to marshal sufficient resources to tackle the fundamental issues of unemployment and public debt. This provided a window of opportunity for opposition parties to attack the right-wing government's poor results.

4.4 François Hollande, 2012–17: Le changement, c'est maintenant?

The 2012 French presidential elections saw the victory of Socialist François Hollande over Nicolas Sarkozy in the second round held on 6 May. Hollande, who never held any ministerial portfolios in his political career but was the party's First Secretary between 1997 and 2008, emerged as the outsider within the Socialist Party following the involvement of IMF Director Dominique Strauss-Khan in a sexual scandal in 2011. He managed to secure the Socialist candidacy after winning the left-wing primary elections held in October 2011 against Lille's mayor (and daughter of Jacques Delors) Martine Aubry, with 56.57 per cent of votes.

Hollande and Sarkozy offered contrasting responses to the Great Recession, and these are worth comparing to understand why Hollande won. His political slogan, 'Change Is Now!' (*Le changement, c'est maintenant!*), illustrated the Socialist Party's strategy of offering an alternative to the politics of austerity introduced by Nicolas Sarkozy. His programme included a total of sixty pledges which mostly focused on the issues of social justice and restoring hope for the younger generations by offering a mix of neo-Keynesian, predistribution, fightback, and social investment policies. Among these was the creation of *contrats de génération* (contracts between younger and older generations) to tackle ageism and youth unemployment by stimulating the creation of fixed-term contracts for younger workers who will be trained by senior employees in a company. Such policies formed the cornerstone of his presidential campaign, along with the renegotiation of the European Fiscal Compact in order to emphasize growth and jobs, and the highly publicized proposal to tax 75 per cent of earnings over 1 million euros.

In contrast, Sarkozy's manifesto entitled 'Strong France' (*La France Forte*) praised the achievements made by the centre-right government since 2007, but his programme focused on moving away from the neo-*dirigiste* approach adopted as a response to the Great Recession in December 2008. The manifesto proposed austerity measures to tackle public deficit, and introduced other reforms aimed at helping low-wage workers such as the suppression of the *Prime pour l'Emploi* (a form of tax credit) replaced by a net wage increase of 70 euros per month, no increase in income tax, and increasing VAT from 19.6 per cent to 21.2 per cent. In addition, even though the percentage of foreign-born population had not increased much in the preceding decade, Sarkozy's programme also included a welfare chauvinist element, by committing to immigration cuts of 50 per cent and allowing immigrants access to some benefits only if they had paid taxes for a minimum of five years. This pledge was made in order to rally the 'hard right' wing of his electorate, who could have been tempted to vote for Marine Le Pen.

One element was common to both candidates, namely the commitment to budgetary balance by the end of the following presidential term at the very latest. This was perceived as a top priority by voters during the campaign. Table 4.1 categorizes the main policies of both candidates during the 2012 presidential election campaign according to the framework for welfare state programmes developed in Chapter 1. The austerity measures proposed by Nicolas Sarkozy as opposed to his initial neo-*dirigiste* response to the crisis proved to be unpopular, and the Socialist Party returned to power after a double victory in the presidential and parliamentary elections.

The new government immediately implemented parts of Hollande's neo-Keynesian agenda in order to tackle the crisis, such as increasing the minimum wage by two per cent and increasing the back-to-school payment by 25 per cent. It also pledged not to increase taxes and even to cut the existing level of income tax by 2015. A new reform of old-age pensions was further approved in 2013 in order to avoid a deficit estimated at €20 billion by 2020, although it is anticipated that discussions about pension reform will continue over the next few years (Naczyk et al. 2014).

The popularity of François Hollande's government fell sharply from 2013. Firstly, in the fourth quarter of 2012, new figures revealed that the youth unemployment rate had reached an all-time high (25.2 per cent) while the general unemployment rate reached the 10 per cent mark in early 2013 (see Figure 4.2). Second, while the government initially pledged not to increase taxes, this promise was abandoned in the 2013 budget; tax increases mainly affected the middle class. Third, the government became divided over policy responses to the Great Recession, as some ministers favoured more state interventionism (for example through the nationalization of the French steel industry) while others favoured more liberal policies. Fourth, while the government attempted to improve transparency and fight against tax evasion as a response to the crisis, the French investigative journal Médiapart revealed that

Table 4.1. Major policy responses associated with the crisis in François Hollande's and Nicolas Sarkozy's 2012 election manifestos

	François Hollande (Socialist Party)	Nicolas Sarkozy (Union for a Popular Movement)
Cuts/austerity	None	• Cutting unemployment benefits as soon as unemployment falls • Administrative cuts: reducing the number of civil service jobs by replacing only half retiring staff • Abolition of tax credit balance by a net wage increase of €70 per month for employees earning €1,000-€1,400 per month
Individual responsibility	None	• Encouraging the development of private medical practices
Neo-Keynesianism	• State-led investment to create 500,000 'generation contracts' • 150,000 new jobs in the social and environmental sectors, mostly in disadvantaged areas • Increasing the minimum wage (SMIC) and indexation based on growth rate (instead of inflation) • Increasing back-to-school payment by 25 per cent	None
Social investment	• Prioritizing and financing training for low-skilled workers and the unemployed	None
Predistribution	• Increasing and improving social housing • Increasing unemployment contributions for companies that abuse precarious jobs • Creation of a 'social credit system'	• Exemption of employer contributions for companies hiring unemployed people over 55 years
Fightback	• Renegotiating the European Fiscal Compact • 75 per cent income tax on earnings over €1,000,000 • 45 per cent income tax on earnings over €150,000	None
Welfare chauvinism	None	• Cutting immigration by half • *Revenu de solidarité* active (RSA) and minimum pension restricted to immigrants who have lived in France for ten years and worked for a minimum of five years

Source: Le Monde (2012)

Minister of the Economy Jérôme Cahuzac held a secret bank account in Switzerland and was accused of tax evasion. Fifth, the government prioritized the divisive issue of same-sex marriage which was heavily criticized by a sizeable conservative group within French society, contributing to a strong decrease in support. Finally, the measures implemented under Ayrault's prime ministership (2012–14) proved to be unpopular not only among voters but also within the parliamentary majority, which created strong divisions and an ideological crisis within the Socialist Party.

Other measures to tackle income inequality were abandoned. For instance, the proposed 'fightback' 75 per cent tax on earnings over €1 million was thrown out by the Constitutional Council in 2012 because it failed to take into account family composition (see André et al. 2015). While Hollande considered his political actions to follow a social democratic ideology, some observers and experts categorized the government's policy as social-liberal or 'Third Way', favouring deficit reduction and business competitiveness in line with policies once advocated by Tony Blair in the UK and Gerhard Schröder in Germany (see e.g. Grunberg 2014; The Economist 2014).

The poor results of the Left in the March 2014 municipal elections led to a major reshuffle in the French cabinet. Prime Minister Ayrault was replaced and the Green Party decided not to participate in the new government, marking their opposition to the direction taken by the Socialist Party. Valls immediately announced his intention to freeze all welfare spending (except in the case of minimum social benefits) in order to reduce the level of public deficit (Grunberg 2014; Le Monde 2014). In the European elections held in May 2014, the Front National became the largest political formation in France, and left-wing parties lost a total of 11 seats (Goodlife 2015). Within the Socialist party itself there was growing discontent and a minority of representatives located to the left of the party, the *frondeurs* (or 'rebels'), refused to support a motion of confidence in the new Valls government. These divergences culminated in August 2014 when three Ministers openly criticized the government's economic policy which focused on deficit reduction rather than on a neo-Keynesian approach to support growth and household demand. As a result of these divergences, the government resigned and a Valls II cabinet was formed, excluding the *frondeurs* and notably including Emmanuel Macron, a non-elected former investment banker, as Minister of the Economy.

In the course of 2015 and 2016 two major reform projects (the Macron and El Khomri bills) dominated the political agenda and contributed to an increase in social unrest.[6] These two reforms, which sparked controversy in France, deserve particular attention as they illustrate the social–liberal turn taken by Francois Hollande's presidency, in contrast to his initial neo-Keynesian, fightback, and predistributive programme.

The Macron bill, which was voted through in July 2015, includes five major changes that aim to stimulate the French economy and 'liberate growth' through deregulation. The first reforms the existing law on working on Sundays and during the night, especially in designated 'international touristic zones' including large cities such as Paris, Nice, Deauville, and Cannes. The second liberalizes long-distance passenger transport by bus as a cheaper alternative to train services, which the government believes will create 'tens of thousands' of jobs outside the heavily unionized state sector. The third is a major reform of collective redundancy rules, which gives more freedom and flexibility to employers. The fourth is the deregulation of the notary and legal professions by reducing barriers to entry. And finally, the Macron bill empowers the government to sell between 5 and 10 billion euros worth of assets without privatizing state-owned companies, to reduce the budget deficit (Le Monde 2015). The Macron bill was heavily criticized by the *frondeurs*, who described it as a 'backward step', while the European Commission praised it as 'a step in the right direction' (EurActiv 2014).

The El Khomri bill extends the Macron bill to 'protect employees, encourage employment, and give more leeway to collective bargaining' (French Government 2016) through deregulation. Among the measures included in this bill is a controversial reform of overtime pay (for work over the legal 35-hour working week): under existing measures overtime is paid as the fixed hourly rate plus a minimum of 25 per cent for the first eight hours and 50 per cent for any that follow. The El Khomri bill would lower these rates to a minimum of 10 per cent upon a collective agreement reached between trade unions and the employer. Workers feared that this would mean the effective end of the 35-hour working week and worsen working conditions in larger firms. Other controversial provisions included measures making it easier for companies to lay off workers, and opportunities for smaller trade unions representing at least 30 per cent of the workers to become involved in collective bargaining through a workforce referendum, thus weakening the French corporatist tradition of social partnerships lead by larger unions.

As a response to the proposed El Khomri bill, trade unions and student associations called for strikes and massive demonstrations all around the country. A youth-led movement named *Nuit Debout* ('Up All Night') and inspired by the Spanish Indignados movement (see Chapter 7) took over the Place de la République in Paris on 31 March 2016. This movement echoes a feeling of despair among traditional left-wing voters, who believe that the Socialist government's actions do not represent the key left-wing values it should advocate.

Between 2015 and 2016 the French government also faced two major contextual issues, which had an impact on policy priorities, the level of public deficit, and the government's popularity. The first one was the rise in terrorist threats following the Île-de-France attacks, including the Charlie Hebdo shooting, and the Paris attacks in 2015 and the Nice attack in 2016. As a response to these attacks, the government raised the level of government security spending, abandoning the deficit targets set up in the Stability and Growth Pact (three per cent of GDP). The second issue that affected France, like other European countries, was the so-called migration 'crisis'. One aspect was the movement of large numbers of undocumented migrants seeking to cross to the Calais area to enter the UK (Rigby and Schlembach 2013: 159). Migrant camps, nicknamed the 'Jungle', increased in size from housing 900 to over 6,000 migrants between 2009 and 2015 and attracted attention from domestic and international media. In response, the French government relocated hundreds of undocumented migrants to different regions, and destroyed most of the camps in March 2016, although informal camps have now sprung up. However, unlike other European countries, the government did not put forward an anti-immigration or welfare chauvinist agenda.

4.5 Conclusion: Future Scenarios and Public Attitudes

Tensions within French society are more pronounced than in other European countries outside the Mediterranean area. The 2012 European Quality of Life Survey (see Figure 4.4) shows strong tensions between the rich and the poor (55.7 per cent), between management and workers (49.3 per cent), and between different racial and ethnic groups (50 per cent). Recent events related to the terrorist attacks and migration have probably increased tensions between different religious groups. A CSA Research (2015) survey showed that 68 per cent of respondents believed that, overall, tensions have increased in France over the course of 2015. Even though income inequality and the overall percentage of people at risk of poverty had not risen over the past

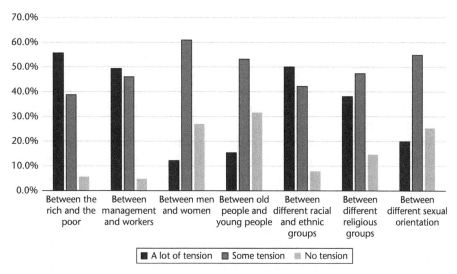

Figure 4.4. Tensions between social groups in France.
Source: European Quality of Life Survey 2012

decade, the same survey also highlighted social inequality as a source of strain in French society, with 72 per cent of respondents believing that French society was not equal enough. Despite this, 53 per cent of respondents stated that social benefits are too generous and benefit cheats are reported as being the main cause of resentment in France (37 per cent).

These results demonstrate deep divisions within French society, and the difficulties that face political elites in tackling the emergence of new cleavages as well as the erosion of existing solidarities. The issues of unemployment (especially among young people) and population ageing have been long-standing problems in France. Projections from the French National Institute of Statistics and Economic Studies suggest that by 2035 30.7 per cent of the population will be 60 or over (against 26.4 per cent in 2020): population ageing is a major policy issue, despite the country's relatively high fertility rate (INSEE 2015). This is likely to put a strain on old-age pensions and health care. Furthermore, governments have failed to address the level of public deficit, which could lead to further retrenchments. There is a strong probability that the pension reforms which began in the early 1990s will intensify in the coming years, though this will trigger public resentment. As demonstrated in section 4.4, the 35-hour working week policy is also under a lot of pressure, and might disappear or be diluted in the near future. It is unclear how far this policy enhanced job creation, productive investment, and economic growth; however, a longer working week could reduce workers' quality of life and increase the share of people in low-paid and less protected employment. Trade unions, which tend to have a very high capacity for mobilization especially within the public sector, are also likely to lose influence following the ratification of the El Khomri law. This could dramatically change the existing French model of corporatism where trade unions are able to veto labour market and social policies, since competition between smaller and larger unions is going to increase. As the French trade unions have historically played a strong role in opposing a general flexibilization of the labour market (see Palier and Thelen 2010), this could pave the way for an increased labour market dualization in France.

In addition, trust in the well-established mainstream political parties hit an all-time low under Hollande's presidency. The aforementioned structural challenges, unpopular policies, and the failure of successive governments to tackle high levels of unemployment have offered a window of opportunity for radical political parties. Even though immigration and income inequality did not rise markedly in recent years (see Figure 4.2), a number of political movements have successfully put these two issues at the top of the political agenda and offer welfare chauvinist (among right-wing parties) as well as further radical fight-back policy alternatives (among left-wing parties). On the radical left side of the political spectrum, the most recent wave of demonstrations and public unrest related to the French labour law changes seems to indicate a resurgence in the popularity of fightback policies, especially among traditional left-wing voters who oppose the government's social–liberal programme. It is too early to tell whether Nuit Debout will succeed in creating a new and successful populist left political party such as Podemos in Spain, though by June 2016 the movement's momentum seemed to be failing. On the radical right side of the spectrum, despite opinion polls suggesting strong support for the Front National in the 2017 presidential election, it is highly unlikely that the party will become a major political force within the French National Assembly and shape the future of the French welfare state. In the French electoral system, the two-round run-off voting system tends to prevent the party from winning major posts, as demonstrated in the 2002 presidential elections and, more recently, the 2015 regional elections, where support for the FN reached a 'toxic ceiling'.

Les Républicains, the main centre-right party in France, now favours a low-tax, low-welfare agenda and might shape the future of the French welfare state within the next decade should the party remain powerful. Social policies in the areas of pensions and the 35-hour working week could be targeted by the party, as demonstrated in the early stages of the 2017 presidential elections and the attack on the Hollande presidency. Welfare chauvinism, advocated by a fringe of the centre-right party led by Nicolas Sarkozy, could also be advocated by the party and implemented in the future.

As far as support for European integration is concerned, there has been an increasing level of public Euroscepticism in recent years, illustrated by the Front National's victory in the 2014 European elections. This is reflected in Sarkozy's recent calls to reform the European Union especially with regards to the Schengen agreement. A poll conducted by the University of Edinburgh in early 2016 revealed that 53 per cent of French respondents would like a referendum on EU membership, following the British example (Eichorn et al. 2016). This was echoed by a minority of elected representatives within the Républicains. The Front National and the radical left Front de Gauch have adopted a 'hard Eurosceptic' agenda following the referendum in the UK on the European Union. In contrast, most members of the political elite regard EU membership as being in France's interest.

As highlighted in the previous sections, the crisis has pushed the French left-wing government towards higher levels of taxation and public spending and led to policies to stimulate growth through labour market flexibility and a reduction in trade union influence. In 2014 the level of social expenditure in France was 31 per cent of the GDP. Throughout Hollande's presidency the economic growth rate remained lower than the OECD average, and unemployment remained high. However, the percentage of people at risk of poverty or social exclusion decreased slightly from 19.3 per cent in 2011 to 18.5 per cent in 2014, while it continued to rise in most EU countries (see Figure 4.5).

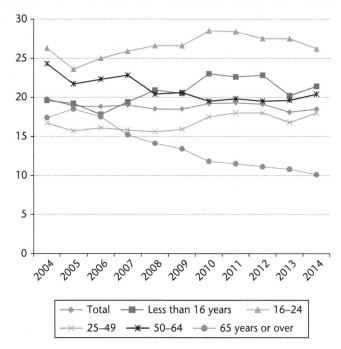

Figure 4.5. Percentage of people at risk of poverty or social exclusion by age in France, 2004–14.

Source: OECD, aggregated data

Looking further ahead, the challenges to the French welfare state outlined at the beginning of this chapter (population ageing, deficit, high unemployment) remain entrenched. Neither right nor left has succeeded in implementing a programme to tackle them decisively. The experience of the 2007–16 period illustrates the general problem across Europe of finding a response to the Great Recession that preserves the main features of existing welfare states and commands electoral support.

In sum, this chapter has outlined France's experience of the Great Recession and demonstrated that replacing a right-wing government by a Socialist-led administration did not produce the change that was hoped for by a majority of the population in 2012. Lasting societal challenges are likely to have an impact on the future of the welfare state and these have not been resolved despite cautious steps towards cutbacks and greater labour market flexibility. Unemployment remains high, the population is getting older, the level of public deficit has not been lowered, the refugee 'crisis' triggered a welfare chauvinistic reaction, and the recent wave of social–liberal reforms angered a significant proportion of the population.

The French welfare state has moved away from the conservative corporatist model, at arm's length from state control, with relatively high public spending, a high standard of childcare provision, influential trade unions, and with low inequality. Immigration is high on the political agenda and there are pressures to ensure that social provision is confined to French nationals. How far the shift in a neo-liberal direction will go is at present unclear, since there is also strong left fightback, but it is unlikely that policies will return to the previous pattern. The French welfare state is, more than ever, at a crossroads.

Notes

1. Associational liberalism is defined by Levy (1999: 9–10) as 'a liberal aversion to the dirigiste state with a countervailing faith in the co-ordinating capacities of societal and local associations'.
2. Income inequality tends to be lower in France than in other European countries. The average income of the richest ten per cent is around seven times as large as for the poorest ten per cent (against an OECD average of 9.5), while the Gini coefficient remained relatively stable (0.282 in 2005 and 0.292 in 2014). France also performs rather well in terms of gender equality compared to other European countries, scoring 57.1 points on the European Index of Gender Equality (against an EU average of 54) and scoring particularly high in terms of Power and Money dimensions (see European Parliament 2015 for further information on France and gender equality).
3. A major public-sector pension reform based on the Juppé Plan was later implemented by the Raffarin government in 2003. For detailed information on pension reforms in France since 1970, see Palier (2003) and Häusermann (2010: 99–123).
4. While this was one of socialist President Francois Mitterrand's electoral pledges back in 1981, he only managed to reduce the working week to 39 hours during his presidency.
5. It is difficult to determine the real impact of the 35-hour working week policy on job creation. The objective was to create 700,000 jobs; however, the best estimate was 350,000 jobs according to Hayden (2006).
6. Both of these laws were adopted by using Article 49-3 of the French Constitution which allows the government to bypass a vote in the French National Assembly.

References

Amable, B. Guillaud, E., and Palombarini, S. (2012) 'Changing French Capitalism: Political and Systemic Crises in France', *Journal of European Public Policy* 18(8): 1168–87.

Ambler, J. S. (ed.) (1991) *The French Welfare State: Surviving Social and Ideological Change*, New York: New York University Press.

André, M., Bozio, A., Guillot, M., and Paul-Delvaux, L. (2015) 'French Public Finances through the Financial Crisis: It's a Long Way to Recovery', *Fiscal Studies* 36(4): 431–52.

Bouget, D. (1998) 'The Juppé Plan and the Future of the French Social Welfare System', *Journal of European Social Policy* 8(2): 155–72.

CSA Research (2015) 'L'état du lien social en France fin 2015', Paris: CSA Research, http://www.csa.eu/multimedia/data/sondages/data2015/opi20151209-ATELIER-CSA-2015.pdf, accessed 10 May 2016.

Eichorn, J., Hübner, C., and Kenealy, D. (2016) 'The View from the Continent: What People in Other Member States Think about the UK's EU Referendum', Edinburgh: Applied Quantitative Methods Network, https://www.aqmen.ac.uk/sites/default/files/TheViewFromTheContinent_REPORT.pdf, accessed 10 May 2016.

Estevão, M. and Sá, F. (2006) 'Are the French Happy with the 35-Hour Workweek?', *IZA Discussion Paper* 2459, Bonn: Leibniz Information Centre for Economics.

Estevão, M. and Sá, F. (2008) 'The 35-Hour Workweek in France: Straightjacket or Welfare Improvement?', *Economic Policy* 23(55): 418–63.

EurActiv (2014) 'Commission Hails French Economic Bill as "A Step in the Right Direction"', Brussels: EurActiv, http://www.euractiv.com/section/euro-finance/news/commission-hails-french-economic-bill-as-a-step-in-the-right-direction/, accessed 10 May 2016.

European Parliament (2015) *The Policy on Gender Equality in France*, Brussels: European Union, http://www.europarl.europa.eu/RegData/etudes/IDAN/2015/510024/IPOL_IDA(2015)510024_EN.pdf, accessed 10 May 2016.

French Government (2016) 'Le Vrai/Faux du Gouvernement sur la #LoiTravail', Paris: French Government, http://www.gouvernement.fr/le-vraifaux-du-gouvernement-sur-la-loitravail-3850, accessed 10 May 2016.

Goodlife, G. (2015) 'Europe's Salience and "Owning" Euroscepticism: Explaining the Front National's Victory in the 2014 European Elections in France', *French Politics* 13: 324–45.

Grunberg, G. (2014) 'Le Socialisme français en crise', *Modern & Contemporary France* 22(4): 459–71.

Häusermann, S. (2010) *The Politics of Welfare State Reform in Continental Europe: Modernization in Hard Times*, Cambridge: Cambridge University Press.

Hayden, A. (2006) 'France's 35-Hour Week: Attack on Business? Win-Win Reform? Or Betrayal of Disadvantaged Workers?', *Politics & Society* 34(4): 503–42.

Hoang-Ngoc, L. (2009) 'La Sarkonomics entre promesses électorales et crise économique: Bilan d'étape fin 2008', *Modern & Contemporary France* 17(4): 423–34.

INSEE (2015) 'Projection de population par grand groupe d'âge en 2060', Paris: INSEE, http://www.insee.fr/fr/themes/tableau.asp?reg_id=0&ref_id=NATTEF02164, accessed 26 June 2016.

Kus, B. (2006) 'Neoliberalism, Institutional Change and the Welfare State: The Case of Britain and France', *International Journal of Comparative Sociology* 147(6): 488–525.

Lafarge, F. (2010) 'La révision générale des politiques publiques: objet, méthodes et redevabilité', *Revue française d'administration publique* 136: 755–74.

Le Bihan, B. and Martin, C. (2010) 'Reforming Long-term Care Policy in France: Private–Public Complementarities', *Social Policy & Administration* 44(4): 392–410.

Le Monde (2012) 'Comparez les programmes de Nicolas Sarkozy et François Hollande', *Le Monde*, 23 Apr. 2012, http://www.lemonde.fr/politique/article/2012/04/23/comparez-les-programmes-de-nicolas-sarkozy-et-francois-hollande_1689558_823448.html, accessed 10 May 2016.

Le Monde (2014) 'Plan d'économies: comment Valls va s'attaquer aux prestations sociales', *Le Monde*, 16 Apr. 2014, http://www.lemonde.fr/politique/article/2014/04/16/valls-donne-un-coup-de-rabot-generalise-sur-les-prestations-sociales_4402571_823448.html, accessed 10 May 2016.

Le Monde (2015) 'Ce que contient (désormais) la loi Macron', *Le Monde*, 6 Aug. 2015, http://www.lemonde.fr/les-decodeurs/article/2015/08/06/ce-que-contient-desormais-la-loi-macron_4714255_4355770.html, accessed 10 May 2016.

Levy, J. D. (1999) *Tocqueville's Revenge: State, Society, and Economy in Contemporary France*, Cambridge, MA: Harvard University Press.

Levy, J. D. (2000) 'France: Directing Adjustment?' in F. W. Scharpf and V. A. Schmidt (eds.) *Welfare and Work in the Open Economy Volume II: Diverse Responses to Common Challenges in Twelve Countries*, Oxford: Oxford University Press, 308–50.

Lewis, J., Knijn, T., Martin, C., and Ostner, I. (2008) 'Patterns of Development in Work/Family Reconciliation Policies for Parents in France, Germany, the Netherlands, and the UK in the 2000s', *Social Politics* 15(3): 261–86.

Marthaler, S. (2008) 'Nicolas Sarkozy and the Politics of French Immigration Policy', *Journal of European Public Policy* 15(3): 382–97.

Milner, S. (2012) 'Fixing France's Broken Social Model? An Assessment of Employment and Labour Market Policy under the Sarkozy Presidency', *French Politics* 10(3): 290–305.

Naczyk, M., Morel, N., and Palier, B. (2014) 'Pensions, Health and Long-Term Care: France', *ASISP Country Document update 2014*, Brussels: ASISP, http://ec.europa.eu/social/BlobServlet?docId=12964&langId=en, accessed 10 May 2016.

OECD (2012) *OECD Public Governance Reviews: France: An International Perspective on the General Review of Public Policies*, Paris: OECD Publishing, http://www.oecd-ilibrary.org/governance/oecd-public-governance-reviews-france_9789264167612-en, accessed 10 May 2016.

Palier, B. (2000) ' "Defrosting" the French Welfare State', *West European Politics* 23(2): 113–36.

Palier, B. (2003) 'Réformer les retraites en France', *French Politics, Culture & Society* 23(3): 51–72.

Palier, B. (2005) 'Ambiguous Agreement, Cumulative Change: French Social Policy in the 1990s', in W. Streeck and K. A. Thelen (eds.) *Beyond Continuity: Institutional Change in Advanced Political Economies*, Oxford: Oxford University Press, 127–44.

Palier, B. and Petrescu, L. (2007) 'France: Defending our Model', in J. Kvist and J. Saari (eds.) *The Europeanisation of Social Protection*, Bristol: Policy Press, 61–76.

Palier, B. and Thelen, K. A. (2010) 'Institutionalizing Dualism: Complementarities and Change in France and Germany', *Politics & Society* 38(1): 119–48.

Rigby, J. and Schlembach, R. (2013) 'Impossible Protest: No Borders in Calais', *Citizenship Studies* 17(2): 157–72.

Sloam, J. (2005) 'West European Social Democracy as a Model for Transfer', *Journal of Communist Studies and Transition Politics* 21(1): 67–83.

The Economist (2014) 'François Hollande, liberal?', *The Economist*, 11 Jan. 2014, http://www.economist.com/news/europe/21593421-french-president-promises-serious-supply-side-reformsagain-fran-ois-hollande-liberal, accessed 10 May 2016.

Thévenon, O. (2005) 'Family Policies in OECD Countries: A Comparative Analysis', *Population and Development Review* 37(1): 57–87.

Vail, M. I. (1999) 'The Better Part of Valour: The Politics of French Welfare Reform', *Journal of European Social Policy* 9(4): 311–29.

Vail, M. I. (2008) 'From "Welfare without Work" to "Buttressed Liberalization": The Shifting Dynamics of Labour Market Adjustment in France and Germany', *European Journal of Political Research* 47: 334–58.

Vail, M. I. (2014) 'Varieties of Liberalism: Keynesian Responses to the Great Recession in France and Germany', *Governance: An International Journal of Policy, Administration, and Institutions* 27(1): 63–85.

5

Changing Scandinavian Welfare States

Which Way Forward?

Jørgen Goul Andersen, Mi Ah Schoyen, and Bjørn Hvinden

5.1 Introduction

The main Scandinavian countries—Denmark, Norway, and Sweden—are highly similar in most respects. They represent the social democratic welfare model. They are small, open economies with proportional electoral systems which frequently result in coalition governments. In practice policy-making has benefited from a stable political climate in which pragmatic decisions and continuity have traditionally prevailed.

Social policy challenges, strategies, and outcomes have also been similar. All three countries have responded to the challenge of an ageing population with reforms of their pension/retirement systems. They have addressed the challenge of globalization by investment in research and infrastructure. Influenced by supply-side economics—and the traditional Scandinavian commitment to employment—they have adopted labour market, social, and tax reforms with the aim of increasing labour supply. They have introduced New Public Management (NPM) in an attempt to enhance efficiency and contain expenditure growth, and brought in new measures to improve the social and labour market integration of immigrants, in particular refugees.

Nevertheless, in their respective challenges, responses, and prospects the countries differ, as they do in the contexts in which the policies for managing the current crisis have developed. Economic constraints have been less stringent in Norway than in the other two countries; floating exchange rates have allowed greater room for manoeuvre to Norway and Sweden than to Denmark, whose currency is pegged to the euro; and Denmark has suffered not only from the Great Recession but also from a self-inflicted financial crisis that led to seven years without economic growth.

In this chapter we first examine conditions before the Great Recession, including economic circumstances, in order to show that pressures are relatively slight compared to those in many other European countries. Next, we compare the challenges and policy changes along key issues, before summarizing country by country and highlighting differences. Finally, we discuss possible future directions based on current trends in policies and public attitudes. Among these directions we consider damage repair, austerity, means-testing, and privatization.

5.2 Preconditions and Outcomes

Before addressing each country individually we summarize common features that reduce *exogenous* pressures for change in the Scandinavian welfare states: Well-balanced economies, prudent economic policies, a long tradition of social investment, and a highly proactive approach to demographic change, including pension reforms.

As regards *the economy*, the Scandinavian countries entered the Great Recession with positive internal as well as external balances and with surpluses on public budgets and current accounts. Norway is exceptional, with its budget surplus peaking at 17–19 per cent of GDP in 2006–8. Sweden and Denmark also exhibited large budget surpluses of 3.3 and 5.0 per cent of GDP respectively in 2007 and positive current account balances of 8.2 and 1.4 per cent.

The Swedish balances were not shaken profoundly by the 2008–9 crisis. Norway followed a Keynesian course by stimulating the economy and managed to avoid a recession, but the fall in oil prices internationally reduced the Norwegian budget surplus. Denmark followed nearly the opposite course as its current account surplus increased to 9.2 per cent of GDP by 2015, well above Norway. However, as this was obtained through lower consumption and investment (in particular in housing), public budgets turned to deficit. Nonetheless, Sweden and Denmark, unlike most EU countries, have met the requirements of the EU stability pact as regards public deficits (3 per cent GDP) and EMU debt (60 per cent GDP) without difficulty.

Permanent current account surpluses indicate high international competitiveness, but the figures also reflect *prudent economic policy*. All the Scandinavian countries are determined to avoid a repeat of the excessive deficits and inflation of the past. Aware of the 'curse of abundant natural resources', Norway has forced itself to save most of its oil revenue in a state fund with the state budget deficit limited to four per cent of the oil fund. This policy

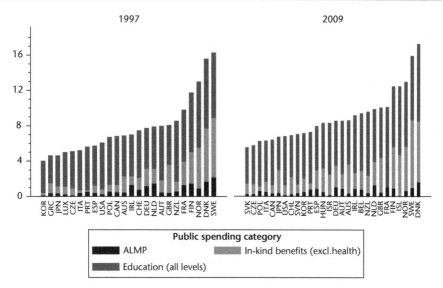

Figure 5.1. Social investment expenditures in OECD countries, 1997 and 2009 (% GDP).
Source: OECD

stands in sharp contrast to that of the UK where no attempt was made to save or invest the proceeds of North Sea oil.

As a third shared characteristic, the Scandinavian countries were early instigators of what is now referred to as *social investment* (Morel et al. 2012). They understood the value of care services for children and the elderly much earlier than other countries. Figure 5.1 shows social investment expenditures. Public childcare and generous parental benefit schemes have made it easier to combine work and family life. Sweden and Norway are consistently counted among the world's four most gender-equal societies. In addition, employment and fertility rates in Scandinavia are among the highest in the Western world.

Social investment contributes to high public spending, as shown in the first two columns of Table 5.1. However, the figures are inflated by high taxation of social transfer incomes (Adema et al. 2011). When taking into account different tax rules, net public expenditure in Scandinavia is not exceptionally high. It is also important to note that low public welfare provision helps promote private welfare. In fact, total welfare costs (public plus private) are at least as high in liberal welfare states like the USA or UK (see Chapter 3).

Statistics that express state expenditure as a proportion of GDP depend as much on the size of GDP as on the amount spent by the state. In relative terms, spending in Norway is close to the OECD average and far below Sweden

Table 5.1. Gross and net public social expenditure, and total social expenditure (public plus private: % GDP)

	2014	2011			
	Gross Public Social Expenditure	Gross Public Social Expenditure	Net Public Social Expenditure	Net Social Expenditure Public+Private	Net Private Social Expenditure
Denmark	30.1	30.1	23.4	26.1	2.7
Sweden	28.1	27.2	22.5	24.6	2.1
Norway	22.0	21.8	18.1	19.3	1.2
OECD -total	21.6	21.4	19.6	21.7	2.1

Source: stats.oecd.org.

and Denmark. But Norway has avoided dramatic cutbacks in social benefits and services, and the figures reflect its large GDP. By the same token, Denmark was ahead of Sweden following 2008–9 as regards relative figures, but while Denmark suffered from economic stagnation after the recession, Sweden's growth rate was among the highest in Europe (Goul Andersen 2011a; 2013).

The fourth trend common to all countries is the *proactive approach to the challenge of ageing*. According to mainstream projections, current welfare programmes in Scandinavia are largely sustainable without increasing taxes or cutting benefits, despite long-term demographic change (Goul Andersen and Hatland 2014). Social investment contributes to high fertility rates (between 1.7 and 2.0 births per woman) which, alongside high net migration, reduce dependency ratios in the future. By 2050 all three countries will face old-age dependency ratios that are in between current ratios in Italy and Japan, and far below the EU average (Figure 5.2). Most importantly, pension systems have been thoroughly reformed, as we shall discuss.

Looking at outcomes, the Scandinavian countries have managed well economically, according to standard measures such as GDP per capita. Figure 5.3 reveals the relative changes between 1990 and 2015, as compared with EU15 and the USA.[1] Norway is unique due to its oil, but Sweden and Denmark have performed at least as well as the EU15 or the US.

As regards employment, Scandinavian employment rates have always been among the highest in Europe. This is still the case, but Scandinavian figures are less exceptional than previously considered since continental Europe is catching up (see Chapter 1).

Finally, the Scandinavian countries follow the global trend towards higher inequality, but Gini coefficients and poverty rates remain among the lowest in the OECD. This reflects the redistribution of the welfare state, but also a low wage dispersion (OECD 2016: 238). Their compressed earnings structures, in turn, reflect high unionization, solidaristic wage agreements (Moene and

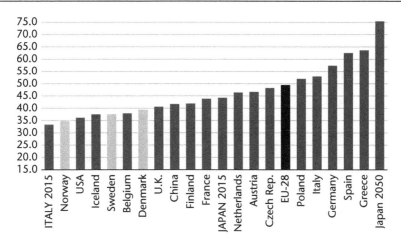

Figure 5.2. Projected old-age dependency ratios 2050: Population 65+ as percentage of population 15–64.

Source: Eurostat; Statistics Japan (2016) + US Census (2010)

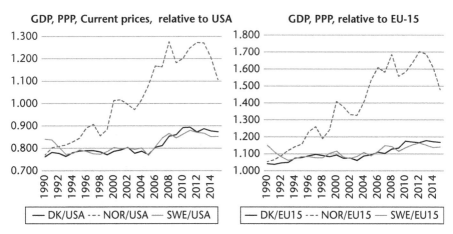

Figure 5.3. GDP in Sweden, Denmark, and Norway, relative to the USA and EU15.

Source: stats.oecd.org (National Accounts—Main Aggregates—Gross Domestic Product)

Wallerstein 2005; Erixon 2010), and coordinated wage setting (Dølvik et al. 2015a). As regards poverty, Denmark, Norway, and Sweden rank two, six, and 12 respectively out of 36 countries (OECD 2015).

One might expect an employment–equality trade-off, but in spite of compressed wage structures with high minimum wages, the Scandinavian countries have maintained comparatively high employment rates among the lowest educated, with unemployment varying less according to education level than in most other countries, including the UK and US (Goul Andersen 2007; 2013).

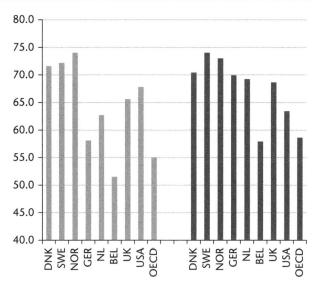

Figure 5.4. Employment rates (percentage) among women, 2000 (grey) and 2015 (black).

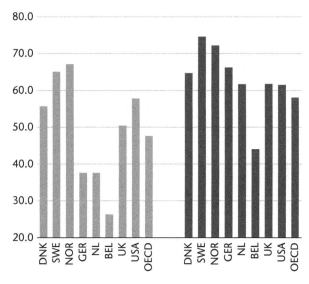

Figure 5.5. Employment rates (percentage) among 55–64 years old, 2000 (grey) and 2015 (black).

As elsewhere, it is common to speak of economic 'challenges' to the welfare state, and by definition there is always the challenge of prioritizing and of making ends meet. But it seems fair to conclude that in the Scandinavian countries economic pressure plays a smaller role as a driver of future welfare state change than in most European countries. Political factors are likely to be more important.

5.3 Recent Developments: Transformation of the Social Contract?

Even though Norway and Sweden were not left entirely unscathed by the Great Recession, the impact was modest. Norway used fiscal policy to avoid a recession, and Sweden rapidly contained the pressures on its economy, helped by significant depreciation of its currency. However, in addition to the recession Denmark was hit by the bursting of a credit and housing bubble and suffered seven years of zero growth, a problem that resulted from an excessive liberalization of credit in the early 2000s. While the crisis did not affect the political agenda dramatically in Norway and Sweden, from 2010 the Danish government used the recession to justify structural reforms that had been planned long before the crisis, all of which aimed at increasing long-term labour supply. The pressures on the economy were aggravated by a strict austerity programme which delayed short-term economic recovery. The 2011–15 Social Democratic government continued this course and alienated former voters (Goul Andersen 2016a). When a Liberal minority government assumed office (2015) it used low economic growth to justify a neo-liberal proposal (not adopted) with tax cuts financed by social retrenchment.

The countries' pre-crisis history, however, was more similar. All three countries were concerned with sustainability vis-à-vis demographic change, and adopted social, labour market, and tax reforms to increase labour supply. However, overall Norway has been more reluctant to impose cuts in benefits and entitlements than the other two countries (Hippe and Berge 2013).

5.3.1 *Pension and Retirement Reforms*

Even though future demographic change is modest because of comparatively high fertility rates and net migration, the pension systems of Sweden, Norway, and Denmark have been thoroughly reformed (Goul Andersen 2011c; Sjögren Lindquist and Wadensjö 2011; Christensen et al. 2012). In Sweden (1994) and Norway (2011) the defined benefit schemes with a basic ('people's') pension and earnings-related supplements were replaced with a notional defined contribution scheme combined with a means-tested guaranteed pension. Future pensions will depend on contributions as well as on average life expectancy. Sweden also has an occupational pension system for all workers and a housing benefit scheme (as does Denmark). Norway has a means-tested housing benefit and made occupational pensions mandatory in 2006.

In Denmark almost universal, fully funded occupational pensions were established by the social partners in 1991. Later reforms linked retirement ages to life expectancy at 60, voluntary early retirement allowances were phased out, and the pension age is expected to increase to at least 70 years for those born after 1970. This is the Danish equivalent of pension sustainability measures in Sweden and Norway (Greve 2007).

The economic challenges of ageing have been addressed with considerable success. The drawback is that there is substantial and significantly increasing class inequality in health and life expectancy (Brønnum-Hansen and Baadsgaard 2012). However, the Danish retirement system has moved from class-graduated retirement age (via voluntary early retirement) towards 'one size fits all'.

Previously, voluntary early retirement provided an early exit opportunity. Working until the age of 70 creates problems for people with deteriorating health, who are often unable to work but fail to qualify for disablement pension. This mostly affects the lower social strata. In Norway the contractual early retirement scheme, initially created to bridge the gap between the age of 62 to the pension age of 67 for worn-out workers, was changed in 2011 to a lifelong (but smaller) pension that can be taken out from the age of 62 alongside working or receiving state pension. The Norwegian reform, although less radical than those in Denmark and Sweden, reflects the same underlying concerns.

5.3.2 *Disability and Sickness Absence*

All Scandinavian countries have made great efforts to reduce sickness absence and limit exit to disability pensions. The political legitimation is that labour market inclusion is the best way to prevent poverty and social marginalization (Bay et al. 2014). The strategy has therefore been to create opportunities for return to part- or full-time work. For those unable to return to work it is essential that social security is adequate. While this was largely the case in Scandinavia in 2000 (Nordlund 2000), and remains so in Norway and to some extent in Sweden, social protection in Denmark has clearly deteriorated.

The Norwegian sickness insurance scheme is the most generous in the world. It covers all workers at full wage compensation (up to a ceiling) without any waiting days for up to one year (NOSOSKO 2015: 62; Hagelund 2014). The system, in place since 1978, has largely resisted government attempts to reduce the replacement rate or tighten eligibility.

In Sweden, cover is provided for a longer period (up to 2.5 years), but with a compensation rate of 80 per cent, falling to 75 per cent after one year. Unless an impairment is permanent and substantial, the employee is protected against dismissal. Employment protection is weak in Denmark: Employees usually lose their jobs if they receive sickness pay for more than 120 days in a year. In 2014 the duration was, in principle, reduced from 52 to 22 weeks, and the benefit ceiling is low. There is then entitlement to a preparatory programme (*jobafklaringsforløb*) at social assistance benefit level, although this is not means-tested. All three countries have introduced schemes to reduce sickness absence via early follow-up of the long-term sick/absent, work capacity assessment, and partial sick leave, but with limited success (Hagelund 2014).

In Norway about ten per cent of the working-age population claim disability benefits, many as an early retirement scheme. The temporary disability benefit introduced in 2004, was replaced in 2010 by a much tighter work assessment allowance (Kann et al. 2013). In Sweden the disability pension scheme was formally abandoned in 2003. Disability benefits (*Sjukersättning*) continued, but the numbers claiming fell from 66,000 to 20,000 between 2004 and 2015. This was partly the indirect effect of efforts to reduce the numbers receiving long-term sickness benefits and partly due to tightening of eligibility. Denmark introduced a so-called flex job scheme in 1998, which allowed disabled people to receive the same wages for a reduced workload. This was cut back in 2013 and eligibility rules for disability pension made more stringent, more than halving the number of pensions awarded (Ankestyrelsen 2016).

Again we find Denmark and Norway at two extremes. Norwegian governments have been cautious. Replacement levels, income ceilings, and benefit periods have remained largely unchanged (Hippe and Berge 2013). In Denmark a deterioration in social security has coincided with greater feelings of insecurity among vulnerable groups (Andersen et al. 2013; 2015; Hede et al. 2009; 2011); poor health has impacted much more strongly on political trust (Goul Andersen 2016b).

5.3.3 *Labour Market Reforms*

Unemployment compensation has been tightened in Scandinavia, as elsewhere. Until the 1990s targets for reform were easy to identify in Denmark and Sweden: the replacement rate was high (at 90 per cent, up to a ceiling), duration was long, and conditions and control were lenient.

Danish reforms in the 1990s cut benefit entitlement from seven to four years. As unemployment was halved in the same period, few people moved onto social assistance. Activation requirements and 'conditionality' (Clasen et al. 2001) were strengthened—especially after 2001 when the new Liberal/Conservative government adopted a 'work-first' approach. As Denmark simultaneously moved towards full employment, however, the social impact was small (Goul Andersen and Jensen 2002; Goul Andersen 2011b). Employment incentives were also strengthened via the introduction of tax credit for those in jobs, but unemployment benefits were maintained. The breaking point came in 2010 when duration was halved to two years, and the requalification requirement was doubled from 26 to 52 weeks of employment; ten to twenty times more unemployed than expected lost entitlement (Pedersen and Andersen 2014: 42). The 2011 Social Democratic government postponed implementation, but the share of (registered) unemployed receiving unemployment benefits dropped from 80 per cent in 2009–11 to 70 per cent in 2012–15. After the 2015 election the three main parties agreed an amendment that made it slightly easier to requalify for unemployment benefits through temporary work.

Conditionality was also tightened substantially in Sweden (Berglund and Esser 2014; Sjöberg 2011), but the most important changes here were the decline in compensation rates, shorter duration, and increasing insecurity. Economic crisis was the reform driver. In 1993 benefits were cut to 80 per cent, and continuing activation lasting throughout the period of unemployment was introduced. But most importantly, the adjustment of benefit ceilings to wages was abandoned in 1993, and up to 2015 the ceiling was only raised twice—the largest reduction of net compensation rates within OECD countries (Dagpengekommissionen 2015a: 45; Sjöberg 2011: 213)—although it was raised again by 2015. Up until 2006 some 60–70 per cent of the unemployed received unemployment benefits. By 2012 this had dropped to about one quarter (Berglund and Esser 2014). The new approach to unemployment under Sweden's centre-right government from 2006 onwards had a dramatic impact.

Norway has a mandatory unemployment insurance scheme, but Denmark and Sweden have maintained the Ghent system of voluntary, state-subsidized unemployment insurance. This was initially a liberal-leaning model that was made universal and decommodifying through higher compensation rates, longer duration, higher subsidies, and elimination of the association between risk and contributions via fixed contributions. However, by changing these parameters the system could also be moved back towards the liberal model (Goul Andersen 2013; Dølvik et al. 2015b). In both Sweden and Denmark efforts were made to increase contributions via removing or limiting tax deductions. In Denmark the tax value of deductions will fall from up to 73 to 25 per cent by 2019. Indexation to wages was maintained, but is being reduced by five per cent between 2016 and 2022 to co-finance the tax cuts of the Social Democratic government in 2012. In both countries private insurance was introduced. By 2014 more than 55 per cent of the insured in Sweden also had private coverage, while the proportion remained much lower in Denmark (Dagpengekommissionen 2015b: 47; Rasmussen 2012).

Norway's administrative system was restructured to integrate various groups of non-employed and, as in Denmark and Sweden, conditions became tighter. The threshold in terms of income and working hours that an unemployed person had to meet to qualify for insurance benefits was raised. Procedures for monitoring job search by unemployed people were tightened (Eurofound 2012). Reforms were limited to cutting entitlement from three to two years in 2003; however, in a full employment economy this had less impact than in Sweden and Denmark.

Since the 1950s an *active labour market policy* (ALMP) was a key element of the Swedish economic strategy to bring together international competition, dynamic growth, and full employment by upgrading and qualifying the labour force. In Denmark ALMP was extended in 1993 as the main instrument against structural unemployment, and as an alternative to lower minimum wages or reduced social protection. Unemployment declined more than expected, but evaluations showed that ALMP was not the main cause (Arbejdsministeriet 2000). Similar findings emerged in Sweden and across OECD countries (Martin and Grubb 2001).

In Denmark activation measures increasingly shifted from a human capital to a disciplinary approach (Larsen and Mailand 2007). Sweden embarked on a 'workfarist' line in which ALMP was downsized, but even in 2014, the Danish expenditure figure remained the highest and the Swedish figure the second highest among the OECD countries.

5.3.4 *Tax Reform*

Norway has also been the most stable country as regards tax reforms. Following the general trend towards broadening the tax base and reducing tax rates, Norway introduced what is labelled 'The Nordic dual income tax' (Sørensen 1994) in a major reform in 1992. This reform separated labour and capital income, with a lower, flat tax rate for capital income (as in Sweden, while Denmark does not follow this consistently), with further minor reforms in 2006 and 2015 (Pirttilä and Selin 2011). The 2015 reform also cut corporate taxes and a provided a small tax relief for most tax payers, and is planned to continue. Unlike Sweden and Denmark, Norway has maintained a wealth tax and has not introduced earned income tax credit (EITC).

The famous Swedish 1991 reform—referred to as the 'tax reform of the century'—was adopted after several years of consensus-building among political elites (Agell et al. 1996). It radically reduced the maximum marginal tax rate on labour to 51 per cent and on capital income to 30 per cent. The reform's timing was a disaster since its anti-inflationary incentive for savings exacerbated the recession of the early 1990s. Although the reform came from a Social Democratic government, it enjoyed most support from the upper social strata—and from men (Svallfors 1992). By 1995 the marginal tax rate for high incomes was increased by a temporary austerity tax which soon became permanent.

The Swedish Conservative-led government in 2006–14 presented itself as centrist but managed to change taxes through small, annual cuts. In 2007 an earned income tax credit was introduced. It is a universal credit with a ceiling, which makes it less redistributive than its Anglo-Saxon counterparts (Aaberge and Flood 2013). By 2008 Sweden had eliminated wealth taxes (like Denmark in 1996) and strongly reduced taxes on real property; in return the capital gains tax for homeowners—a distinctive Swedish tax—was increased from 20 to 22 per cent.

Denmark also adopted a series of seven big tax reforms since 1985. The typical Danish formula, like that in Sweden, consisted of revenue-neutral reforms that would broaden the tax base, reduce marginal taxes, and only have small distributional effects (Goul Andersen 2013), but the distributional impact was cumulative. The 2012 reform was co-financed by welfare retrenchment. This was even more prominent in a new government proposal in 2016 which failed to gain support in parliament; a new proposal is being announced in 2017. Between 1985 and 2013 the highest marginal tax rate was reduced from 73 to 55.6 per cent, and the income bracket raised. A proposal to cut this by 5 per cent failed in parliament. An income tax credit for the employed—as in Sweden, a universal credit with a ceiling—was introduced in the 2003 reform and expanded in 2009 and 2012 to about the Swedish level.

5.3.5 New Public Management

One of the important waves of welfare reform in the public sector, New Public Management (NPM) was introduced in Scandinavia in the 1980s to control expenditure growth and raise efficiency in state services. Norway has adopted NPM rather more reluctantly than the other countries (Lægreid et al. 2013). Denmark managed to gain control over public service expenditure in the 1980s, but it largely abstained from market solutions until 2001 (Christiansen 1998; Green-Pedersen 2002). By contrast, the Swedish government in 1991–4 launched a 'choice revolution' in the public sector and invited private suppliers in childcare, schools, healthcare, and elder care (Hansen 2013; Kristiansen 2015). This reform also involved large for-profit companies in childcare and schools, even more successfully than anticipated, especially in the education and child-care sectors. It now seems almost irreversible since citizens are reluctant to abandon an opportunity for greater choice.

The central question from a welfare perspective is whether marketization leads to market inequalities. It should be underlined that even though the Swedish school system involves private for-profit providers, in principle all children receive the same service (West 2014). The ideals of universalism and citizenship are not therefore immediately undermined (Blomqvist 2013). So far, privatization of childcare, schools, and elder care in Scandinavia has not involved a breach with universalism. The state invites private providers, but the state foots the bill, and all citizens receive the same service. If private actors deliver higher quality for the same money they attract more users.

Healthcare insurance differs as it offers a supplementary or supposedly better service. There has been an expansion of private (or occupational) health insurance in Scandinavia, especially in Denmark (Berge and Hyggen 2010), but except for some treatments at the margins of conventional healthcare, one cannot buy better treatment. Previously, the main incentive to buy private insurance was to jump the queue, but treatment guarantees in the public system have greatly reduced waiting times. It is difficult to imagine private insurance as a threat to universal, 'best possible' standards in health care.

Still, it is feared that privatization may undermine social cohesion. Private welfare in Sweden has also been criticized for its high profits, much of which has been channelled to tax havens (Burström 2015).

Whether privatization involves efficiency gains, lower quality, or a worse work environment will probably remain a matter of ideological dispute. A meta-evaluation concludes that there is little real knowledge in this area (Helby Petersen and Hjelmar 2014), except that privatization may bring some cost savings and quality improvements in elder care. However, as we will argue, if the quality of public service provision falls there may be strong institutional feedback effects.

5.3.6 Immigration

Until the 1960s there was little immigration to the Scandinavian countries, except for Finns working in Sweden. From the mid-1960s until the early 1970s, all three allowed a modest immigration of 'guest workers', mainly from Yugoslavia, Turkey, and Pakistan, some of whom settled and brought over their families. Although the 'guest worker' population expanded, the size and composition of immigration only began to change radically in the 1980s.

Apart from some refugees from Chile and Vietnam in the 1970s, the Scandinavian countries had traditionally granted asylum to a few resettlement (quota) refugees and to a few refugees from Eastern Europe. However, in Denmark and Norway, the number of refugees multiplied tenfold in the early 1980s (Pedersen 1999), and a decade later the Yugoslav wars led to an enormous increase in the number of asylum seekers. Since the 1980s wars and civil wars in Asia, Africa, and the Middle East have contributed waves of refugees. By 2000 the foreign-born population had increased to 11.3 per cent in Sweden, 6.5 per cent in Norway, and 5.6 per cent in Denmark.

By 2015 the civil war in Syria contributed to the highest number of asylum seekers recorded. 2015 was an exception, however, and during the early 2000s asylum seekers were few. Nonetheless, immigration peaked shortly before the Great Recession because of labour migration from Eastern Europe, or via green card arrangements. In 2016 the largest immigrant group in Denmark and Norway was the Poles.[2] Immigration from Western Europe also increased, but this settlement tends to be more temporary (Pedersen 1999). By 2016 the foreign-born population was 17.0 per cent in Sweden, 13.4 per cent in Norway and 9.5 per cent in Denmark.

Unlike labour force immigration, the immigration of refugees seldom benefits a country economically. In addition to low qualifications, many refugees have health problems, and, accordingly, low employment rates. Political claims that the costs constitute a threat to the welfare state are exaggerated, however. In Denmark net costs are typically calculated to 0.5–1 per cent of GDP (Wadensjö and Orrje 2002; Schultz-Nielsen and Tranæs 2014). There are also concerns that immigration could undermine the high minimum wages, but unions have largely prevented this.

Not surprisingly, the approach of the Scandinavian welfare states, at least since the 1990s, has been to promote the integration of immigrants in the labour market. Introduction programmes have been adopted in all three countries (Breidahl 2012) to ensure that immigrants learn the country's language, history, and culture, and a variety of ALMP measures have been applied. Nearly all pre-school immigrant children are enrolled in kindergartens (Goul Andersen 2007), and this is generally understood as an investment since it improves educational outcomes. Second-generation immigrants, especially women, also achieve better results in the education system (Tranæs 2008; Ministry of Children, Equality and Social Inclusion 2011), but many still do not progress beyond compulsory schooling.

Immigrants generally enjoy the same social rights and public services as natives in the universal Scandinavian welfare states, except in the area of pensions. Denmark is an exception, however, as regards income replacement. From 2002 to 2011 new immigrants from countries outside the European Economic Area received a much reduced social assistance (called 'introductory assistance') for the first seven years after arrival. From 2006 married social assistance recipients were obliged to work for 300, later 450, hours (in an unsubsidized job) for two years to maintain eligibility for social assistance. These 'poverty schemes', as they were dubbed by the new government, were abandoned in 2011 but reintroduced in 2015 when the Liberals returned to office. In 2016 the lower introduction allowance was extended from new immigrants to apply to all social assistance recipients with fewer than seven years' residence, but the government here sought to target groups mainly composed of non-Western immigrants.

Denmark and Sweden have markedly different degrees of political conflict over the issue of immigration. In Denmark the anti-immigration Progress Party, and later the Danish People's Party, mobilized on the issue in the mid-1980s and were soon joined by centre-right parties (Green-Pedersen and Krogstrup 2008). However, the mainstream parties in Sweden have sought to isolate the nationalist Sweden Democrats, except for an opening in 2016 by the conservatives (Moderaterna)—which was certainly not rewarded in opinion polls. In Norway the Progress Party formed a coalition government with the Conservatives in 2013.

In sum, the idea that welfare states are resilient to change is by no means confirmed in the case of the Scandinavian countries. All three have adapted proactively to the future of an ageing society, even though prospective age pressures are comparatively modest. They have adopted tax and welfare reforms to increase labour supply, often redefining social problems as employment problems, and they have experimented with NPM and privatization and the changes have been most far-reaching in Denmark and Sweden. Finally, immigration has moved rapidly up the policy agenda and all three countries have moved in 2015–16 to curtail benefit rights for asylum seekers. Globalization has provided an extra stimulus to investment in research, education, and infrastructure.

5.4 Still a Scandinavian Family?

As underlined above, the Scandinavian welfare states have each developed differently. Norway has remained loyal to the Nordic welfare model. There are fewer instances of severe cuts in social protection or of changes in social protection systems, and Scandinavian full employment policy has been maintained. By contrast, the Swedish and Danish welfare states have undergone quite significant changes. Both countries have shortened the duration of unemployment benefits and cut compensation levels. The Ghent system has been pulled in a more liberal direction with the higher net contributions after tax. Until the 2015 adjustment the decline of the compensation level in Sweden was the largest within OECD countries, and this encouraged supplementary private insurance provided by the trade unions. A greater proportion of the unemployed—most dramatically in Sweden—was left without unemployment benefits. Even though introducing EITC in the tax system is a softer approach than benefit cuts to 'making work pay', it still reduces the compensation rate.

Table 5.2. Cumulative growth in public consumption, 2002–10 and 2011–15 (%)

	2002–10	2011–15
Denmark	17.5	1.8
Sweden	10.3	7.5
Norway	21.9	8.5
Germany	12.1	7.4
UK	23.2	5.9
EU(28)	18.7	2.6
USA	18.2	−4.9

Source: stats.oecd.org and Quarterly National Accounts vol.2016 (3).

Public consumption expenditure, however, has continued to increase in Sweden and Norway throughout the crisis. In Sweden, the use of vouchers and outsourcing to provide services through a variety of public and private providers has been pursued extensively. As regards cash benefits, the generosity index of Scruggs et al. (2014; quoted in Dølvik et al, 2015b: 93) reveals status quo in Norway, but a steep decline in Sweden after 2005. The Danish figures only reveal modest decline 2005–10, but in 2010 Denmark embarked on radical structural reforms of the cash benefit systems. These include tighter economic incentives to mobilize people into work, tougher sanctions, and strict work tests that reduce entitlements for those who fail to pursue jobs with sufficient vigour. More people with long-term unemployment or health issues have ended up in difficult circumstances, receiving social assistance. The high number of social assistance recipients has in turn served as an argument for tightening the eligibility rules for this group. In addition to impaired income security, the Danish welfare state is distinctive in Scandinavia with its severe retrenchment in public consumption since 2010. Privatization has been more modest in this country than in Sweden, where the voucher system has produced the greatest changes.

Public consumption as well as cash benefit generosity remains comparatively high, even in Sweden and Denmark (Dølvik et al. 2015b: 93). Moves towards the privatization of welfare services have not included private financing. Unemployment is modest by comparative standards and, especially in Sweden, aggregate unemployment rates are inflated by the large number of foreigners with employment problems. These reservations aside, only the Norwegian welfare state remains fully intact whereas the Swedish and Danish welfare states have become less distinct than previously, and inequality and poverty rates have increased significantly.

In Denmark this has been aggravated by a political discourse increasingly hostile to immigrants, and, since 2010, increasingly likely to stigmatize social assistance recipients regardless of origin. Moreover, the low economic growth—mostly rooted, as already mentioned, in neo-liberal policy failures of the past such as credit liberalization before the recession and austerity afterwards—ironically became a justification for more radical neo-liberal policy proposals of the Liberal minority government in 2016.

5.5 Possible Trajectories for the Future

Considering possible future directions, we have to bear in mind not only public opinion (generally favourable to welfare) but also the trajectories that emerge from recent policy changes. Public opinion is always policy contingent: opinion formation takes place in a situational context in which options are limited. Moreover, people adapt their attitudes to political messages and to institutions; institutions may even shape people's behaviour, for example as users of welfare services, and this, in turn, may affect their attitudes.

5.5.1 Damage Repair: Rebuilding Nordic Welfare

One scenario is that Denmark and Sweden take a step back from their far-reaching reforms, not by repealing the reforms but by repairing the damage to social protection. In the absence of severe economic pressure, this remains likely. We have already seen steps in this direction. Sweden raised the unemployment benefit ceiling significantly in 2015. In Denmark the 2014 labour market reform modified the conditions for requalifying for unemployment benefits.

A similar retreat might also apply to public service reform. The Danish negative growth in public consumption per capita over 2011–16 is highly unusual and would previously have been considered impossible to maintain against pressures from voters, public employees, and user groups. In Sweden growth in public consumption was maintained throughout the recession, but the privatization of welfare services has been a source of debate; a questioning of the quality of private welfare was stimulated by the decline in the positon of Swedish students in the global PISA tests. Also, the Social Democratic government has attacked the profits made by private sector providers, an attack supported strongly by the public (Ohlsson et al. 2016). More generally, schemes that can be presented as offering freer choices are difficult to repeal, but decision makers can introduce heavy regulations that make private investment in this field unattractive.

Importantly, the negative social consequences of recent cutbacks, not least in Denmark, affect groups that score high on any 'deservingness' criterion (van Oorschot 2000). If their experiences are covered in the media, they tend to generate widespread identification, as happened when large numbers lost unemployment benefits in Denmark in 2013–14. However, it is also noteworthy that when the Social Democrats were out of office and the case was closed politically following a compromise between the Social Democrats, the Liberals, and the Danish People's Party, the media became silent on the problems, even though they were far from solved.

5.5.2 Prolonged Austerity

It seems unlikely that the welfare state will ever return to the growth rates of the golden age in the 1960s. However, these growth rates were driven by the changed division of labour between state and family as regards child and elder care, and by an explosion in education. This process is now complete. In the future, there will be demographically determined increases in expenditures, but these are by and large financed already; there is no need to raise taxes or to cut service levels due to ageing populations.

As regards the economic future, Norway may face a challenge to restructure its economy as oil production declines even further and becomes less profitable. Moreover, several observers (such as the IMF) fear that the housing bubble will burst. In 2015–16 the Norwegian current account surplus declined conspicuously, and the exploitation of oil revenues for current state expenditures—and tax cuts—seem to reach unprecedented heights in 2017. In short, the Norwegian economy will probably become more like those of other European countries, but in general, there is nothing to indicate that the Scandinavian countries will face severe economic challenges. If austerity is to prevail, it will be mainly for political reasons.

In Denmark, the Liberal government in 2016 presented a '2025 plan' that would mean tax cuts and permanent austerity in the public sector, regarding both cash benefits and welfare services, justified as a means of breaking a decade of economic stagnation. This idea of a neo-liberal revolution would seem impossible to carry through in parliament, and even more difficult to justify to the voters. However, if it was carried through one cannot automatically infer that the government would be defeated in the next election, and the decisions repealed. There is also the possibility that people would adapt to the new conditions by turning to the market for private alternatives for themselves and thereby crowd in private welfare.

5.5.3 *Privatization: Promoting or Undermining State Welfare?*

Privatization can develop in several directions. One is the *mixed economy of welfare* which we have hinted at above; another is *new public management* which has introduced quasi-markets within the public sector; finally there is the conventional meaning of *state vs market* responsibility. Undoubtedly, responsibility for welfare in Scandinavia has become more divided— between the state, the individual, the third sector, the social partners, and even corporate social responsibility. However, there seems to be an underlying consensus that voluntary work should not replace ordinary paid work, and that the inclusion of other actors does not reduce state responsibility for outcomes. As regards *new public management*, Scandinavian countries have had positive and negative experiences, and, as elsewhere, there is increasing focus on the negative side effects. But implications for welfare would seem modest. In Scandinavia, new public management was never really aimed at scaling down public responsibility for welfare, and consumer influence (exit) has always been mixed with user influence (voice) in what Hernes (1988) dubbed 'activist' welfare states (Goul Andersen and Rossteutscher 2007).

The important issue is whether one can imagine an expansion of private market solutions that would imply a break with universalism in the sense that affluent people could buy better welfare services (or income security) than the public sector provides (Beland et al. 2014). So far this has not been an issue, with the same standards applying to all regardless of the type of supply (private or public). However, this might present a challenge in the future, and Scandinavian 'consumers', already socialized to choose between providers of welfare, might also choose to pay a little more to obtain better services. This presupposes that private provision is affordable for a substantial number of people, that state provision is considered unsatisfactory, and that there are institutional opportunities for establishing private alternatives with service levels that meet the demand.

In Denmark there are few institutional barriers for private alternatives, if the quality of public services is considered inadequate. Such behavioural adaptations would even appear likely if the government should manage to execute its initial 2025 plan with its small annual reductions in service costs per capita (despite rapid population growth and a 45 per cent increase in the number of people aged 75 and older). In principle it is even possible that people would opt for tax cuts in order to be able to afford better welfare for themselves. The government's 2025 plan would amount to path-breaking change. 2010–15 witnessed an unprecedented decline of public consumption per capita, and the plan anticipated negative growth per capita for the entire period 2010–25.

A similar scenario in Sweden would require changes in the institutional set-up. But more importantly, it would presuppose that the government breaks away from its increases in public service expenditure. This is even more the case in Norway, the country with probably the highest proportion of citizens able to pay for higher quality, but here state provision has so far been acceptable.

In summary, privatization is not the most likely future for Scandinavian welfare, but the possibility exists: a successful neo-liberal attack against the welfare state could not only generate a political counter-reaction, as at present (Goul Andersen 2013); it might also generate behavioural adaption to the new realities. Recent political and institutional changes, especially in Denmark, could in principle usher in a silent revolution of privatization as people choose to take up private services.

5.5.4 Targeting

The welfare state is sometimes criticized for its high costs and limited effectiveness because the state supports everybody rather than focusing on those most in need. Danish data reveal that voters are ambivalent: they seem to support the idea that welfare should be targeted at the poor, but at the same time refuse all conceivable specific proposals that would make social security and services more targeted. Moreover, there is virtually no relationship between the specific pro-targeting attitudes and the general more generous stance, except in a few, very marginal cases (Goul Andersen 2013).

The socialization of the population into universal institutions aside, however, there is a further impediment to policy change: the interaction between marginal income tax rates and means-tested benefits generates very high marginal tax rates. This is a solid correction mechanism if means-testing is expanded: in universal schemes there is a strong bias towards maintaining the status quo. Accordingly, the chances of moving in the same direction as the UK (Chapter 3) by targeting more and more benefits would appear slim.

5.5.5 Welfare Chauvinism

In the last two decades waves of asylum seekers and migrant workers from Eastern Europe have driven discussions about who are 'deserving' in relation to welfare protection. This is understandable from ordinary 'deservingness' criteria (van Oorschot 2000)—not least the criterion of reciprocity—and people do think about the welfare state in national terms. There is the economic challenge of immigration, but as mentioned, this is relatively marginal. More important are the symbolic aspects, as illustrated by the 2013 Danish debate about migrant workers receiving child benefit for their children who remained at home. The amount of money involved was negligible, and if any immigrant group provides a surplus, it is workers from EU countries who leave their family behind: they pay taxes and receive little in return. Nonetheless, the Social Democratic government faced extremely strong, firmly rooted opposition, even among its own supporters.

In Denmark, since 2002 (with an interruption in 2011–15), welfare chauvinism has been institutionalized in the shape of lower social assistance for immigrants for the first seven years and tighter eligibility and entitlement criteria which de facto target non-Western immigrants (Goul Andersen 2007). Since 2015 this has accelerated, also supported by the Social Democrats; such proposals are now a standard element of party competition in Denmark.

It is possible that Sweden and Norway could move in the same direction. The Swedish parties remained united against the nationalist Sweden Democrats, but in 2016 the conservative party tried to modify its position.

In Norway the Progress Party is a government coalition partner. And in Denmark, the Danish People's Party became the second largest party in the 2015 election. Even if countries should embark on this nationalist path, the universal welfare states of Scandinavia will still ensure far-reaching inclusion of immigrants, and depriving immigrants of equal access to social services and other cash benefits has never been discussed. However, it is possible to restrict entry to the country—and here the Scandinavian countries have taken action, with new regulations that limit the number of asylum seekers who can enter and conditions that make it much harder for family members to come into the countries.

5.6 Conclusion

All Scandinavian countries recognized the long-term economic, social, and political pressures on their welfare states and responded with measures that improved the quality and availability of their labour forces, contained pressures on pensions through adjustments to pension age and entitlement, and helped ensure that more disabled and unemployed people moved into jobs. They responded to the 2008–9 crisis with some constraints on public spending but retained their distinctive social democratic approach. Overall social spending remains high, there is a high degree of inclusive, universal provision, and the government provides high-quality health, social care, education and childcare services and active support to help unemployed people into paid work.

There are also national differences. Denmark made the deepest spending cuts and has moved towards a work-first benefit system for those of working age. Sweden has also cut benefits for unemployed people and introduced more stringent targeting of welfare. It has expanded the use of private market services, largely state-financed and within a strict regulatory framework. Norway, protected to a considerable extent by its oil wealth, has done least to cut back its welfare state. Denmark has moved to limit immigration. Sweden and Norway remain more welcoming to immigrants than other European nations. However they have also introduced restrictions on asylum seekers in the very recent past in response to the demands of right-wing parties.

Scandinavian social democracy has experienced real pressures as a result of the great recession and the growth of right-wing populism. It retains considerable strength and appears likely to sustain its distinctive approach to state welfare, perhaps suffering from erosion at the margin, into the future.

Notes

1. The comparison is based on PPP in current prices. This measure captures changes in volume as well as changes in relative prices. Flexible exploitation of niches is a competitiveness factor. In Denmark the terms of trade have improved steadily for 70 years (Statistics Denmark 2014). This is not captured by PPP *in fixed* prices. In addition, it should be noticed that relying on GDP measures rather than Gross National Income (GNI) ignores that fact that for Norway and Denmark substantial incomes from net investments abroad contribute to these countries' wealth.
2. Source: Statistics Denmark, Norway and Sweden. In Sweden the Polish ranked fourth, after the Finns, the Iraqis, and the Syrians.

References

Aaberge, R. and Flood, L. (2013) 'U.S. versus Sweden', Statistics Norway Research Department Discussion Papers no. 761, https://www.ssb.no/en/forskning/discussion-papers/_attachment/145526?_ts=141fe2a5468, accessed 6 Feb. 2017.

Adema, W., Fron, P., and Ladaique, M. (2011) 'Is the European Welfare State Really More Expensive?', *OECD Social, Employment and Migration Working Papers*, No. 124, OECD Publishing, http://dx.doi.org/10.1787/5kg2d2d4pbf0-en, accessed 31 Jan. 2017.

Agell, J., Englund, P., and Södersten, J. (1996) 'Tax Reform of the Century: The Swedish Experiment', *National Tax Journal* 49(4): 643–64.

Andersen, J., Hede, A., and Goul Andersen, J. (2013) *Danskernes hverdagsproblemer. Tryghedsmåling 2013*, Copenhagen: TrygFonden, http://vbn.aau.dk/da/publications/danskernes-hverdagsproblemer-tryghedsmaaling-2013(b8b9e78b-dffd-4c1e-8ea8-490a279be6e4).html, accessed 7 Feb. 2017.

Andersen, J., Hede, A., and Goul Andersen, J. (2015) *Den lange vej ud af krisen. Tryghedsmåling 2015*, Copenhagen: TrygFonden, http://vbn.aau.dk/da/publications/den-lange-vej-ud-af-krisen(4ea6c661-80f4-475c-9bc9-90a834831208).html, accessed 7 Feb. 2017.

Ankestyrelsen (2016) Ankestyrelsens årsstatistik om afgørelser på arbejdsskadeområdet 2015, Copenhagen: Ankestyrelsen, file:///C:/Users/ptg/Downloads/Arbejdsskade-statistikken%202015.pdf, accessed 9 Feb. 2017.

Arbejdsministeriet (2000) *Effekter af aktiveringsindsatsen*, Copenhagen: Arbejdsministeriet.

Bay, A.-H., West Pedersen, A., and Finseraas, H. (2014) 'Comfort in Numbers?', *European Journal of Social Security* 16(4): 290–308.

Béland, D., Blomqvist, P., Goul Andersen, J., Palme, J., and Waddan, A. (2014) 'The Universal Decline of Universality?', *Social Policy & Administration* 48(7): 739–56.

Berge, Ø. M. and Hyggen, C. (2010) *Fremveksten av private helseforsikringer i Norden*, Fafo-Notat 2010: 11, http://www.fafo.no/index.php/nb/zoo-publikasjoner/fafo-notater/item/framveksten-av-private-helseforsikringer-i-norden, accessed 6 Feb. 2017.

Berglund, T. and Esser, I. (2014) *Modell i förändring. Landrapport om Sverige*, NordMod 2030, Delrapport 8, Fafo-rapport 2014:10, http://docplayer.se/116874-Delrapport-8-tomas-berglund-ingrid-esser-modell-i-forandring-landrapport-om-sverige-nordmod.html, accessed 6 Feb. 2017.

Blomqvist, P. (2013) 'Citizenship, Choice and Social Equality in Welfare Services', in K. Svedberg Helgesson and U. Mörth (eds.) *The Political Role of Corporate Citizens*, Houndsmills: Palgrave, 166–89.

Breidahl, K. N. (2012) *Når staten lærer: En historisk og komparativ analyse af statslig policy læring og betydningen heraf for udviklingen i den arbejdsmarkedsrettede del af indvandrerpolitikken i Sverige, Norge og Danmark fra 1970 til 2011*, Aalborg: Institut for Statskundskab, Aalborg Universitet.

Brønnum-Hansen, H. and Baadsgaard, M. (2012) 'Widening Social Inequality in Life Expectancy in Denmark', *BMC Public Health* (2012) 12: 994. doi: 10.1186/1471-2458-12-994, accessed 7 Feb. 2017.

Burström, B. (2015) 'Sweden: Recent Changes in Welfare State Arrangements', *International Journal of Health Services* 45(1): 87–104.

Christensen, A. M., Fredriksen, D., Lien, O. C., and Stølen, N. M. (2012) 'Pension Reform in Norway', in R. Holzmann, E. Palmer, and D. Robalino (eds.) *Nonfinancial Defined Contribution Schemes in a Changing Pension World*, Washington DC: The World Bank, i, 129–54.

Christiansen, P. M. (1998) 'A Prescription Rejected', *Governance* 11(2): 273–95.

Clasen, J., Kvist, J., and van Oorschot, W. (2001) 'On Condition of Work', in M. Kautto et al. (eds.) *Nordic Welfare States in the European Context*, London: Routledge, 198–231.

Dagpengekommissionen (2015a) *Dagpengekommissionens samlede anbefalinger*, Oct. 2015, Copenhagen: Dagpengekommissionen, http://www.denoffentlige.dk/dagpengekommissionens-samlede-anbefalinger, accessed 7 Feb. 2017.

Dagpengekommissionen (2015b) *Privat forsikring, supplerende ydelser og fratrædelsesgodtgørelser*, Arbejdspapir no. 9, Copenhagen: Dagpengekommissionen.

Dølvik, J. E., Goul Andersen, J., and Vartianen, J. (2015a) 'The Nordic Social Models in Turbulent Times', in J. E. Dølvik and A. Martin (eds.) *European Social Models from Crisis to Crisis*, Oxford: Oxford University Press, 246–86.

Dølvik, J. E., Fløtten, T., and Hippe, J. M. (2015b) *The Nordic Model towards 2030*, NorMod Final Report, Fafo Report 2015:07, http://www.fafo.no/index.php/en/publications/fafo-reports/item/the-nordic-model-towards-2030-a-new-chapter, accessed 6 Feb. 2017.

Erixon, L. (2010) 'The Rehn-Meidner Model in Sweden: Its Rise, Challenges and Survival', *Journal of Economic Issues* 44(3): 677–715.

Eurofound (2012) *Norway: Social Partner's Involvement in Unemployment Benefits Regimes*, EurWORK, 20 Dec. 2012, http://www.eurofound.europa.eu/observatories/eurwork/comparative-information/national-contributions/norway/norway-social-partners-involvement-in-unemployment-benefits-regimes, accessed 30 Jan. 2017.

Goul Andersen, J. (2007) 'The Danish Welfare State as "Politics for Markets"', *New Political Economy* 12(1): 71–8.

Goul Andersen, J. (2011a) 'From the Edge of the Abyss to Bonanza—and Beyond', *Comparative Social Research* 28: 89–165.

Goul Andersen, J. (2011b) 'Denmark—Ambiguous Modernisation of an Inclusive Unemployment Protection System', in J. Clasen and D. Clegg (eds.) *Regulating the Risk of Unemployment*, Oxford: Oxford University Press, 187–207.

Goul Andersen, J. (2011c) 'Denmark: The Silent Revolution toward a Multipillar Pension System', in B. Ebbinghaus (ed.) *The Varieties of Pension Governance: Pension Privatization in Europe*, Oxford: Oxford University Press, 183–209.

Goul Andersen, J. (2013) *Krisens Navn. Bekæmper regeringen den forkerte økonomiske krise?*, Copenhagen: Frydenlund Academic, https://www.frydenlund.dk/varebeskrivelse/3208, accessed 6 Feb. 2017.

Goul Andersen, J. (2016a) 'Reformpolitik, politisk mistillid og vælgere på vandring 2011–2015', in J. Goul Andersen and D. Shamshiri-Pedersen (eds.) *Vælgere på vandring 2011–2015. Fra krisevalg til jordskredsvalg*, Copenhagen: Frydenlund Academic, 321–41, https://www.saxo.com/dk/fra-krisevalg-til-jordskredsvalg_joergen-goul-andersenditte-shamshiri-petersen_haeftet_9788771187199, accessed 6 Feb. 2017.

Goul Andersen, J. (2016b) 'Stigende politisk mistillid', in J. Goul Andersen and D. Shamshiri-Pedersen (eds.) *Vælgere på vandring 2011–2015. Fra krisevalg til jordskredsvalg*, Copenhagen: Frydenlund Academic, 277–320, https://www.saxo.com/dk/fra-krisevalg-til-jordskredsvalg_joergen-goul-andersenditte-shamshiri-petersen_haeftet_9788771187199, accessed 6 Feb. 2017.

Goul Andersen, J. and Hatland, A. (2014) 'Meeting the Demographic Challenges', in P. Kettunen, S. Kuhnle, and R. Yuan (eds.) *Reshaping Welfare Institutions in China and the Nordic Countries*, NordWel Studies in Historical Welfare State Research 7, Helsinki: NordWel, 257–88, https://helda.helsinki.fi/bitstream/handle/10138/45403/nordwel7.pdf?sequence=1, accessed 7 Feb. 2017.

Goul Andersen, J. and Jenson, P. (2002) *Changing Labour Markets, Welfare Policies and Citizenship*, Bristol: Policy Press.

Goul Andersen, J. and Rossteutscher, S. (2007) 'Small-Scale Democracy: Citizen Power in Domains of Everyday Life', in J. W. van Deth, J. R. Montero, and A. Westholm (eds.) *Citizenship and Involvement in European Democracies: A Comparative Analysis*, London: Routledge, 221–54.

Green-Pedersen, C. (2002) 'New Public Management Reforms of the Danish and Swedish Welfare States', *Governance* 15(2): 271–94.

Green-Pedersen, C. and Krogstrup, J. (2008) 'Immigration as a Political Issue in Denmark and Sweden', *European Journal of Political Research* 47(5): 610–34.

Greve, B. (2007) *Occupational Welfare: Winners and Losers*, Cheltenham: Edward Elgar.

Hagelund, A. (2014) 'From Economic Incentives to Dialogic Nudging', *Journal of Social Policy* 43(1): 69–85.

Hansen, H. F. (2013) 'NPM in Scandinavia', in T. Christensen and P. Lægreid (eds.) *The Ashgate Research Companion to New Public Management*, Farnham: Ashgate, 113–29.

Hede, A., Goul Andersen, J., and Andersen, J. (2009) *Danskernes tryghed på verdenskrisens og bandekrigenes tid. Tryghedsmåling 2009*, Copenhagen: TrygFonden.

Hede, A., Goul Andersen, J., and Andersen, J. (2011) *Danskernes tryghed i krisens år 3. Tryghedsmåling 2011*, Copenhagen: TrygFonden.

Helby Petersen, O. and Hjelmar, U. (2014) 'Marketization of Welfare Services in Scandinavia', *Scandinavian Journal of Public Administration* 17(4): 3–20.

Hippe, J. M. and Berge, Ø. M. (2013) *Ombyggingens periode. Landrapport om Norge 1990–2012*, Normod 2030, Fafo-rapport, http://www.fafo.no/index.php/nb/

zoo-publikasjoner/fafo-rapporter/item/ombyggingens-periode-landrapport-om-norge-1990-2012, accessed 6 Feb. 2017.

Kann, I. C., Kristoffersen, P., and Thune, O. (2013) 'Arbeidsavklaringspenger—gjennomstrømning og avgang', *Arbeid og Velferd* 2013(1): 41–57.

Kristiansen, M. B. (2015) 'Management by Objectives and Results in the Nordic Countries', *Public Performance and Management Review* 38: 542–69.

Lægreid, P., Dyrnes Nordø, Å, and Rykkja, L. H. (2013) *Public Sector Reform in Norway*, Country Report Norway, COCOPS Research Project, http://www.cocops.eu/wp-content/uploads/2013/06/Norway_WP3-Country-Report.pdf, accessed 6 Feb. 2017.

Larsen, F. and Mailand, M. (2007) 'Danish Activation Policy', in A. Serrano Pascual and L. Magnusson (eds.) *Reshaping Welfare Regimes and Activation Regimes in Europe*, Brussels: Peter Lang, 99–126.

Martin, J. and Grubb, D. (2001) 'What Works and for Whom', *Swedish Economic Policy Review* 8(2): 9–56.

Ministry of Children, Equality and Social Inclusion (2011) *Welfare and Migration*, Norwegian Official Report (Green Paper) 2011:7, https://emnbelgium.be/sites/default/files/publications/nou_2011_7_perspective_andsummary.pdf, accessed 9 Feb. 2017.

Moene, K. O. and Wallerstein, M. (2005) *The Scandinavian Model and Economic Development*, Development Outreach Special Report, Washington DC: World Bank Institute, https://www.frisch.uio.no/publikasjoner/pdf/TheScandinavianModelandEconomic Development.pdf, accessed 7 Feb. 2017.

Morel, N., Palier, B., and Palme, J. (2012) *Towards a Social Investment Welfare State? Ideas, Policies and Challenges*, Bristol: Policy Press.

Nordlund, A. (2000) 'Social Policy in Harsh Times', *International Journal of Social Welfare* 9(1): 31–42.

NOSOSKO (2015) *Sickness Absence in the Nordic Countries*, Copenhagen: Nordic Social Statistical Committee, http://norden.diva-portal.org/smash/get/diva2:811504/FULLTEXT06.pdf, accessed 6 Feb. 2017.

OECD (2015) *In It Together: Why Less Inequality Benefits All*, Paris: OECD Publishing, http://dx.doi.org/10.1787/9789264235120-en, accessed 7 Feb. 2017.

OECD (2016) *OECD Employment Outlook 2016*, Paris: OECD Publishing.

Ohlsson, J., Oscarsson, H., and Solevid, M. (2016) 'Ekvilibrium', in Ohlsson, Oscarsson, and Solevid (eds.) *Ekvilibrium. SOM-undersökningen 2015*, SOM.rapport nr 66, Gothenburg: SOM-Institutet, 11–46.

Pedersen, L. and Andersen, S. K. (2014) *Reformernes tid. Regulering af arbejdsmarked og Velfærd siden 1990. Dansk landerapport*, NorMod delrapport no. 7, Oslo: FAFO rapport 2014:31, http://www.fafo.no/index.php/nb/zoo-publikasjoner/fafo-rapporter/item/reformernes-tid-regulering-af-arbejdsmarked-og-velfaerd-siden-1990-dansk-landerapport, accessed 6 Feb. 2017.

Pedersen, S. (1999) 'Migration to and from Denmark during the Period 1960–97', in D. Coleman and E. Wadensjö *Immigration to Denmark: International and National Perspectives*, Aarhus: Aarhus University Press, 148–90.

Pirttilä, J. and Selin, H. (2011) 'Income Shifting within a Dual Income Tax System', *Scandinavian Journal of Economics* 113(1): 120–44.

Rasmussen, P. (2012) 'The Politics of Restraining Options', MA thesis, Aalborg University, 2012.

Sjöberg, O. (2011) 'Sweden: Ambivalent Adjustment', in J. Clasen and D. Clegg (eds.) *Regulating the Risk of Unemployment: National Adaptations to Post-Industrial Labour Markets in Europe*, Oxford: Oxford University Press, 208–31.

Sjögren Lindquist, G. and Wadensjö, E. (2011) 'Sweden', in B. Ebbinghaus (ed.) *The Varieties of Pension Governance*, Oxford: Oxford University Press, 240–61.

Sørensen, P. B. (1994) 'From the Global Income Tax to the Dual Income Tax', *International Tax and Public Finance* 1(1): 57–79.

Statistics Denmark (2014) *65 år i tal*, Copenhagen: Statistics Denmark, http://www.dst.dk/Site/Dst/Udgivelser/GetPubFile.aspx?id=19228&sid=65aarital, accessed 6 Feb. 2017.

Statistics Norway (2016) *Key Figures for Immigration and Immigrants*, Oslo: Statistics Norway, https://www.ssb.no/en/innvandring-og-innvandrere/nokkeltall/immigration-and-immigrants, accessed 25 Feb. 2016.

Svallfors, S. (1992) 'Uppskattad reform?', *Sociologisk Forskning* 29(2): 13–29.

Tranæs, T. (2008) *Indvandrere og det danske uddannelsessystem*, Copenhagen: Gyldendal/Rockwool Foundation Research Unit.

Van Oorschot, W. (2000) 'Wfho Should Get What, and Why?', *Policy & Politics* 28(1), 33–48.

West, A. (2014) 'Academies in England and Independent Schools (fristående skolor) in Sweden', *Research Papers in Education* 9(3): 330–50.

6

The Future of the Slovenian Welfare State and Challenges to Solidarity

Maša Filipovič Hrast and Tatjana Rakar

6.1 Introduction

Slovenia is a small country that once formed part of Yugoslavia and was ruled by a communist regime until 1990. Due to the specific circumstances by which modern Slovenia developed from a formerly socialist society, a special type of welfare system has evolved in the country: a state socialist welfare system in which the state plays a dominant role. The state was initially the owner, financer, and controller of every institution and organization that provided services or paid for the provision of social protection and citizen welfare.

An important fact is that during the 1990s transition period Slovenia did not experience a so-called welfare gap, in contrast to some other countries (Kolarič et al. 2009; 2011). Instead, welfare reforms followed a gentler path, maintaining strong state involvement in the provision of services and in regulating the economy through state ownership of many companies and banks. Bohle and Greskovits (2007) claim that the neo-corporatist regime established after Slovenia's independence exhibited a firmly institutionalized balance between marketization (liberalization, privatization, and market-oriented institution-building) and social protection (based on a welfare system and economic protectionism), and that this balance differs markedly from the neo-liberal brand of capitalism that emerged concurrently in the Baltic and Visegrad states.

From the time that it declared its independence from Yugoslavia in 1990 until the beginning of the global recession in 2008, Slovenia was one of the most successful post-socialist transition countries and featured both strong economic growth and a comparatively high standard of living. It was also among the first of the former Eastern Bloc territories to enter the EU following

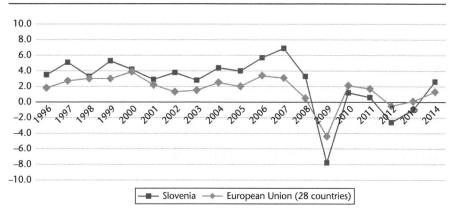

Figure 6.1. Slovenia's real GDP growth rate (percentage change on previous year).
Source: Eurostat

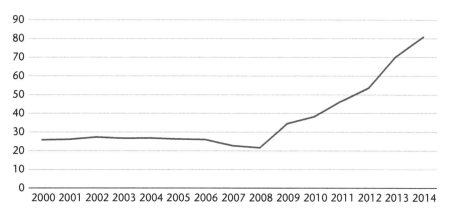

Figure 6.2. The Slovenian government's consolidated gross national debt (as a percentage of GDP).
Source: Eurostat

the 2004 'big bang enlargement', joining the Eurozone in 2007. However, recently the country's well-developed social system has come under increasing pressure due to the global economic crisis. Indeed, in 2009 Slovenia faced one of the most pronounced recessions in the OECD (see Figure 6.1). The country has been slower to recover than others in the EU28. The government's gross national debt has risen sharply, growing from 22 per cent of GDP in 2008 to more than 80 per cent of GDP by the last quarter of 2014 (IMAD 2015a; see Figure 6.2). The crisis has revealed critical weaknesses in Slovenia's pre-crisis economic strategy, structural inconsistencies within its welfare system, and a limited ability to innovate. This has forced its government to take significant steps to restructure the welfare system, leading to discontent among Slovenia's citizenry.

This chapter first describes the past development of the welfare state in Slovenia. It then discusses policy responses to the Great Recession and presents the current changes in the welfare system, followed by a discussion of possible future developments. We use the framework for analysing the responses that is set out in Chapter 1. This distinguishes neo-liberal austerity policies, which have dominated across Europe (see van Kersbergen et al. 2014; Borosch et al. 2016) and are usually linked to greater individual responsibility and privatization; counter-cyclical policies following a neo-Keynesian logic; social investment, which emphasizes the importance of state welfare in societal development through investments in human capital via education, lifelong training and active labour market policies (Greve 2015); pre-distribution—policies which seek to maintain market incomes and control prices; fightback policies confronting austerity, which are not strongly evident in Slovenia; and welfare chauvinism, protecting welfare standards for the existing population against immigrants.

Slovenia has a strong tradition of social investment and social protection. This has been scaled back as austerity measures have set the tone of social policy, with moves towards greater individual and family responsibility, but is still significant. There are also indications of neo-Keynesian counter-cyclical policy-making, pre-distribution through raising the minimum wage, very limited fightback, and, more recently, the emergence of welfare chauvinism in the face of strong migration flows. The chapter will examine the extent to which policies have shifted from universality to selectivity and determine which population groups have been most affected by austerity and which have been most 'sheltered' from the state's cutbacks. We will link these findings to the politics of welfare and consider likely future developments.

6.2 Gradual Welfare State Reforms After Independence

In the first decade following its transition to self-rule and democracy, Slovenia's governments mainly consisted of left-oriented coalitions. Under the country's liberal democratic party (*Liberalna demokracija Slovenije*), with bipartisan governments or grand coalitions, coalition compromises were hard to achieve and reforms were often incomplete. However, this political option rejected the reform recommendations based on the principle of shock therapy advocated by experts from international monetary institutions (Kolarič et al. 2011). As emphasized by Guardiancich (2011), Slovenia's transition from socialism to a market economy was gradual, path-dependent, and characterized by the preservation of existing power balances. Slovenia adopted a multi-party system in which powerful social partners, such as leading trade unions, played important roles in coalition-building. Social partnerships and the involvement of trade unions have been established in Slovenia's welfare system for a long period. Despite a decline in union membership after the country declared its independence,[1] Slovenia stood out among other Central and Eastern European countries for having a workforce that remained overwhelmingly unionized and for having a collective-agreement coverage rate at close to 100 per cent, due to its extensive legal framework and functioning system of social dialogue (Crowley and Stanojević 2011).[2]

These contextual factors therefore meant that welfare system reforms in Slovenia were invariably built on the pre-independence systems, were gradual, and were based on the consent of the governments' coalition partners, especially that of the country's trade unions. Trade union agreement was needed whenever the government wished to implement changes in areas such as the pension system, minimum wage, and labour market regulations. The welfare system that consequently emerged retained a strong role for the state in providing public services, such as education, childcare, healthcare, and social services. It also provided a relatively high level of benefits while preserving universal rights (linked to residence in Slovenia) for some benefits and services, including healthcare and certain family benefits such as a large family allowance and a childbirth grant. Further, the ceilings for means-tested benefits were relatively high so that, for example, child benefits were almost universal and received by the vast majority of families. In general, the welfare system was based on the principle of social justice (in the sense of providing equal opportunities to access certain levels of social protection and certain amounts and types of services), upgraded with a meritocratic principle and the principles of solidarity and equity (Kolarič et al. 2009).

Slovenia's transition to a market economy was relatively soft. Inequalities did not become significantly pronounced and remained far less severe than in many other Central and Eastern European countries (Flere and Lavrič 2003; Malnar 2011). In fact, inequality grew only marginally after the transition period, with Slovenia's Gini index rising from 21.5 points in 1987 to around 26 points by the mid-1990s; however, the index had dropped to around 23 points before the 2008 financial crisis (Filipovič Hrast and Ignjatović 2012). Social welfare policies such as social assistance and child benefits schemes are important in achieving this, but so too are the minimum wage (introduced in 1995), unemployment benefits, and the progressive personal income tax system. The personal income tax system remained practically unchanged between 1991 and 2004 when a new tax code was passed. However, considerable public discussion in Slovenia has focused on tax reforms due to the high taxes on labour and complicated set of tax codes. Slovenia is among those EU countries which have the highest taxes on labour (Majcen et al. 2009).

The centre-left retained control over the Slovenian government for more than a decade after independence. This was labelled the 'comeback (or just "persistence") of the left' by some (Pikalo 2000: 203), as those in power were, for the most part, the same individuals who had held power under the previous regime; in fact, it was not until 2004, under Prime Minister Janez Janša (leader of the conservative Slovenian Democratic Party, *Slovenska demokratska stranka*), that a genuine break with the socialist past happened. The right-wing political elite designed and partly implemented reforms which were more in line with the neo-liberal doctrines of most international monetary institutions. For the most part, these planned reforms pursued re-commodification, re-familialization, and the establishment of for-profit and non-profit organizations as carriers of insurance schemes and service providers. Yet strong resistance from the trade unions and the general public stopped the proposed reforms being implemented and contributed to the defeat of the rightist political elite in the elections in 2008 (Kolarič et al. 2011).

Another crucial issue faced by Slovenia after its independence was labour market policy reform. At the beginning of the transition, the country's economic restructuring led to high unemployment. An important policy introduced to tackle this problem was an early-retirement scheme, which exacerbated sustainability issues by placing an additional burden on the national pension system. Employment increased as the economy grew, but these gains were somewhat illusory as the Slovenian labour market over the past twenty-five years has become increasingly segmented between those who have secure, permanent employment and those who have flexible (short-term or part-time) jobs (Ignjatović 2011; Kajzer 2011). In terms of employment, the most vulnerable parts of the population included the young, 69 per cent of whom have a fixed-term contract, the highest proportion in the EU. In the decades since Slovenia's independence, the unemployment insurance system has become ever more based on social assistance as the duration of benefit entitlement has been reduced and the maximum payment cut, and the rights of workers have become more closely related to their responsibilities. Active labour market policy has been increasingly emphasized (Ignjatović et al. 2002), although it could be labelled as a social investment of a 'lean' type since the funds for these programmes have constituted a small share of welfare spending.

Moreover, family policies have played a central role in supporting high labour market participation among women, a tradition in Slovenia for over half a century. This has been sustained through the development of a widespread network of childcare services, the introduction of insurance-based social security schemes for parenthood, such as maternity and parental leave, and other family-related benefits. Women's participation in the labour market in Slovenia was first stimulated by the rapid post-war growth of industry and the equally fast expansion of the service sector in the 1970s.

However, when it comes to domestic work, a large burden was placed on women and, in relation to care for the elderly, on social networks, especially the family. Further, the high employment level of women (and, by extension, the number of dual-earner households) became an essential part of the prevailing employment conditions in Slovenia as the country's cost of living quickly outpaced average wages.

Slovenia's social spending as a percentage of GDP was near the OECD average. It in fact fell between 2005 and 2008, but, as elsewhere in Europe, rose sharply in 2009 and 2010. By function, the greatest proportion of social spending is allocated to old age, followed by sickness and disability and family and children (see Figure 6.3). However, despite the largest share being targeted at older people, their economic situation has deteriorated since 2001, with those aged 75 and over the most affected (Kump and Stropnik 2009; Stropnik et al. 2010). It is therefore unsurprising that Slovenians' evaluations of the quality of the pension system are relatively negative, according to data from the European Quality of Life Survey.

Meanwhile, unlike many other European countries, immigration has not been a major political issue in Slovenia. Immigration into the country has been growing steadily since independence, although the biggest increase came in the period between 2004 and 2008 when the number of immigrants from other countries rose from 10,171 to 30,693. However, after 2009 the number has dropped significantly and in 2010 and 2014 the flows of emigration exceeded those of immigration. The share of foreign-born population in

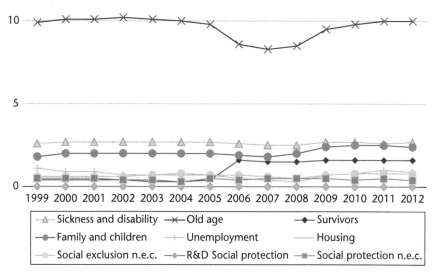

Figure 6.3. Total general government expenditure on social protection (as a percentage of GDP), 1999–2012.

Source: Eurostat

Slovenia is comparatively high, 11.4 per cent in 2014 (Eurostat), but has been quite stable and has risen by only 0.3 per cent since 2011. The vast majority are immigrants from other former Yugoslav republics who relocated to Slovenia after World War II, and again after 1991 as refugees or economic migrants. In terms of public attitudes, welfare chauvinism is stronger in Slovenia than in Europe as a whole, but is weaker than in other post-socialist countries (see Mewes and Mau 2013). Perhaps the most politically contested issue linked to immigrants is the issue of the 'erased'. This group encompasses citizens of former Yugoslavia who live in Slovenia, do not hold Slovenian citizenship, and are classed as 'aliens' (Deželan 2011). The current migration trends may see immigration issues become more prominent, as will be discussed in 6.3.

6.3 Current Issues: Policy Responses to the Great Recession

The global financial and economic crisis has hit Slovenia particularly hard. The government's initial response to the crisis was to soften its impact on the labour market with two temporary measures: (1) a partial subsidy of full-time work for part-time workers; and (2) the introduction of a 'temporary waiting-to-work' benefit for those temporarily laid off. These responses reflect neo-Keynesian ideas of stimulating the economy by promoting high employment and purchasing power. As a direct response to the crisis, intervention legislation was adopted that introduced temporary austerity measures. These policies are to remain in force until one year after national economic growth exceeds 2.5 per cent of GDP. The acts of intervention limited outflows from the public budget, the budgets of municipalities, and those of the Health Insurance Institute and Pension Insurance Institute by limiting the indexation of transfers, public employee salaries and the share of co-investments with municipalities. These policies clearly indicate that austerity was the main response to the crisis, an approach reinforced by further reforms of the welfare system.

In the first stages of a more structural response to the crisis, the government tried to tackle the sustainability of social spending with pension and labour market reforms and, during the second stage, welfare and family policy reforms were also adopted. The biggest changes to welfare policy after 2010 involved new social legislation that came into force on 1 January 2012, as embodied in the Exercise of Rights to Public Funds and the Financial Social Assistance acts, which together with the aforementioned austerity laws introduced substantial changes to social and family benefits. These became more targeted measures with stricter criteria. Universal rights were abolished and extensive means-testing adopted, increasing selectivity. Further, austerity laws lowered the level of some benefits also with regard to social insurance-related benefits such as leave policies.

The economic crisis also marked a period of political instability, with changes to both the left- and right-wing coalitions in parliament. From November 2008 until early 2012 the Social Democrats (Socialni demokrati) led a left-wing coalition government. Then, during the next preliminary elections, a right-wing government came to power, only to lose public support again in 2013 and be replaced by a centre-left government that lasted until August 2014, when the newly formed Modern Centre Party (*Stranka modernega centra*) won enough national support to form a second, centre-left coalition. These changes to government have been seemingly continual, swift, and momentous. However, both rightist and leftist governments have acted to curb government spending, viewing the discharge of the state's responsibility for social protection and the wellbeing of its citizens as the dominant way out of the country's difficult economic and financial circumstances (Kolarič et al. 2011). With the austerity discourse prevailing in the political arena, the austerity measures introduced were therefore seen more as a necessity than as having clear ideological roots in any electoral mandate. This is in line with Armingeon's (2012) findings concerning fiscal responses to the crisis— retrenchment responses that were, in fact, so dominant in European economic thinking that the political party in power hardly mattered.

Retrenchment and neo-liberal responses in Slovenia during the crisis have been particularly evident in the area of family policy where, with the introduction of strict means-testing, a shift towards 'social care' is apparent. This shift is best seen in the paradigm shifts that have occurred with regard to the purpose and function of child benefits, which no longer serve to cover children's extra expenses but have instead become a primary income source for poor families. These changes to child benefits and the austerity policies have reduced the number of child benefit recipients and cut spending in this area by tightening the eligibility criteria. It should be noted, however, that for the first time since Slovenian independence family policy has been affected by austerity measures. Only when it came to services such as child-care were no austerity measures introduced. Nonetheless, austerity affected childcare subsidies as a result of the government's new calculations of family income, and the requirement that a second child concurrently enrolled in preschool incurred a reduced fee rather than being free-of-charge. Likewise, leave policies were affected to some extent as wage compensation for parental and paternity leaves was lowered and an upper ceiling for the maternity-leave benefit was introduced. In early April 2014 a new Parental Protection and Family Benefits Act was enacted. In line with earlier social investment strategies, it introduced more gender-equal leave policies, changing parental leave from a family entitlement to an individual entitlement for each parent, thereby making it consistent with the EU Directive on Parental Leave introduced in 2010. The new law also responded to the increases in poverty among single-parent households by increasing benefits for such parents. Despite these minor expansionary measures, the predominantly neo-liberal crisis-related reforms weakened the defamilializing effects of social and family policy in Slovenia (Blum et al. 2014; Rakar 2015).[3] However, the relatively limited changes to the public provision of childcare, as well as the absence of, or only small, changes in the education and active labour market policies, indicate that social investment is perceived as an important direction to pursue.

In the labour market the economic crisis also precipitated several policy reforms. In general, these reforms emphasized the concept of flexicurity and the activation principle. In an attempt to overcome the increasing dualization of the labour market, the government introduced a new Minimum Wage Act (2010) along with the Labour Market Regulation (2010) and Employment Relationship (2013) acts, reducing the degree of protection for most workers under permanent contracts, and increasing protection for more vulnerable workers. The government's attempts to improve conditions for vulnerable workers were most evident in raising the national minimum wage and softening the eligibility criteria for receiving unemployment benefits so that those in more irregular, flexible jobs became eligible also. Further, the government increased the level of unemployment benefit, introduced 'partial unemployment' to enable the unemployed to work in 'mini-jobs', reduced the incentive for employers to use fixed-term contracts by raising contributions, limited to two the number of fixed-term contracts an employee could be employed under, and introduced severance-pay requirements for employees dismissed under a fixed-term contract. These changes are in line with the predistribution response, strengthening regulations in the labour market in relation to more vulnerable groups. Some of the policies could also be labelled neo-Keynesian as they encouraged the employment of the most vulnerable groups, such as the long-term unemployed and young people, through subsidies to employers.

Still, many of these positive developments were reversed by austerity measures, which again reduced the amount of unemployment benefit and shortened benefit durations, hence following a neo-liberal paradigm. In addition, further policy changes limited some of the existing rights of the most protected workers even more, specifically by simplifying employment-termination rules, limiting the protected category to older workers, and reducing the notice period required for terminations. These changes have come in addition to the government's implementation of active labour market policies, especially with regard to training and educating the unemployed and also introducing activation principles for social-benefit recipients.

Lastly, demographic changes represent one final, crucial challenge to the transformation of Slovenia's welfare state. Initial responses to the economic crisis consisted of cost-containment measures that froze pension indexation. Austerity laws in 2012 also rejected pension adjustments. It should be emphasized that the long-lasting pension reform has been highly controversial. The first proposed major reform (adopted by the government in 2010) was rejected in a referendum in 2011. In 2012 negotiations took place between the social partners and policy-makers, and the reform was again successfully adopted as the Pension and Disability Insurance Act of 2012. The most significant changes included increasing the retirement age, further strengthening bonuses and penalties to stimulate labour market participation among elderly workers, and implementing different calculations for the pension base, establishing it over a longer period. Further, a neo-liberal response has been evident in the abolition of state pensions with the introduction of new social legislation. Previously, such pensions were a universal right and functioned as support for elderly persons not eligible for insurance-based pensions. These persons have now become dependent on social assistance and on the supplementary allowance; the latter has been made a social assistance benefit, thereby significantly reducing the number of persons eligible to receive it (Trbanc et al. 2014).

In summary, to paraphrase van Kersbergen et al. (2014: 885), Slovenia's retrenchment and cost containment in response to the Great Recession has affected every aspect of the country's welfare system. Expansions were rare and mainly occurred during the first stages of reform or under delayed implementation. In addition, as the present analysis shows, the most significant retrenchments have concerned Slovenia's long-standing social protection policies—although its social investment policies have also been modified. Increased selectivity and the retrenchment of universal schemes have been the most obvious trends in all areas of Slovenian welfare policy.

These neo-liberal responses have impacted the lower middle class especially hard. Medium-income families are now 'not (much) better off than the low income families' (Stropnik 2014: 19). This can also be observed in the fact that wages have stagnated at the lower end of the spectrum. More than two thirds of employees receive below-average wages and one quarter receive less than 60 per cent of the average wage (Trbanc et al. 2014), and the proportion on the minimum wage has risen. Moreover, the share of Slovenians earning less than 105 per cent of the minimum wage was 19 per cent in 2010. This was followed by a significant increase in the number of claimants for exceptional social assistance,[4] showing the rise of the 'working poor' class, as claimants are often ineligible for regular (means-tested) social assistance. Similarly, the number of beneficiaries of regular social assistance has risen, the majority of whom are single persons, a fact that can be linked to the low income and property

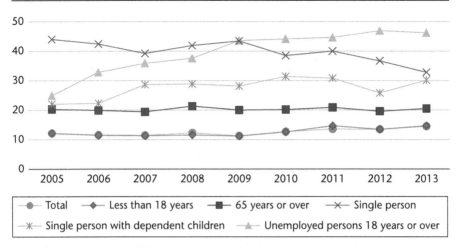

Figure 6.4. At-risk-of-poverty rates for select groups, 2005–13.

Note: The cut-off point is 60 per cent of median, equivalized income after social transfers.

Source: Eurostat

criteria for receiving benefits. In addition, new social legislation introduced a strict hierarchy for assessing benefit entitlement. Child benefits are claimed first and often increase the family's household income above the social assistance threshold.

These changes to the country's social legislation have worsened the financial situation and wellbeing of some of the country's most vulnerable groups, including single-parent families, those with large loans, families with school-age children, large families, elderly persons, and couples without children (Dremelj et al. 2013). Consequently, Slovenia's poverty rate rose from 11.5 per cent in 2007 to 14.5 per cent in 2013, with those at the highest risk of poverty remaining the unemployed and elderly, single persons, and single-parent households. Indeed, while the risk of child poverty in Slovenia was long one of the lowest in the EU (Stropnik 2014; UNICEF Office of Research 2014), in 2011 the at-risk-of-poverty rate for children in Slovenia (14.7 per cent) exceeded that of the total population (13.6 per cent) for the first time; according to the latest available figures, this trend was also evident in 2013 (see Figure 6.4).

6.4 The Politics of Welfare and Possible Welfare State Futures

As we have argued, Slovenia's welfare reform strategy since the start of the Great Recession has primarily favoured retrenchment and cost containment in the context of a European discourse dominated by calls for austerity. This will most likely continue, not only because of the country's slow economic recovery but because of the government's decision to prolong most austerity measures,[5] even though Slovenia's GDP growth rate rose to 2.6 per cent (IMAD 2015b)—which is above the level required by a number of laws to discontinue the austerity measures and introduce expansionary reforms. This raises the question of whether some of the temporary austerity measures are now becoming permanent. Predictions of Slovenia's GDP growth in the coming years are less optimistic and below the required growth rate: for 2015, the estimated real growth rate as a share of GDP is predicted to be 2.4 per cent; for 2016, 2.0 per cent; and for 2017, 2.1 per cent (IMAD 2015b).

Currently, the policy of financing benefits through high social security contributions[6] continues to enjoy strong support among Slovenians. However, in response to growing public dissatisfaction with the present government's policies and ongoing reforms concerning welfare spending and service efficiency, this might change in the future. This dissatisfaction has been further exacerbated by the government's attempts to find additional income sources to finance the public budget. One measure already implemented is the increased value-added tax enacted in 2013. Other possible new taxes include a real-estate tax that was once adopted but later rejected by the Constitutional Court. Compared with other EU nations, Slovenians show less support for increased taxation to cover the costs of increased social spending, and this is characteristic of people who view their government as inefficient and of low quality (Svallfors 2012).

Meanwhile, social investment policies have remained less affected by the government's austerity measures, and this trend will most likely continue into the future, especially in the context of the EU's emphasis on social investment (Bonoli and Natali 2012; Cantillon and van Lancker 2013; Hemerijck 2013). Slovenia's history of post-crisis reforms thus far indicates that, although it already predominates, 'retrenchment is not the only game in town', as is also the case for several other EU countries (see van Kersbergen et al. 2014). Reforms in line with a social investment strategy such as long-term care and active labour market policies are still being pursued, but remain relatively weak compared with those established in the past, for example childcare and education. This might be framed as social investment of the 'lean' type, and it goes hand-in-hand with retrenchment (van Kersbergen et al. 2014: 894). Further, several authors have pointed out that social investment strategies are less redistributive and less protective of the most vulnerable (Cantillon 2011; Vandenbroucke and Vleminckx 2011; Cantillon and van Lancker 2013). Slovenians are increasingly critical of the country's welfare system and of whether it has been successful in managing the risks its citizens face. This is reflected in the strong political discontent that has spread across the Slovenian electorate (see Social Watch Report 2014). Slovenia has the lowest trust in parliament and political parties among the EU28, with only nine per cent of respondents trusting the parliament, and only six per cent trusting the political parties. Moreover, with regard to trust in the national government and local political authorities, Slovenia is at the bottom of the scale (Eurobarometer 2014). The government's welfare reforms in the short term should therefore be seen in a context of political instability as the public's distrust in politicians and public institutions is rising and political participation is declining.

At the end of 2012 civil protests flared up on the local level and then, in 2013, spread across the country. While revolt against key political figures was the dominant mobilizing factor, protestors also called for systemic changes such as the government's resignation and an end to the theft of public goods, the exploitation of workers, and corruption. New political parties emerged after these protests, including the Modern Centre Party which won a majority at the last elections (in August 2014), as well as the radical left Unified Left party (*Združena levica*) which also won seats in the Slovenian parliament. Consequently, the current centre-left government coalition confronts an opposition that is even more leftist, which could further incline the short-term future of welfare reforms towards a fightback response. An illustration of such a response is the remission of debts for the most deprived population in relation to unpaid bills for electricity, heating, health insurance, taxes, child-care, and school meal payments. This was initially proposed by the opposition party, the Unified Left, and then adopted by the Social Democrats within the ruling coalition.

As far as inequality issues are concerned, there is a long-standing belief in the importance of equality and intense support for the state's role in pro-moting greater equality (see Figure 6.5). This is, undoubtedly, linked to the country's past and is a sentiment shared by the populations of the majority of post-Communist countries (Svallfors 2012). However, despite the high income equality in the country at present there is a strong prevalence of low wages, as already discussed. Accordingly, equality issues might become even more exacerbated in the future since the welfare reforms have mostly squeezed the middle class and are perceived as having been ineffective in preventing old social risks—especially in preventing poverty. In a European Social Survey conducted in 2012, a large majority (70 per cent) of respond-ents felt the state does not protect people from poverty, and a similarly high share (63.2 per cent) felt the state does not take measures to decrease income inequality.

Slovenia is also facing strong demographic pressures. The old-age depend-ency ratio was 24.4 per cent in 2012, slightly below the EU27 average. How-ever, this is projected to rise rapidly to 57.6 per cent by 2060, above the projected old age-dependency ratio for the EU27 (52.5 per cent; Eurostat).

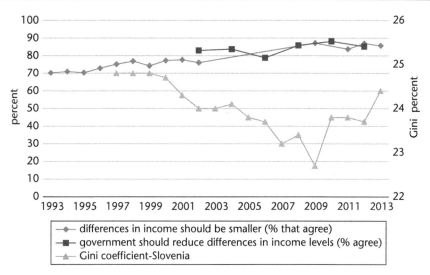

Figure 6.5. Attitudes to income inequality and the Gini coefficient.
Sources: SJM (2013), ESS (2012), SURS

Despite the many reforms carried out since the crisis to address this issue, several problems must still be addressed, such as how to ensure the sustainability of the healthcare and the underdeveloped long-term care systems, while also pushing through further reforms of the pension system. There is strong support for providing welfare to the elderly. In addition, the elderly have a strong political presence as their party, the Democratic Party of Slovenian Pensioners (*Demokratična stranka upokojencev Slovenije*, also known as DESUS), has been part of every government coalition since the earliest years of independence (1996). Thus, cutting social spending on the elderly is exceedingly difficult. Nevertheless, several cuts have been made, resulting in a significant rise in the number of elderly persons suffering financial vulnerability. In this context, future possible cleavages in solidarity could develop as the young are being ever more squeezed by the labour market conditions and the poorly adapted welfare system to compensate for social costs, while the elderly are trying to protect their rights and are also being increasingly pressed.

The equality of the distribution of welfare spending between young and old might serve as one point of contention in the future. This situation, however, might be alleviated by solidarity and the transfer of burdens to the private sphere—moves already characteristic of Slovenia (Filipovič et al. 2009; Kolarič 2011; Mandič 2012)—indicating a trend towards increased familialism. We can link this push towards the private sphere to the increased emphasis on individual responsibility in ensuring personal (or familial) wellbeing. However, strengthening the role of the family could have a negative effect on work-life balance and gender equality.

Another important issue in the context of the health and long-term care reforms will be the future of public services relative to possible trends towards privatization and a larger role for third-sector organizations, supporting the trend towards individual responsibility. This is an especially pressing issue since some services are financed at the local level by municipalities (for example elder care, childcare, and social housing), and funding for these services has decreased in the wake of the Great Recession. Privatization trends are especially strong in the healthcare sector, having already begun in the 1990s. In general, Slovenians seem to support the government's assuming a greater role in all areas, including the provision of services. However, problems with these services' efficiency as well as perceptions of relatively high levels of corruption in the public sector[7] might shift people's support away from state provision and possibly towards stronger support for other actors.

New massive migration flows were seen in 2015, which affected Slovenia as part of the so-called Balkan route from Greece to Western European countries. In order to limit migration Slovenia erected a fence in November 2015 along the border with Croatia. Despite the mass migration flows through Slovenia (from 16 October 2015 to 1 March 2016 a total of 476,184 migrants crossed into the country), only a small share of the refugees applied for asylum. While Austria's and later Germany's stricter regulations on entry have led to an increased number of asylum seekers in Slovenia (2015 in total saw 277 asylum seekers while there were already 287 by March 2016), numbers are still relatively low. Enforcement of the Schengen regime on the border caused a significant drop in the number of refugees and of migrants in the country's accommodation centres (currently around 400; MNZ 2016). These trends have also highlighted issues linked with welfare chauvinism. This is evident in the proposed changes to the asylum legislation to introduce stricter criteria for asylum seekers and tighten the criteria for receiving financial aid for private accommodation; it also plans to abolish one-off social assistance and aid for accommodating the family members of asylum seekers. Another change illustrating this direction is to make state scholarships conditional upon holding citizenship (previously linked to temporary or permanent residence in the country) and limiting child benefits only to children actually living in Slovenia, as introduced already by the new social legislation in 2012.

6.5 Conclusion

As we have shown, Slovenia is a highly egalitarian society in which great emphasis is put on the redistributive role of the state. Stemming from its socialist origins, centre-left governments, and the strong roles the social partners have played in reforming the welfare state since its independence,

Slovenia's transition to a free-market economy has been gradual. Social protection and investment policies have frequently remained in place or have, in some cases, been further expanded. The Great Recession has profoundly affected many Slovenians, and led to several structural reforms along with ad hoc and temporary measures intended to stabilize public finances. The combination of these structural changes and austerity measures has triggered drastic changes in the country's welfare programmes, which have been subject to retrenchment and cost containment through greater needs-testing and tighter qualification criteria as well as the abolition of some universal rights. Although some structural reforms, for example of the labour market, have attempted to increase protection for the country's most vulnerable workers and raised the minimum wage, indicating a pre-distributionist approach, the main policy changes have been neo-liberal, pursuing austerity, cuts, and cost containment. There seems to be a limited trend towards increasing the protectionism of citizens as against immigrants, as evident in some legislative changes and proposed amendments to the asylum legislation. Due to the currently stable share of foreign-born people in the population and the low number of asylum seekers (despite the large migration flows), this remains a less present issue in Slovenia, although it is one with the strong potential to become more salient.

The current trend towards diminishing the state's role in protection against social risks runs contrary to public expectations concerning the role of government in providing a safety net and preventing inequality. It is thus unsurprising that there is increased dissatisfaction with the welfare state, especially its efficiency. The legitimacy of the welfare state not only depends on the impact of these developments but also on which interventions actually work (Greve 2015: 206). Issues of efficiency with regard to the welfare state providing high-quality services and protections against social risks will therefore most likely be vital to future developments, potentially also raising the question of whether or not the privatization of welfare programmes and diversification of welfare services amongst other actors will occur. The consequences of retrenchment and cost containment have been to weaken the defamilializing effects of social and family policies in Slovenia, and this can be linked to the enhanced role of intermediary institutions in securing welfare (see Daly 2011). This development is a consequence of the neo-liberal approach in increasing individual responsibility for welfare. In the meantime, the growth of interpersonal dependence has not resulted in wider social solidarity but in the formation of islands of loyalty and trust (Iglič 2014: 22), which could have a negative impact on intergenerational solidarity (outside the family) and on solidarity between different societal groups. In addition, the increased role of the family could also lead to further issues in terms of gender equality and the work-life balance.

As Farnsworth and Irving (2011: 271) have emphasized, the outcomes for and responses of welfare states to crises have been quite varied, and the process of welfare change remains as unpredictable as it is fluid: 'Challenging times are as likely to widen the scope for progressive welfare state building as they are to diminish it, and how states respond is a matter of political struggle and political choice' (Farnsworth and Irving 2011: 278). In Slovenia's politically unpredictable environment, where new parties have recently formed and won the last two national elections, the future of welfare state reform is perhaps even less certain.

Notes

1. Before Slovenian independence in 1989, 69 per cent of workers were members of trade unions. In 1994 approximately 58.6 per cent were still members; this figure dropped again to 42.8 per cent in 1998. A sharp decline (10 per cent) came between 1994 and 1995 (Stanojević 2000: 39), after which unionization stayed approximately on the same level at around 40 per cent, followed by a sharp decline after Slovenia joined the EU from 43.7 per cent in 2003 to 26.6 per cent in 2008. With the economic crisis there was a further drop in trade union membership to 22 per cent in 2013 (Stanojević 2015).
2. The comparable coverage rate for other post-communist EU member states was 27.4 per cent, whereas the average coverage rate for the EU15 was 78.8 per cent. Moreover, collective bargaining in Slovenia still takes place predominantly at the sector level and is framed by income policy agreements; almost all bargaining elsewhere in Eastern Europe takes place at the company level (Crowley and Stanojević 2011).
3. Indeed, additional modifications to the new legislation did come in 2014, yet, as shown by several studies (Trbanc et al. 2014; Rakar 2015), these changes were minor and mostly served as 'cosmetic makeovers' to satisfy the public. It should be stressed as well that these corrections were not new but were policies that existed before the introduction of the new social legislation.
4. This benefit is granted in exceptional circumstances. It can also be granted when the ceiling set for financial social assistance is surpassed but the applicant is found to be in financial distress for reasons beyond their control.
5. However, changes in abolishing some temporary austerity measures and some minor expansion reforms were introduced, such as raising the ceiling for state scholarship, raising the child benefit for some income groups back to the level before austerity law, raising the minimum income, and prolongation of paternity leave.
6. In Slovenia, social contributions account for 40.1 per cent of total tax revenue and are the fourth-highest in the EU, while employees' social contributions are the highest in the EU (Eurostat).
7. In the latest research (2013) more than half of respondents believe that corruption in public services is widespread (Toš et al. 2014).

References

Armingeon, K. (2012) 'The Politics of Fiscal Responses to the Crisis of 2008–2009', *Governance: An International Journal of Policy, Administration, and Institutions* 25(4): 543–65.

Blum, S., Formánková, L., and Dobrotic, I. (2014) 'Family Policies in "Hybrid" Welfare States after the Crisis: Pathways between Policy Expansion and Retrenchment', *Social Policy & Administration* 48(4): 468–91.

Bohle, D. and Greskovits, B. (2007) 'Neoliberalism, Embedded Neoliberalism and Neo-Corporatism: Towards Transnational Capitalism in Central Eastern Europe', *West European Politics* 30(3): 433–66.

Bonoli, G. and Natali, D. (eds.) (2012) *The Politics of the New Welfare State*, Oxford: Oxford University Press.

Borosch, N., Kuhlmann, J., and Blum, S. (2016) 'Opening up Opportunities and Risks? Retrenchment, Targeting and Activation as Main Trends of Recent Welfare State Reforms across Europe', in K. Schubert, P. de Villota, and J. Kuhlmann (eds.) *Current Challenges to European Welfare Systems*, New York: Springer Publishing, 769–91.

Cantillon, B. (2011) 'The Paradox of the Social Investment State: Growth, Employment and Poverty in the Lisbon Era', *Journal of European Social Policy* 21(5): 432–49.

Cantillon, B. and van Lancker, W. (2013) 'Three Shortcomings of the Social Investment Perspective', *Social Policy & Society* 12(4): 553–64.

Crowley, S. and Stanojević, M. (2011) 'Varieties of Capitalism, Power Resources and Historical Legacies: Explaining the Slovenian Exception', *Politics and Society* 39(2): 268–95.

Daly, M. (2011) *Welfare*, Cambridge: Polity Press.

Deželan, T. (2011) 'Citizenship in Slovenia: The Regime of a Nationalising or a Europeanising State?' *CITSEE Working Paper Series* 2011/16, Edinburgh: University of Edinburgh.

Dremelj, P., Smolej, S., Boškić, R., Narat, T., Rihter, L., and Kovač, N. (2013) *Ocena učinkov izvajanja nove socialne zakonodaje, končno poročilo*, Ljubljana: Social Protection Institute of the Republic of Slovenia, http://www.irssv.si/upload2/Ocena_ucinkov_socialna_zakonodaja_IRSSV_2013.pdf, accessed 20 Apr. 2015.

Eurobarometer (2014) *Standard Eurobarometer 82*, Autumn 2014, Brussels: European Commission, http://ec.europa.eu/public_opinion/archives/eb/eb82/eb82_anx_en.pdf, accessed 25 May 2016.

Farnsworth, K. and Irving, Z. (2011) 'Responding to Challenges: Some Concluding Remarks on Welfare Futures in Changed Circumstances', in Farnsworth and Irving (eds.) *Social Policy in Challenging Times: Economic Crisis and Welfare Systems*, Bristol: Policy Press, 271–8.

Filipovič Hrast, M. and Hlebec, V. (2009) 'Medgeneracijska solidarnost v Sloveniji in tranzicijske spremembe', in V. Tašner, I. Lesar, M. G. Antić, V. Hlebec, and M. Pušnik (eds.) *Brez spopada: kultur, spolov, generacij*, Ljubljana: Pedagoška fakulteta, 195–214.

Filipovič Hrast, M. and Ignjatović, M. (2012) *Country Report on Growing Inequalities Impacts in Slovenia, GINI Report 2012*, Ljubljana: Faculty of Social Sciences.

Flere, S. and Lavrič, M. (2003) 'Social Inequalities in Slovenian Higher Education', *International Studies in Sociology of Education* 13(3): 281–90.

Greve, B. (2015) *Welfare and the Welfare State: Present and Future*, London: Routledge.

Guardiancich, I. (2011) 'Slovenian Social Policy in a Consensual Political System: The Dilemmas of a Delayed Transition', in M. Sambolieva and S. Dohnert (eds.) *Welfare States in Transition: 20 years after the Yugoslav Welfare Model*, Sofia: Friedrich Erbert-Stiftung, 310–44.

Hemerijck, A. (2013) *Changing Welfare States*, Oxford: Oxford University Press.

Iglič, H. (2014) 'The Crumbling or Strengthening of Social Capital? The Economic Crisis' Impact on Social Networks and Interpersonal Trust in Slovenia', *Družboslovne razprave* 30(77): 7–26.

Ignjatović, M. (2011) 'Slowenien: Konsolidierung oder Erosion des Arbeitsmarktes', in W. Reiter and K. H. Müller (eds.) *Arbeitsmärkte und Sozialsysteme nach der Krize: strukturelle Veränderungen und politische Herausforderungen*, Vienna: Echoraum, Bundesministerium für Arbeit, Soziales und Konsumentenschutz, 91–7.

Ignjatović, M., Kopač, A., Svetlik, I., and M. Trbanc (2002) 'Slovenia's Navigation through a Turbulent Transition', in J. Goul Andersen (ed.) *Europe's New State of Welfare: Unemployment, Employment Policies and Citizenship*, Bristol: Policy Press, 195–216.

IMAD (2015a) *Ekonomski izzivi 2015*, Ljubljana: Institute for Macroeconomic Analysis and Development, http://www.umar.gov.si/fileadmin/user_upload/publikacije/izzivi/2015/EI_2015-splet.pdf, accessed 25 May 2016.

IMAD (2015b) *Ekonomsko ogledalo, 6 (XXI)*, Ljubljana: Institute for Macroeconomic Analysis and Development, http://www.umar.gov.si/fileadmin/user_upload/publikacije/eo/2015/EO_06_15.pdf, accessed 25 May 2016.

Kajzer, A. (2011) 'Vpliv gospodarske krize na trg dela v Sloveniji in izzivi za politiko trga dela', *IB revija* 4: 13–21.

Kolarič, Z. (2011) 'Medgeneracijska solidarnost v primežu reform evropskih držav blaginje', in S. Mandič and M. Filipovič Hrast (eds.) *Blaginja pod pritiski demografskih sprememb*, Ljubljana: Fakulteta za družbene vede, 205–25.

Kolarič, Z., Kopač, A., and Rakar, T. (2009) 'The Slovene Welfare System: Gradual Reform instead of Shock Treatment', in K. Schubert, S. Hegelich, and U. Bazant (eds.) *The Handbook of European Welfare Systems*, London: Routledge, 444–61.

Kolarič, Z., Kopač, A., and Rakar, T. (2011) 'Welfare States in Transition: The Development of the Welfare System in Slovenia', in S. Dehnert and M. Stambolieva (eds.) *Welfare States in Transition: 20 Years after the Yugoslav Welfare Model*, Sofia: Friedrich Ebert Foundation, 288–309.

Kump, N. and Stropnik, N. (2009) 'Socialno-ekonomski položaj starejšega prebivalstva', in V. Hlebec (ed.) *Starejši ljudje v družbi sprememb*, Maribor: Aristej, 77–94.

Majcen, B., Verbič, C., Bayar, A., and Čok, M. (2009) 'The Income Tax Reform in Slovenia: Should the Flat Tax have Prevailed?', *Eastern European Economics* 47(5): 5–24.

Malnar, B. (2011) 'Trendi neenakosti v Sloveniji med statistiko in javnim mnenjem', *Teorija in praksa* 48(4): 951–67.

Mandič, S. (2012) 'Spreminjanje sistema blaginje v post-socialističnih državah in primer Slovenije', *Teorija in praksa* 49(4–5): 611–25.

Mewes, J. and Mau, S. (2013) 'Globalization, Socio-Economic Status and Welfare Chauvinism: European Perspectives on Attitudes toward the Exclusion of Immigrants', *International Journal of Comparative Sociology* 54(3): 228–45.

MNZ (2016) 'Statistical Data on the Number of Migrants Having Entered Slovenia by 12 am on 1 March 2016', *Ministry of the Interior Reports*, http://www.policija.si/eng/index.php/component/content/article/13-news/1729-a-new-webpage-on-police-activities-re-current-migration-flows-set-up-available-informations, accessed 25 May 2016.

Pikalo, J. (2000) 'Vrnitev (ali samo vztrajanje) levice na Slovenskem', in D. Fink-Hafner and M. Haček (eds.) *Demokratični prehodi I*, Ljubljana: Fakulteta za družbene vede, 203–10.

Rakar, T. (2015) 'Country Report for Slovenia, Eurofound Project "Families in the Economic Crisis: Mapping Policy Responses in Five European Member States"', *Eurofound Work Programme 2013–2016*, Ljubljana: IRSSV.

Social Watch Report (2014) 'Slovenia: Gotovi ste!—You're finished!', Ljubljana: Humanitas, http://www.socialwatch.org/node/15975, accessed 25 May 2016.

Stanojević, M. (2000) 'Slovenian Trade Unions: The Birth of Labour Organisations in Post-Communism', *Družboslovne razprave* 16(32–3): 39–52.

Stanojević, M. (2015) 'Sindikalne strategije v obdobju krize', *Teorija in praksa* 52(3): 394–416.

Stropnik, N. (2014) *Investing in Children: Breaking the Cycle of Disadvantage. A Study of National Policies: Slovenia*, Ljubljana: Institute for Economic Research, http://csdle.lex.unict.it/docs/labourweb/Investing-in-children-Breaking-the-cycle-of-Disadvantage-A-study-of-national-policies-Country-Report/4885.aspx, accessed 20 Apr. 2016.

Stropnik, N., Kump, N., Filipovič Hrast, M., Hlebec, V., Vezovnik, A., and Kavčič, M. (2010) *Revščina in materialna deprivacija starejšega prebivalstva: projekt v okviru Ciljnega raziskovalnega programa Konkurenčnost Slovenije 2006–2013 v letu 2006*, Ljubljana: Institute for Economic Research.

Svallfors, S. (2012) 'Welfare attitudes in Europe: Topline Results from Round 4 of the European Social Survey', *ESS Topline Results Series 2*, ESS ERIC, Centre for Comparative Social Surveys at City University, London, https://www.europeansocialsurvey.org/docs/findings/ESS4_toplines_issue_2_welfare_attitudes_in_europe.pdf, accessed 25 May 2016.

Toš, N. et al. (2014) *Slovensko javno mnenje 2013, longitudinalni projekt, pregled in primerjava rezultatov*, Ljubljana: FDV.

Trbanc, M., Smolej, S., Dremelj, P., Črnak Meglič, A., Kobal Tomc, B., and Kovač, N. (2014) *Socialni položaj v Sloveniji 2013–2014, končno poročilo*, Ljubljana: Social Protection Institute of the Republic of Slovenia, http://www.irssv.si/upload2/Koncno%20porocilo%20(dopolnjeno-februar15).pdf, accessed 15 Feb. 2016.

UNICEF Office of Research (2014) 'Children of the Recession: The Impact of the Economic Crisis on Child Well-Being in Rich Countries', *Innocenti Report Card 12:*

Children in the Developed World, Florence: UNICEF Office of Research, https://www.unicef-irc.org/publications/pdf/rc12-eng-web.pdf, accessed 10 Jan. 2016.

Van Kersbergen, K., Vis, B., and Hemerijck, A. (2014) 'The Great Recession and Welfare State Reform: Is Retrenchment Really the Only Game Left in Town?' *Social Policy & Administration* 48(7): 883–904.

Vandenbroucke, F. and Vleminckx, K. (2011) 'Disappointing Poverty Trends: Is the Social Investment State to Blame?', *Journal of European Social Policy* 21(5): 450–71.

7

Spain and Italy

Regaining the Confidence and Legitimacy to Advance Social Policy

Ana M. Guillén and Emmanuele Pavolini

7.1 Introduction

Spain and Italy are respectively the fifth- and fourth-largest economies in the European Union, the latter also a member of G8. Since their accession to the EU (Italy a founder member of the European Economic Community from 1957, Spain joining in 1986), a deep process of Europeanization has taken place in both member states. In fact, enthusiasm for the EU was the norm among both populations and elites prior to the Great Recession.

It is not an easy task to place the Spanish and Italian political economies on the continuum between liberal market and coordinated market economies. The existing literature tends to classify them as mixed-market economies, the main difference lying in the fact that the Spanish labour market shows a much more intense pro-cyclical behaviour than the Italian one in the creation and destruction of employment. This is related to the production model and heavy reliance on fixed-term contracts (about one third of all contracts during the past few decades).

Similarly the Spanish and Italian welfare states do not fit neatly into any of the three regimes identified by Esping-Andersen (1990): social democratic, conservative corporatist, and liberal. There is much debate on whether and how far they represent the so-called Mediterranean model, even more so after divergences among Southern social protection systems during the crisis (see Petmesidou and Guillén 2014; Guillén and Pavolini 2015). What may be defended is that both welfare states have come to constitute a mixed model of the three traditional principles: income maintenance remains close to conservative corporatist principles, healthcare and education follow the social democratic/universalist approach, and social assistance and social care remain grounded in liberal means-tested principles. The two countries have also faced massive immigration flows from the turn of the millennium, the refugee crisis currently affecting Italy more than Spain.

Spain and Italy were among the European countries most affected by the Great Recession and have not yet recovered fully. Strong austerity measures have been applied in the macroeconomic, labour, and social protection spheres. Even if such measures have not been as harsh as in bailed-out economies, they have had substantial impact, so that one can speak of intense external pressures in reform processes since 2010 (Pavolini et al. 2015).

From the 1990s onwards the countries pursued major economic and social reforms in order to meet the standards of the European Monetary Union. More recently the EC and ECB response to the crisis (particularly in the case of Spain which obtained an ECB loan in 2012), coupled with more general pressures to reduce government deficits, have led to more critical perceptions of the EU.

Pressures from the EU, both formal and informal (see Sacchi 2015; De La Porte and Natali 2014; Heins and De La Porte 2015), and other developments in government have led to a sharp decline in trust in political institutions, hindering consensus on social policy reform. Welfare state retrenchment is widely seen as an external imposition rather than an outcome of national policy directions. Policy responses associated with the crisis (Table 1.2, Chapter 1) have constituted a mix of initial neo-Keynesianism, followed by cuts and austerity, enhanced individual responsibility, and interventionism, while welfare chauvinism has remained absent in Spain and less influential in Italy than elsewhere.

The main challenges confronting the Spanish and Italian welfare states in the near future are re-fleshing out the policy-making process and overcoming the institutional crisis. Once this is achieved, groups supporting different policies may find a way to negotiate and decide on future directions. The list of options is constrained to finding a balance between the increased traditional redistributive intervention (irrespective of expenditure), advocated by the traditional left and new populist social movements and parties, and market-friendly and/or retrenchment measures, defended weakly (because of the high electoral cost) by conservatives and liberal democrats in Spain, but more decidedly in Italy.

The chapter is organized in five sections. Following this contextual introduction, section 7.2 analyses the development of policy before the crisis. Section 7.3 examines social policy responses to the Great Recession and changes in the policy-making process. Section 7.4 focuses on the evolution of trust in national/sub-national institutions and salient policy actors, emerging policy cleavages, and subsequent challenges for the future of social protection policies. The chapter closes by gathering the main conclusions on likely future scenarios.

7.2 Pre-crisis Policies and Issues in Spain and Italy

The Spanish and Italian welfare states were established according to the conservative-corporatist model. Both have traditionally been grounded on the 'male breadwinner' and 'transfer heavy/service lean' approaches. During the late 1970s and 1980s an intense process of decentralization to the regions took place.[1] Also, path-breaking reforms occurred in compulsory education (5–16) years and healthcare, increasing coverage to the whole of the population. The full implementation of national healthcare services entailed a drastic change not only in access but also in financing: income tax rather than social contributions became the main source of funding for health and social care.

As to childcare, coverage was greatly improved during the 1990s with the introduction of three years of voluntary pre-schooling with universal access and subject to the same regulations and conditions as elementary schooling. Almost all children between three and five years old are in school at present. Provision of care for under-threes was traditionally meagre, but it grew significantly to reach a coverage rate of 38 per cent (Spain) and 28 per cent (Italy) in 2008.

Social assistance also expanded. In the 1990s new non-contributory pension schemes were put in place and minimum income policies were introduced at the regional level, more broadly in Spain than in Italy, but access remained means-tested. Adaptation to the post-industrial context meant confronting the challenge of overcoming the breadwinner model and paying increased attention to new social risks (Taylor-Gooby 2004), a challenge that has only been partially tackled to date (Guillén and Luque 2016).

Pathways of social protection reform differed in Italy and Spain during the two decades prior to the onset of the Great Recession. In the case of Italy reforms were largely concerned with retrenchment. Cuts in traditional policy fields (pensions and labour market) were not matched by any real recalibration as to new social risks (Ascoli and Pavolini 2015). Spain cut spending, but also recalibrated so that cost containment and rationalization measures in the more traditional social and employment domains coexisted with the introduction of policies dealing with new social risks (Guillén 2010; Rodríguez Cabrero 2011).

Italy has been rightly defined as a 'pension welfare state' (Fargion 2009). Despite two wide-ranging restrictive pension reforms of the 1990s, per-capita expenditure in 2007 was still around 19 per cent higher than the EU15 average. However, per capita expenditure on pensions in Spain was already lower than the EU15 average in 2000, thanks to several rationalization reforms introduced since 1985 (Eurostat). On the recalibration front, a number of bills were passed in Spain before 2010 with the aim of improving income maintenance (including pensions and unemployment benefits) for the self-employed, and salaried agrarian and domestic workers.

The Dependence Law of 2006 established universal access to care and/or cash benefits for all people unable to carry out everyday chores. Legislation on gender equality in 2007 improved work-life balance. Both acts were backed up by broad political agreements and were to be implemented in stages, beginning with the most highly dependent. Still, it has to be underscored that the debate on these measures was never related to social investment. The implementation of both reforms was slowed (and some aspects discontinued) by the crisis (León and Pavolini 2014). In Spain expenditure on care for the elderly increased from 0.16 per cent of GDP in the 1990s to 0.45 in 2008, while in Italy it remained at around 0.1 per cent of GDP (Eurostat).

As Marí-Klose and Moreno-Fuentes (2013) point out, both countries were already directing their welfare state institutions away from an emphasis on old risks before the crisis, especially Spain. This modernization process may well be slower in Italy because, among other factors, fewer women are engaged in paid work and female social roles and the values surrounding them changed more slowly (Calzada and Brooks 2013; Moreno and Marí-Klose 2013).

When comparing Italy and Spain it is also to be noted that, despite showing many similarities as political economies, the origins of the Great Recession and the prior economic situation differed. This posed dissimilar challenges as to available resources for cushioning the social needs generated by the Great Recession. The specificities of Italy and Spain in macroeconomic terms are even clearer when compared with the other three large West European economies: Germany (Chapter 2), the United Kingdom (Chapter 3), and France (Chapter 4).

From 1995 to 2007 Spain enjoyed the most rapid economic growth among the five countries, with the lowest level of deficit and government debt (after the UK), enabling expansionary social protection measures to be pursued (OECD 2016). Italy showed a totally different pattern: the lowest economic growth (together with Germany), matched by the highest, by far, public debt and deficit. GDP per capita in 1995 was similar to that in Germany and France and higher than in the UK and especially Spain. By 2007 Germany had moved ahead, the UK had overtaken Italy, and Spain was getting closer: only France found itself closer to the Italian case. In terms of GDP per capita, economic growth, and government debt, Italy and Spain were at opposite ends of the continuum. Public sector deficits, however, in the two countries were drawing closer and growth was built on shaky foundation (especially for Spain with its huge construction sector), as the crisis soon proved.

The political systems of both countries also differ. The Spanish electoral system is proportional but renders majoritarian results, due to the application of the D'Hondt law in the transformation of votes into seats, and the small number of political parties. As a result, the two major political parties tend to alternate in office. In Italy, a proportional electoral system (corrected since the 1990s in a majoritarian direction) usually renders very fragmented electoral results due to the existence of an extremely pluralist political party spectrum. Social pacts are traditionally made among social partners in order to achieve the legitimization of major welfare reforms.

Finally, according to Eurostat data, the proportion of the population born abroad had grown rapidly in less than fifteen years. It stood at 12.8 per cent in Spain and 9.4 per cent in Italy in 2015. Around half a million immigrants left Spain during the crisis, but the immigration flow was positive again in 2016 (INE 2016). The number of refugees asking for asylum in Italy increased rapidly during the last decade from 9,000 in 2005 to 64,000 in 2014. At the beginning of 2016, around 100,000 refugees were housed in Italian residential accommodation for a total cost of around 1.1 billion euros (0.1 per cent of Italian public expenditure: Fondazione Leone Moressa 2016). Spain received many fewer, about 17,000 asylum seekers and refugees in 2015 (UNHCR 2016). Antagonism towards immigrants both from within and from outside the EU is very high in Italy, but relatively low in Spain (European Commission 2015: 151–6). These pressures have not so far led to anti-immigrant policies.

7.3 The Great Recession Hits the Spanish and Italian Welfare States: Restrictive Policy Reforms and Rescaling of the Policy-Making Process

The public deficit and debt crises were in part related to internal structural rigidities and problems in both countries, and in part the outcome of staggering private debt (twice the GDP) and the bursting of the real estate bubble in Spain. GDP growth collapsed and deficits skyrocketed in Spain, whereas Italy showed greater stability despite huge and increasing public debt. This section analyses the extent of social policy reform and changes in the policy-making process.

7.3.1 Social Policy Reform

If previous trends in economic growth and public debt together with different choices in relation to welfare state innovation and restructuring led to different trajectories for Italy and Spain, the responses to the Great Recession as far as social and labour market policy reforms are concerned have been very similar in content and timing (León et al. 2015). Policies of fiscal consolidation and market liberalization, in conjunction with the implementation of harsh austerity measures and budgetary cuts in relation to welfare state issues, were at the heart of the reform programme in both countries. This demonstrates the salience of external pressures, despite different challenges. In other words, similar reforms were applied regardless of national differences.

Social policy changes took two different forms: radical institutional changes in the main two traditional pillars of the welfare state (pension and labour market policies), and severe cuts, without paradigmatic institutional changes, in the other social policy fields, but with a potential 'transformative' effect in the medium term (for instance, growing waiting lists jeopardizing universal access to welfare services).

Pension reforms (both enacted in 2011) cut back the generosity of the programmes and strengthened the insurance principle. The statutory retirement age was raised and access to early retirement limited, indexation became less generous or was ended, the means-testing of basic pensions was tightened, and contributions and entitlements were more closely linked (Natali and Stamati 2014). The implementation of the reforms was phased in. It hardly affects current pensioners, but will have a major impact in the future.

As has been the case in a majority of EU member states, Italian and Spanish pensioners (over 65) have been better sheltered than the working-age population during the crisis. In fact, at-risk-of-poverty rates for over 65s were significantly reduced: from 2008 to 2015 they halved in Spain, from 25.5 to 12.3 per cent of the age group, and fell by just over six percentage points in Italy, from 20.9 to 14.7 per cent. However, budgetary cuts on healthcare and social services had an impact on older people's quality of life (European Commission 2016). Unemployment rose rapidly and poverty among the general population increased from 24 to 29 per cent in Spain and from 26 to 28 per cent in Italy (Eurostat 2016). Further, pensioners have in many cases pooled their resources with unemployed younger family members. The impact of freezes and discontinuities in inflationary indexation has to be taken into account. Spanish pensioners lost seven per cent of their purchasing power between 2008 and 2016 (INE 2016).

Although cuts to unemployment benefits have taken place, their impact seems to have been less severe than in the field of employment protection. Access to unemployment benefits was not restricted; rather, what has taken place is a combination of reduced generosity for labour market insiders and attempts to expand protection to previously unprotected groups.

Meanwhile, more flexibility for core workers was introduced in the labour market by reforms approved in 2011–12 in both countries. For the first time in decades, reforms were not at the margins, given that the intention of the reforms was to reshape the overall functioning of the labour market and, especially, the position of the insiders. Moreira et al. (2015) show how traditionally segmented and dualized labour markets like those in Spain and Italy are changing rapidly. In particular, the position of the traditional 'winners' has been weakened both in terms of security in employment (lower protection against dismissals) and security in unemployment (protection against drops in the income provided by unemployment insurance and assistance).

Low-wage earners (as a proportion of all employees) for the period 2006–10 have increased from 13.36 to 14.66 per cent in Spain and from 10.27 to 12.36 per cent in Italy, while the Euro area (EA) average increased only slightly. The in-work at-risk-of-poverty rate has also grown, from 11.3 to 13.1 per cent in Spain and from 9.0 to 11.5 in Italy between 2008 and 2015 (Eurostat 2016). As a consequence, labour market change is what Ferrera (2012) would term 'subtractive recalibration' or 'levelling down': differences between outsiders and insiders have decreased not because the former are better treated by new labour regulations, but rather because the latter have become less protected.

Public sector employees are traditionally included among the 'insiders' in the Spanish and Italian labour markets. Austerity measures focused prominently on them through administrative reforms as to enhancement of performance management and reinforcement of a results-based culture. As Sotiropoulos (2015) states, the response to the crisis was similar in both countries also in this respect. To different extents, reforms involved a reduction in the size of public employment, in the cost of labour, and a shift towards performance criteria. During the central years of the crisis, cuts were implemented in public employment through none or minimal replacement of retirees, hiring freezes, and non-renewal of fixed-term contracts (followed, in the case of Spain, by dismissals of permanent employees). In Spain the absolute number of public employees reached its historical peak in 2010 because of high increases since 2005, and then, due to public sector rationalization, in 2015, it fell to a figure similar to that of 2007 (around 14 per cent of the total labour force in 2015, the corresponding figure for Italy amounting to just over 17 per cent: OECD 2015).

Labour market reforms have been coupled with changes in the regulation of industrial relations (Eurofound 2015; León et al. 2015). In Spain the 2012 labour market reform enhanced the capacity of employers to unilaterally modify employees' working conditions by opting out of the clauses contained in collective agreements (see also French reforms for small firms: Chapter 4). In 2013 the 'ultra-activity principle' of Spanish law, guaranteeing the continuation of a collective agreement even after its expiry date, was abolished, so that a maximum period of validity for a collective agreement was set at one year after its official expiry date. In Italy a shift towards decentralized collective bargaining has taken place in recent years. In particular the tripartite Pact on Productivity of November 2012 focused on the bargaining of a productivity wage at plant level, fostered through a reduction of the tax wedge.

If radical reforms took place in pension and labour market policies, all other policy fields were mainly affected by severe budgetary cuts starting from 2010. In Spain policy implementation as to new social risks was either halted or slowed down (León and Pavolini 2014). Healthcare, education, as well as social assistance and family policies were all affected. The only exception is the recent trend to increased access to childcare for children under three in Spain. In 2013 the percentage of children younger than three years in formal childcare was two per cent higher than the EU15 average of 35 per cent enrolment. This expansion is related to the 'Educa3' program set up in 2008. In contrast, in Italy, the percentage was 12 per cent lower (León and Pavolini 2014).

The overall result of internal devaluation and austerity in recent years is a process of substantial retrenchment of citizens' rights with almost non-existent hints of recalibration, from which pensioners have remained better protected. Poverty has increased sharply for those of working age (while it has fallen even more rapidly for pensioners) and austerity policies accounted for a major part of that increase (see estimates by Matsaganis and Leventi 2014). At-risk-of poverty rates for the population as a whole grew more slowly, from 19.8 to 22.1 per cent in Spain between 2008 and 2015, the corresponding figures for Italy amounting to 18.9 and 19.9 (Eurostat 2016). However, the crisis changed the composition of the population in poverty. Poor people were mainly pensioners before 2007 and the austerity programme. Now they are more likely to come from younger age groups and to be unemployed or low paid. The very poorest are now considerably poorer than those occupying the same position before the crisis.

While housing deprivation has not increased, homelessness, although remaining at low levels, has grown in both countries. A similar proportion of households had mortgage or rent arrears in both countries before the crisis (around 4.4 per cent in 2008). This figure grew by only 11 per cent in Italy (worst year 2011) but by almost 80 per cent up to 2015 in Spain and then started to fall (Eurostat 2016). Food banks and Caritas (the biggest Catholic network of non-profit organizations in Spain dealing with poverty and social exclusion) report major expansion in demand during the crisis. All this speaks of deeper cleavages along the lines of advantaged versus disadvantaged groups and also intergenerational ones.

We now move on to consider the political forces behind these reforms.

7.3.2 Changes in the Policy-Making Process

The economic crisis has led to a shift in the structure of the political field. The rise of new political actors, novel alignments of old and new political issues and the implementation process for social policy reform in both countries become of paramount importance. Equally important, though, is the consideration of novel positions on the role and direction of social policies stemming from the birth of social movements and political parties.

In Lijphart's influential classification (Lijphart 2012), Spain is a 'majoritarian democracy' (with a strong role for the executive), similar to France. Italy comes from a 'consensus democracy' tradition. The parliament has traditionally played a central role in policy-making (Cotta 1991). Both countries are federal states and regions enjoy considerable autonomy, of somewhat narrower scope in Italy, but the main difference amounts to the existence of special status regions (asymmetrical devolution) in Spain.

Before 2010 the typical EU approach in social and labour policies was based on multi-level and flexible governance grounded on tools such as the Open Method of Coordination. This was matched in much of Europe and also in the South by a relevant role for national parliaments (as expressions of different societal and political interests), social partners, and sub-national governments, given the heavily institutional decentralization process in the previous years and decades. During the crisis, reforms across the European Union became increasingly top-down with two key central players: non-elected supranational authorities (the EU and the ECB) and the executive of the national governments. All the other main traditional players (parliaments, social partners, sub-national governments, and civil society organizations) lost much of their former influence on national policy-making.

From mid-2010 onwards this structure changed. On the one hand, a major shift took place in EU supranational governance towards strict and binding conditions for those states (for example Italy and Spain) in need of financial help. On the other hand, partisan politics, parliamentary debates, interaction with organized interests, and sub-national governments came to a standstill at the national level.

Although Italy enjoys a consensus democracy tradition, several reforms have taken place since the 1990s aimed at shifting the system towards a majoritarian model. The reforms of election rules have fostered the consolidation of a 'two-coalitions' system. Moreover, in recent years and even before austerity, governments have increasingly taken the lead in legislation: around 80 per cent of the most important laws passed between 2008 and 2013 were started by a government initiative (Marangoni and Tronconi 2014).

If Lijphart's 'Executive-Parties' dimension differentiates Italy and Spain, in relation to his second 'Federal-Unitary' dimension the countries' differences narrow down: both initiated a process of decentralization in the mid- to late 1970s, which has been more pronounced in the case of Spain but has been very relevant in Italy as well, especially after the Constitutional Reform of 2001. Political decentralization has relied on high support from the population in both countries.

Given the differences in their institutional settings, the transformation of policy-making has had a different impact on the two countries. In a majoritarian democracy such as Spain, the stronger role of the government meant an intensification of a specific way of decision-making that was already part of the way in which democracy worked. Conversely, in Italy, this transformation appears as a stronger departure from the traditional consensual model, which was already under transformation before the crisis. In this respect, in Italy, the crisis has provided a window of opportunity for forcing a shift in the model of decision-making towards an enhanced role of the government that different veto players were previously trying to impede.

In particular, the executive has been strengthened, especially in Italy, in two ways. The Prime Minister's Office has become central in promoting and monitoring the reforms, acting as a strong gatekeeper in the coordination between ministries and increasingly responsible for reporting to EU institutions. At the same time, the Ministry of Finance, committed to fiscal consolidation, has taken charge of administrative and welfare state reforms. This has led to a perception of imposed (as opposed to democratically adopted) restrictive social protection reforms, hard to accept even if governments have repeatedly used a 'there is no alternative' strategy to justify their decisions.

Still, change occurred not only as to how governments work internally but also as to how they interact with parliaments and social partners. Parliaments have been sidelined as far as possible: an approach based on 'legislating by fiat', as Sotiropulos (2015) terms it, is evident in both countries. Social partners were also pushed aside (Luque Balbona and González Begega 2015). During the 1990s and the 2000s an increase in forms of collaboration and social pacts between social partners and governments had taken place. Since 2010 governments explicitly stated a change of attitude, declaring that concertation was over, especially in Italy. Consultation (devoid of any real veto opportunity) became the new buzzword. A generalized drift from 'bargaining to imposition' can be seen with regard to socio-economic governance at the national level (Molina and Miguélez 2013). This trend is now starting to reverse in Spain, especially at the regional level.

Not only have social partners, particularly trade unions, been sidelined, but, as already emphasized, new legislation shifts regulation of the employment contract from the level of collective national negotiations to decentralized arrangements, curtailing labour protection and trade unions' capacity to represent workers. The result is that, since 2010, the limited confrontation between the actors turned into a clash of 'trade unions against governments' (Hamann et al. 2013). Strikes and protests have not been able to block reforms so far.

The loss of influence in the policy-making process has also affected subnational governments. Much decision-making has been re-centralized. There have been severe cuts in the resources transferred by central government to regional/local authorities, despite the delegation to the latter of several new tasks (see Bolgherini 2014 and Morlino and Della Piana 2014 for the Italian case, and Viver 2010 for Spain). Sub-national governments have been forced to accept significant cuts and greater control or supervision of their budgets by central governments. Two-thirds of regional budgets are spent on social policies, and regional and local welfare systems have inevitably been affected both in scope and in the way in which decisions are made.

Looking comparatively at how welfare state expenditure changed from 2007 to 2012, both in Spain and Italy, sub-national governments were the ones that paid the highest price in terms of expenditure cuts: while central government expenditure rose slightly (by about one per cent) and social security funds witnessed robust increases (almost three per cent in Spain and one per cent in Italy), spending by sub-national governments fell by 1.3 per cent on average (Del Pino and Pavolini 2015), mainly affecting healthcare and education and impacting most severely on those less able to resort to private provision.[2]

Spain experienced greater overall political stability than Italy from 2011 to 2015. This situation has now been reversed: the last two elections in Spain failed to produce a viable coalition and a minority government was only established in October 2016.

Growing discontent and unrest among those social groups worst hit by the crisis has led to an upsurge of social movements, reflecting the deepening cleavage between the worse and the better off. The latter have crystallized into populist left parties, namely the Five Star Movement in Italy (established in October 2009) and Podemos in Spain (founded in January 2014 and originating in the May 2011'14-M' protest). The Five Star Movement defines itself as a free association of citizens rather than a political party since it is positioned against the traditional political system. It initially defined itself as an ecological, anti-Euro and partially Eurosceptical movement (Ceccarini and Bordignon 2016; Bordignon and Ceccarini 2013). In turn, Podemos seeks the renovation of 'the left of the left' and then the conquering of the whole space of the left. Supporters and voters came originally from among those better off but indignant about the social impact of the crisis, and later incorporated many of the worse off (Politikon 2015; Fernández Albertos 2015). These political parties/movements claim that eradication of corruption among political elites and the discontinuing of austerity policies (in both the social protection and labour market domains) would liberate enough resources to expand the welfare state and provide a universal basic income to all citizens.

To sum up, the crisis period has witnessed retrenchment measures and an upward 'rescaling' process of decision-making, leading to a reconfiguration of the set of 'appropriate' actors for dealing with social problems (who decides and how), and repartition of competencies among different actors and layers of government, with regional and local governments finding themselves in dire straits, scarcely able to provide the services and transfers for which they are responsible, namely, healthcare, education, minimum income, active labour market policies, social care, and social inclusion. The Great Recession has also witnessed the upsurge of new social movements and political parties trying to represent the worse off and the disillusioned and to advance their interests. Official state policies are neo-liberal and austerity-based, but include some social investment. They are vigorously contested by a political fightback. These changes have led to major instability in the political system in Spain.

7.4 The Institutional Crisis and Future Scenarios

To examine more closely the development of public attitudes and emerging cleavages we analyse here the performance of governments in controlling corruption (the source of all social evil according to new populist movements and political parties), and the evolution of trust in national governments and trade unions. The collapse of political trust poses great challenges for debate, negotiation, and decision-making in social policy. On the other hand, anti-immigrant feelings are high in Italy, but not necessarily tantamount to welfare chauvinism, and largely absent in Spain so far, but future developments here are hard to predict.

The World Bank (2016) Control of Corruption indicator reflects perceptions of the extent to which public power is exercised for private gain, including both petty and grand forms of corruption, as well as seizure of the state by elites and private interests (Figure 7.1). As perceived by citizens, Spanish and, especially, Italian governments have been less successful in controlling corruption than those of France, Germany, and the UK. Italy also scores consistently worst of all five countries on the Transparency International index of corruption in public administration. Public confidence has also declined over time (Transparency International 2016).

Figure 7.2 compares the evolution of trust in national governments in Germany, France, the UK, Italy, and Spain. It shows that the effect of the crisis is more visible in Spain than in Italy, where trust has been consistently low. Trust in the central government in Spain was higher than in the other four countries until 2008. Trust in local and regional governments was also relatively high (at least as much as in France). The collapse of trust in these three institutions in Spain, starting in 2008, has followed a downward path not reflected in any of the three other countries considered in the comparison. In fact, Spanish institutional (dis)trust has reached levels similar to that in Italy. Trust levels diverge in the five countries after 2008. The UK and, especially,

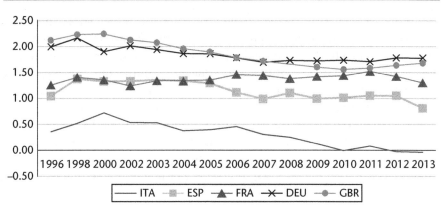

Figure 7.1. Control of corruption by governments.

The values of the indicators above range from approximately −2.5 (weak) to 2.5 (strong) governance performance. The Worldwide Governance Indicators (WGI) from the World Bank summarizes the views on the quality of governance provided by a large number of enterprise, citizen, and expert survey respondents.

Source: World Bank 2016

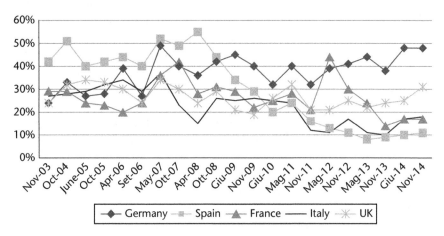

Figure 7.2. Evolution of trust in national government (2003–14).

Source: EC 2003–14

Germany show relatively higher institutional trust levels while Spain and Italy have relatively lower levels. France appears closer to Southern Europe than to Germany and the UK.

The crisis in trust has affected not only public bodies in the countries in which trust in government has declined but also some of the main socio-economic institutions which play an important role in the labour market and welfare state policy arena. Spain shows the fastest deterioration in trust in trade unions since the onset of the crisis: around 65 per cent of Spaniards trusted trade unions at the end of 2007, whereas already in winter 2010 this percentage had fallen to 28 per cent. In Italy corresponding figures are 58 and 40 per cent. In Germany trust in unions remained stable (60 and 57 per cent respectively) and in France it fell somewhat from 57 to 48 per cent (European Commission 2003–14).

Corruption scandals, diminishing trust in institutions and political elites, and growing inequalities have all reinforced support for new parties critical of the traditional left, such as Podemos and the Five Star Movement. In Spain, Podemos has often attacked national and sub-national political elites, supra-national institutions, and trade unions, but has not engaged in welfare chauvinism. In Italy, regional parties as the Lega Nord and Fratelli di Italia have adopted a strong anti-immigrant stance.

To sum up, challenges for the future of the welfare state in Spain and Italy stem from the political transformations analysed in Section 7.3, namely, upward rescaling of the policy-making process (including EU conditionality), loss of influence of the traditional political actors, and deepening cleavages between the worse and the better off resulting from restrictive labour and social protection reforms. This section shows that perceptions of a declining government capacity to control corruption and the erosion of trust in institutions are at least equally important. Support for new directions in social policy in the Spanish and Italian welfare states in the future depends on the recovery of legitimacy and trust through participatory decision-making. It will be impossible to address them effectively through policies that are developed without such a process.

7.5 Conclusion

Our analysis shows that in spite of differences in the pre-crisis macroeconomic circumstances and distinct social protection macro-institutional configurations, the path of welfare state reform, based on retrenchment and austerity (with some limited social investment), and of change in the policy-making process during the Great Recession shows a high degree of similarity between Italy and Spain. External conditionality, together with the urgency of reform, has played a prominent role in explaining how social policy developed during the crisis, although institutional problems started to emerge even before the Great Recession.

The ensuing main cleavages in social protection terms are, in both cases, between advantaged and disadvantaged social groups but also between pensioners and active-age citizens. Currently, Italy and Spain are facing parallel socio-economic and political crises. To the extent that the deepening of the politico-institutional crisis is the result of the responses to the socio-economic crisis, the two cannot be examined in isolation. Both these crises are transforming traditional understandings of political actors and institutions, elicited by increasing disaffection towards formal democratic institutions and traditional actors and the emergence of alternative politics.

The political management of the economic crisis deepened already growing distrust in political institutions. Such distrust is based mainly on negative perceptions of the responsiveness of institutions, strengthened by the perception of corruption among politicians. Governmental management of the crisis pressed citizens to question the legitimacy of democratic institutions and political representatives.

In general, in recent years, old problems (persistent inequalities), new ones (the economic crisis and its impact on millions of workers and households), and the upward rescaling of policy decisions have all converged, creating the basis for political tensions, protests, and (potential) changes. In both countries trust in parties and politicians and support for the EU have fallen sharply. Public protest has become an important component of the socio-political dynamics. Resistance movements have gathered momentum and have stimulated public debate. New or traditionally peripheral parties have entered the political arena gaining space and electoral support.

Transformations of the welfare states of the two countries have been possible given the upsurge of strong internal and external pressures on institutional environments to react to the crisis and to answer previous problems of governance. This has pushed through a different model of policy-making, which has proved only partially successful in persuading voters of the absence of real alternatives to harsh austerity as the only way to recover economic stability and growth, and of the virtues of reforms led by EU/national executives. In Spain, traditional political parties have so far paid a high electoral price and must face intense competition with new parties. In Italy the situation is more fluid, although parties and movements expressing strong resistance against austerity (and the EU) are gaining support for their protest and their political platform.

External conditionality, coupled with increasingly powerful national executives, corruption scandals, and perceived lack of responsiveness, has resulted in a situation in which overcoming the economic and financial crisis has become just one of the challenges for the future. Re-conquering citizens' trust in institutions at all levels of governance (including the EU), political elites, and interest groups has become essential. This is crucial for the attainment of a new social agreement allowing for (re)negotiation of the path of reform of social protection policies and redistribution.

Strategic options for the future remain difficult to elicit. Analysis of the social policy responses to the crisis and of the changes in the decision-making process tells us that welfare state reform is hardly following a planned strategy. It rather resembles the result of a list of last-minute unavoidable decisions to regain the confidence of the international financial markets. In other words, no clear strategy of reform, be it social investment, pre-distribution, emphasis on new social risks, or enhancement of individual responsibility, is fought for, whether by traditional political forces or by emerging ones. While labour markets, industrial relations, social concertation, and retrenchment of social protection have followed a neo-liberal reform trajectory during the crisis, the fact remains that the imposition of these policies by national and supranational executives is not what the populations wish for.

The generational divide could be overcome by coupling the implementation of already enacted restrictive reforms of pension systems (although poverty among the elderly is likely to rise) to the introduction of increased protection for new social risks. This would result in a better balance between active and non-active populations (and, indirectly, children), and, probably, would narrow inequalities among those better and worse off. However, both of the approaches advocated by current political positions—either reversing the reforms enacted during the crisis and increasing expenditure irrespective of deficits to return to the previous position (termed the 'fightback strategy' in Chapter 1) or going further along the neo-liberal path—are unrealistic: the first for economic reasons in a globalized international context, and the second in electoral terms. Whether the Spanish and Italian welfare states will be able to undergo recalibration in a direction that satisfies their populations and results in enhanced trust is yet to be seen.

Notes

1. Healthcare, education (fully in Spain and partially in Italy), and social services are in the hands of regional governments, while pensions and passive unemployment protection schemes have remained centralized.
2. Given that regional debt in Catalonia was one of the highest in the country, this may have enhanced the region's desire for independence. It is also the case than Catalonia benefited most from the public regional rescue fund, so that the issue remains a matter of heated discussion with little agreement in media, political, or academic debates.

References

Ascoli, U. and Pavolini, E. (eds.) (2015) *The Italian Welfare State in a European Perspective: A Comparative Analysis*, Bristol: Policy Press.

Bolgherini, S. (2014) 'Can Austerity Lead to Recentralization? Italian Local Government during the Economic Crisis', *South European Society and Politics* 19(2): 193–214.

Bordignon, F. and Ceccarini, L. (2013) 'Five Starts and a Cricket: Beppe Grillo Shakes Italian Politics', *South European Society and Politics* 18(4): 427–49.

Calzada, I. and Brooks, C. (2013) 'The Myth of Mediterranean Familism', *European Societies* 15(4): 514–34.

Ceccarini, L. and Bordignon, F. (2016) 'The Five Stars Continue to Shine: The Consolidation of Grillo's Movement Party in Italy', *Contemporary Italian Politics*, 8(2): 131–59.

Cotta, M. (1991) 'Il parlamento nel sistema político italiano: Mutamenti instituzionali e cicli politici', *Quaderni Costituzionali* 2: 201–23.

De la Porte, C. and Natali, D. (2014) 'Altered Europeanization of Pension Reform during the Great Recession: Denmark and Italy Compared', *West European Politics* 37(4): 732–49.

Del Pino, E. and Pavolini, E. (2015) 'Decentralization at a Time of Harsh Austerity: Multilevel Governance and the Welfare State in Spain and Italy Facing the Crisis', *European Journal of Social Security* 17(2): 246–70.

Esping-Andersen, G. (1990) *The Three Worlds of Welfare Capitalism*, Cambridge: Polity Press/Princeton, NJ: Princeton University Press.

Eurofound (2015) *Collective Bargaining in Europe in the 21st Century*, Luxembourg: Publications Office of the European Union, https://www.eurofound.europa.eu/publi cations/report/2015/industrial-relations/collective-bargaining-in-europe-in-the-21st-century, accessed 23 Sep. 2016.

European Commission (2003–14) *Standard Eurobarometers* 60 to 82, Brussels: European Commission, http://ec.europa.eu/COMMFrontOffice/publicopinion/index.cfm/Sur vey/index#p=1&instruments=STANDARD, accessed 23 Sep. 2016.

European Commission (2015) *Public Opinion in the European Union, Standard Barometer* 83, Spring 2015, Brussels: European Commission, http://ec.europa.eu/public_opinion/ archives/eb/eb83/eb83_publ_en.pdf, accessed 23 Sep. 2016.

European Commission (2016) *Fighting Poverty and Exclusion through Social Investment: A European Research Perspective*, Brussels: European Commission, http://bookshop. europa.eu/en/fighting-poverty-and-exclusion-through-social-investment-pbKI0116761/, accessed 23 Sep. 2016.

Eurostat (2016) *ESSPROS Database*, Luxemburg: Eurostat, http://ec.europa.eu/eurostat/ statistics-explained/index.php/Social_protection_statistics, accessed 23 Sep. 2016.

Fargion, V. (2009) 'Italy: Still a Pension State?', in P. Alcock and G. Craig (eds.) *International Social Policy*, New York: Palgrave, 171–89.

Fernández Albertos, J. (2015) *Los votantes de Podemos: del partido de los indignados al partido de los excluidos*, Madrid: Catarata.

Ferrera, M. (2012) 'Verso un welfare più europeo? Conclusioni', in M. Ferrera, V. Fargion, and M. Jessoula (eds.) *Alle radici del Welfare State all'italiana*, Venice: Marsilio, 323–44.

Fondazione Leone Moressa (2016) *La buona accoglienza. Analisi comparative dei sistemi di accoglianza per richiendenti asilo in Europa*, Venezia: Fondazione Leone Moressa, http:// www.fondazioneleonemoressa.org/newsite/wp-content/uploads/2016/01/LA-BUONA-ACCOGLIENZA-20_01_2016.pdf, accessed 25 Sep. 2016.

Guillén, A. M. (2010) 'Defrosting the Spanish Welfare State: The Weight of Conservative Components', in B. Palier (ed.) *A Long Good-Bye to Bismarck: The Politics of Welfare*

Reforms in Continental Welfare States, Amsterdam: Amsterdam University Press, 143–62.

Guillén, A. M. and Luque, D. (2016) 'Adjusting to the Post-Industrial Era: How Have the Spanish and Italian Welfare States Performed?', paper presented at the 23rd International Conference of Europeanists, Philadelphia, Apr. 2016.

Guillén, A. M. and Pavolini (2015) 'Welfare States under Strain in Southern Europe: Overview of the Special Issue', *European Journal of Social Security* 17(2): 147–57.

Hamann, K., Johnston, A., and Kelly, J. (2013) 'Unions against Governments: Explaining General Strikes in Western Europe, 1980–2006', *Comparative Political Studies* 46(9): 1030–57.

Heins, E. and De la Porte, C. (2015) 'The Sovereign Debt Crisis, the EU and Welfare Reform', *Comparative European Politics* 13(1): 1–7.

INE (2016) *Instituto Nacional de Estadística*, www.ine.es, accessed 23 Sep. 2016.

León, M. and Pavolini, E. (2014) 'Social Investment or Back to Familism: The Impact of the Economic Crisis on Family and Care Policies in Italy and Spain', *South European Society and Politics* 19(3): 353–69.

León, M., Pavolini, E., and Guillén, A. M. (2015) 'Welfare Rescaling in Italy and Spain: Political Strategies to Deal with Harsh Austerity', *European Journal of Social Security* 17(2): 182–201.

Lijphart, A. (2012) *Patterns of Democracy: Government Forms and Democracy in Thirty-Six Countries*, 2nd edn, New Haven and London: Yale University Press.

Luque Balbona, D. and González Begega, S. (2015) 'Austerity and Welfare Reform in South-Western Europe. A Farewell to Corporatism in Italy, Spain and Portugal?', *European Journal of Social Security* 17(2): 271–91.

Marangoni, F. and Tronconi, F. (2014) 'La rappresentanza degli interesi in parlamento', *Rivista italiana di Politiche Pubbliche* 9 (3): 557–88.

Marí-Klose, P. and Moreno-Fuentes, F. J. (2013) 'The Southern European Welfare model in the post-industrial Order', *European Societies* 15(4): 475–92.

Matsaganis, M. and Leventi, C. (2014) 'The Distributional Impact of Austerity and the Recession in Southern Europe', *South European Society and Politics* 19(3): 393–412.

Molina, O. and Miguélez, F. (2013) 'From Negotiation to Imposition: Social Dialogue in Austerity Times', *ILO Working Paper* No. 51, Geneva: International Labour Organization, 1–32.

Moreira, A., Alonso, A., Antunes, C., Karamessini, M., Raitano, M., and Glatzer, M. (2015) 'Austerity-Driven Labour Market Reforms in Southern Europe: Eroding the Security of Labour Market Insiders', *European Journal of Social Security* 17(2): 202–25.

Moreno, L. and Marí-Klose, P. (2013) 'Youth, Family Change and Welfare Arrangements', *European Societies* 15(4): 493–513.

Morlino, L. and Della Piana, D. (2014) 'Economic Crisis in a Stalemated Democracy: The Italian Case', *American Behavioral Scientist* 58(12): 1657–82.

Natali, D. and Stamati, F. (2014) 'Reassessing South European Pensions after the Crisis: Evidence of Two Decades of Reform', *South European Society and Politics* 19(3): 309–30.

OECD (2015) *Government at a Glance*, Paris: OECD, http://www.oecd.org/gov/govataglance.htm, accessed 23 Sep. 2016.

OECD (2016) *OECD Statistical Database*, Paris: OECD, https://stats.oecd.org/, accessed 23 Sep. 2016.

Pavolini, E., León, M., Guillén, A. M., and Ascoli, U. (2015) 'From Austerity to Permanent Strain? The EU and Welfare State Reform in Italy and Spain', *Comparative European Politics* 13(1): 56–76.

Petmesidou, M. and Guillén, A. M. (2014) 'Can the Welfare State as We Know It Survive? A View from the Crisis-Ridden South European Periphery', *South European Society and Politics* 10(3): 295–307.

Politikon (2015) *Podemos: la cuadratura del círculo*, Madrid: Debate.

Rodríguez Cabrero, G. (2011) 'The Consolidation of the Spanish Welfare State (1975–2010)', in A. M. Guillén and M. León (eds.) *The Spanish Welfare State in European Context*, Farnham: Ashgate, 17–38.

Sacchi, S. (2015) 'Conditionality by Other Means: EU Involvement in Italy's Structural Reforms in the Sovereign Debt Crisis', *Comparative European Politics* 13(1): 77–92.

Sotiropoulos, D. (2015) 'Southern European Governments and Public Bureaucracies in the Context of Economic Crisis', *European Journal of Social Security* 17(2): 226–45.

Taylor-Gooby, P. (2004) 'New Social Risks and Welfare States: New Paradigm and New Politics?' in Taylor-Gooby (ed.) *New Risks, New Welfare: The Transformation of the European Welfare State*, Oxford: Oxford University Press, 209–38.

Transparency International (2016) *Corruption Perceptions Index 2016* website: http://www.transparency.org/, accessed 1 Aug. 2016.

UNHCR (2016) *Population Statistics* [database], Geneve: UNHCR, http://popstats.unhcr.org/en/overview#_ga=1.1490737.1410439585.1452783218, accessed 23 Sep. 2016.

Viver, C. (2010) 'Impact of the Financial Crisis on the Territorial Power Structure in Spain', paper presented at the conference 'Federalism and the Global Financial Crisis: Impact and Responses', Philadelphia, Sep. 2010.

World Bank (2016) *Worldwide Governance Indicators*, Washington: World Bank, http://data.worldbank.org/data-catalog/worldwide-governance-indicators, accessed 23 Sep. 2016.

8

Welfare Reform in Greece

A Major Crisis, Crippling Debt Conditions and Stark Challenges Ahead

Maria Petmesidou

8.1 Introduction

Among the countries of the European periphery, Greece has been hit hardest and longest by the sovereign debt crisis following the Great Recession. In 2010 Greece entered into a 'rescue-deal' with the so-called troika (the three international lenders: the European Commission, the International Monetary Fund, and the European Central Bank) conditional on implementing austerity-driven structural adjustment. This exacerbated an already serious recession. Between 2009 and 2013 GDP contracted by about a quarter; anaemic growth of 0.7 per cent in 2014 came to an end in 2015 due to political and economic instability, leading to two snap general elections, a referendum, and the signing of a new bailout package deal in mid-July. GDP fell by 0.2 and 0.1 per cent in 2015 and 2016. Unemployment nearly tripled from 9.6 per cent in 2009 to 25 per cent in 2015. It slightly fell to 23.5 per cent in 2016 yet the Greek General Confederation of Labour (INE-GSEE 2017: 17) estimates the real unemployment rate at about 30 per cent). Youth unemployment has been hovering around 50 per cent. Job losses since the recession now exceed the total number created between 1993 and 2008.

Three factors are crucial for understanding the politics of welfare in Greece and assessing the effects of austerity-driven measures. First, Greece contains a 'small, quasi-closed economy' producing mostly for internal consumption (Gros et al. 2011; Barslund and Andersen 2015). Although exports account for nearly a third of GDP this is mainly oil and shipping. Added value in both is low, since Greece does not produce but simply trades in oil and runs shipping lines which employ few Greek workers (Barslund and Andersen

2015: 2). Interestingly, in the 2000s, when the country experienced sustained economic growth of over three per cent annually (up to 2007), growth had come almost entirely from the 'non-tradeable' sector (local services and construction). This sector has persistently been larger than tradeables (manufacturing, agriculture, and raw materials). The small size of the latter and the fact that it contracted faster than the former during the crisis raise doubts as to whether the internal devaluation imposed by structural adjustment will succeed in triggering growth.

Secondly, the economy consists of very small firms (96 per cent with less than five employees), and self-employment is comparatively high (over a third of the economically active population; Athanasiou 2015: 21–2). The tertiary sector expanded rapidly from the 1970s onwards, associated with rising educational qualifications and an expanding professionalization of the labour market. Men and (particularly) women made significant inroads into professional, technical, and managerial occupations, yet the shift towards services was accompanied by comparatively weak development of the services typical of a post-industrial economy: producer services (business services, finance, insurance) and social services requiring high-end skills. Instead it was traditional services that developed (utilities, tourism, retail, and public administration: Petmesidou 2011a).

Thirdly, rent-seeking statist–clientelistic practices which undermine the politics of solidaristic support for collective welfare dominated society for much of the post-war period (Petmesidou 2011b). This is closely linked with the way in which political parties have related to their social base through clientelistic exchanges to ensure electoral support. Moreover, party patronage has persistently involved trade union cadres as well. Trade unions have tended to fragment along party political lines, and industrial relations are highly conflictual, often within a framework of maximalist demands. This pattern of state–society relationships differs significantly from both the coordinated and liberal types of capitalism (as defined by Hall and Soskice 2001, in the *Varieties of Capitalism* approach). Rent-seeking behaviour by those with access to political power has persistently influenced the distribution of income and resources. Union density is low and the unions that take a leading role in industrial action are mainly those of state sector employees (teachers, public administrators, and workers in public utilities). In this socio-political configuration, the 'logic of populism' combined with electoral overbidding in clientelist concessions and rent-seeking behaviour (see Kovras and Loizides 2014) has for a long time produced institutional sclerosis and administrative inertia. This limits opportunities to rationalize the system. Public debt has grown as governments borrowed to fund clientelistic payouts but found it hard to levy extra taxes.

The crisis imposed huge restrictions on resources for clientelism by political parties. Trust in parties and trade unions and their political legitimacy declined significantly, triggering the reshuffling of the political scene. The two main parties that ruled the country in the period after the restoration of democracy (the centre-right New Democracy and the centre-left Panhellenic Socialist Party) reached their lowest point in opinion polls in early 2012. New party formations have emerged out of the collapsing post-dictatorship party political system based on the centre-right/centre-left cleavage, and electoral volatility has increased.

The rise to power of a previously marginal left-wing party, SYRIZA, in the snap election of late January 2015, has brought to the fore many of the failures of structural adjustment under the bailout deal and opened up debate on alternative scenarios to neo-liberal austerity, and on the need for a European-wide backlash against such measures. However, after five months of fruitless talks with the international lenders, increasing economic uncertainty that threatened to cause financial chaos, and a dubious referendum held in early July on whether to accept or not a proposal by the creditors (for a fresh bailout), the coalition government of SYRIZA and a small conservative–nationalist party, ANEL, made a U-turn and agreed painful reforms in exchange for a new loan. The new 'austerity deal' was approved by the Greek parliament with the support of the mainstream pro-European opposition parties, but a significant number of SYRIZA's MPs voted against it. This led to the revolt and the defection of the left-wing of SYRIZA in order to form a new party (Popular Unity). The government resigned and SYRIZA was again victorious in the snap election on 20 September 2015.

This chapter examines current welfare state reforms in Greece, the background to them and likely future developments. Section 8.2 briefly sketches the main characteristics of the social welfare model which prevailed in the country for a considerable period. This combined rent-seeking statist practices with a welfare system extensively relying upon the family. We emphasize the deadlocks of the system reflected in the extent of unmet need and the gaps in protection against old and new social risks, and highlight direct and indirect influences from the EU in the 1990s and 2000s up to the crisis in 2008.

Section 8.3 tracks the unfolding of the crisis and examines the main policy reform options in the context of the conditions imposed by the 'rescue-deals'. Underlying the crisis were the structural rigidities of the economy, and particularly an economic structure based primarily on internal consumption (and benefiting from the inflow of EU structural funding into the country), profligate borrowing by successive governments to pay for current provision, leading to a current account deficit—in tandem with weak revenue collection and adverse demographics. Current reforms must tackle these issues. At the centre of this analysis is a raft of significant reforms since 2010 in labour market policies, social insurance, and health and social care. These are assessed according to whether and to what extent fiscal consolidation has been balanced with concerns about improving protection and redressing inequalities, or whether standards of social protection have been forced ever lower.

Taking into consideration the overall explanatory framework developed in Chapter 1, an attempt will be made to throw light on social inequalities, social cleavages, and solidarities, vis-à-vis the ongoing welfare state reforms and prospective changes under the bailout deal. Undoubtedly, neo-liberal austerity is the mantra of social adjustment under the successive bailout agreements. A fightback stance rejecting austerity and its neo-liberal assumptions in an attempt to reassert neo-Keynesianism acquired broad political significance with SYRIZA's rise to power, which tapped into the discontent resulting from the harsh austerity measures. However, the government's failure to translate the anti-austerity stance into a realistic economic policy and negotiate a better deal for Greece seriously narrows the scope for reform towards a sustainable redistributive welfare state.

Section 8.4 raises a number of questions as to the future of welfare. The overall orientation of 'structural adjustment' towards liberalization and significant wage and benefit compression in order to turn a quasi-closed economy into a competitive, outward-facing one is a crucial issue. How will these changes impact upon the social structure, social cleavages, and conflicts? More importantly, how will they impact on the relatively large Greek middle class? Will the outcome be 'a race to the bottom' in wages and social welfare? Could, instead, a socially embedded form of liberalization and flexibilization be followed (for example, along the lines of social investment)? The conclusion summarizes the main arguments developed in this chapter with an emphasis on the effects of the protracted crisis and future possibilities for social welfare.

8.2 The Context: The 'Lagged' Development of the Welfare State in the 1980s and Reform Pressures before the Sovereign Debt Crisis

The historical origins of public welfare lie in the late nineteenth and early twentieth centuries when the first social insurance funds were established for particular professions and the armed forces. For a long time coverage remained limited, highly fragmented, and unequal. In the 1950s and 1960s, when the country experienced fast economic growth and structural changes boosting industrialization, no major developments in public welfare were recorded. The same holds for the period of authoritarian rule (1967–74; see Petmesidou 2006; 2015). The restoration of democracy, and particularly the coming to power of PASOK in 1981, unleashed pent-up pressures for expanding social protection. Social expenditure as a percentage of GDP almost doubled between 1981 and 1990 (from 12 to 22 per cent). It decreased in the first half of the 1990s, after which it resumed a slightly upward trend until the eruption of the financial and economic crisis in 2008.

In the mid-1990s Ferrera (1996) described the main features of the 'South European welfare regime'. He identified a bias in spending towards pensions (which crowds out resources for support to families at earlier stages of the life cycle), undeveloped social safety nets, high labour market segmentation, and great inequalities in social insurance coverage. Such traits are particularly evident in the 1980s and early 1990s which can be considered as the era of 'the peak of commonalities' among the South European welfare states. Yet since the early to mid-1990s 'South European welfare capitalism has become increasingly dissimilar in the four countries, putting into question the existence of a distinctive model' (Petmesidou and Guillén 2015: 9).

Due to the strong populist current during the 1980s in Greece, welfare policies came to be a crucial instrument in clientelistic–particularistic exchanges that characterized socio-political integration in the country. The growing size and political weight of the middle class since the mid-1970s intensified social fragmentation and the contradictions of Greek statism (Petmesidou 1991). Public spending rapidly increased, but conflicts along clientelist lines severely hampered reforms aimed at redistribution on the basis of need. Public deficits and indebtedness soared dramatically during this period, partly because of a rapid expansion of benefit schemes such as favourable retirement provisions for some socio-professional groups, early retirement schemes, disability pensions, and other more or less discretionary benefits. These substituted for more comprehensive, rights-based welfare arrangements. By the mid-1980s the total deficits of social insurance funds reached 16.7 per cent of their revenue and three per cent of GDP.

Expansion and reform during the 1980s and 1990s consolidated a hybrid social protection system, combining different organizing principles across major policy areas (social security, health and social care) that embrace elements from all three 'welfare regimes' distinguished in the well-known typology documented in the work of Esping-Andersen (1990: compare Spain and Italy, Chapter 7). 'Density of historical time' is another key characteristic. Greece has attempted to implement social rights, which have taken north-western Europe more than half a century to achieve, in one decade.

A Bismarckian, extremely fragmented, and highly unequal social insurance system was combined with an incomplete shift to social-democratic healthcare, with the establishment of a national health service in 1981, while statutory social care remained rudimentary. In addition, a dualization pattern along the formal/informal economy divide was prevalent. Deep inequalities in terms of funding, scope, and level of provision characterized the more than 130 social insurance funds covering those employed in the formal sector, while workers in the informal economy were at an even greater risk of income loss. In healthcare, inequalities in coverage among social groups were sustained and private health spending remained high (about 40 per cent of total health expenditure by the end of the 2000s). This is mostly due to the fact that a mixed system continued to operate in terms of both funding and service delivery: an occupation-based health insurance system was combined with a national health service, but private provision kept expanding too. More importantly, private expenditure in Greece consists of out-of-pocket payments. These amounted to more than 90 per cent of total private health expenditure in the mid- to late 2000s (OECD 2015a: 2). Extensive reliance on out-of-pocket payments (part of it being under-the-table payments) and indirect taxation (by the mid-2000s about a fifth of total health expenditure was financed by taxation, with indirect taxes accounting for a large part of it) renders the system highly regressive. Furthermore, the main obstacles to building a truly national health system in Greece have always been a serious lack of support by major social actors, conflicting interests within the medical community, discretionary privileges to particular social insurance funds, and complex ties between the public and private sector fostering corruption and waste of resources.

As to social assistance and social care, these are chronically ailing policy areas. The family has traditionally been the main provider of care and support. Growing demand for care services, due to changes in family patterns and a rise in women's employment, until the crisis erupted, combined with an ageing population and a steadily rising number of lone elderly people, was met by female migrant workers employed informally as domestic carers (Guillén and Petmesidou 2008: 75). Such arrangements, however, turned out to be highly fragile under the impact of the economic crisis. Increasing hardship among low-income (but also middle-income) households made it difficult for them to afford a paid carer and strongly exacerbated the need for a new framework for sharing of public/private responsibility in social care.

Statist–clientelistic practices have for a long-time been a major influence on the politics of welfare, hindering a modernization path towards the development of rational–bureaucratic structures and universalist social citizenship values. Both the required machinery and personnel for carrying out systematic policy planning and implementation were lacking, even though state intervention was virtually all pervasive. During much of the 1980s public expenditure amounted to 50 per cent of GDP even though state provision was far from comprehensive (Petmesidou 2006: 39). There is a sizeable critical literature on the deficiencies of public administration and planning in Greece. Monastiriotis and Antoniades (2009) sum up these deficiencies as a 'failing reform technology' in the country or, in other words, an absence of a (more or less) systematic process of research and evidence-informed policy-making. Hence the Greek pathologies, namely that plans developed are barely implemented and 'reform activism' remains on paper with little effect in terms of policy processes and outcomes.

The economic recession in the first half of the 1990s and the serious fiscal pressures and challenges linked to a range of hard and soft EU requirements (prominently the core convergence criteria of the Maastricht Treaty and participation in the Eurozone: see Chapter 1) brought imbalances to centre stage. Yet, despite prolific legislation in various policy fields, major issues were barely touched. These issues included the hybrid healthcare system (with an overlap of universalist and corporatist organizing criteria), the blurred line between social insurance and assistance, the fragmentation and inequality of coverage, with major challenges from an ageing population, the absence of an income support safety net, and growing informal privatization with respect to social care (care provided within the family by informal carers, mostly legal and/or illegal female migrants).

In the field of social security, legislation passed in the early 1990s (by the New Democracy government) aimed primarily to restore financial equilibrium in the short and medium term with regard to the public and social security deficits, but the measures left problems of fragmentation and inefficiency intact. In the early 2000s, two ambitious plans to reform pensions drastically and to overhaul ESY (the National Health Service) by decentralizing decision-making, integrating primary and secondary care, rationalizing funding and management, and introducing a purchaser–provider split sparked mass protest. The pension reform plan was withdrawn and a diluted healthcare reform approved by parliament abandoned the ambitious objectives of the original plan.

Responses to EU-initiated policies and options, such as the guidelines and targets of the Open Method of Coordination in the social and employment policy fields, have been high in rhetoric but low in practice. As Zartaloudis stresses (2013: 86), it is mostly the financial conditionality of the EU Structural Funds that pushed through some novel approaches and measures, for example the personalized approach and activation in labour market policies. Although these have repeatedly been acknowledged in successive legal reforms, there has been no substantial impact on implementation.

An argument often expressed is that rising social spending contributed to the crisis, as though the Greek welfare state grew to a level that the country could not afford (Matsaganis 2011). Over the last three decades, spending increased rapidly and profligate borrowing by successive governments (combined with EU funding flowing into the country) significantly boosted expenses. However, Greece started from a very low spending level in the early 1980s (about 12 per cent of GDP). Despite a remarkable rise in social expenditure over the 1990s and 2000s, per capita social spending (measured in Purchasing Power Standards) remained below 80 per cent of the EU15 average; conversely, GDP per capita almost converged to the EU15 average on the eve of the crisis. Contrary to the 'overspending' argument, this indicates that the country underspent in social protection in terms of its wealth (Petmesidou 2013: 599).

Markedly, actual redistribution has been limited. This is most clearly reflected in the persistently high poverty rate over the 1990s and 2000s, until just before the crisis (about 21 per cent; EU15 average of about 16 per cent), and the strikingly low redistributive effects of all other social transfers except pensions, namely, sickness, family, unemployment, and social assistance benefits. Thus when the crisis broke out Greece was characterized by a 'gridlocked system' (Petmesidou & Guillén 2015: 12).

8.3 The Sovereign Debt Crisis, Protracted Austerity, and Welfare Reform

The intractable sovereign crisis that engulfed the country since the late 2000s demands reform. The critical question is whether the crisis can be a spur to rationalizing social protection with the aim of improving institutional/ administrative capabilities and social redistribution, or whether austerity will instead dismantle social rights and drive welfare standards to the lowest common denominator.

From spring 2010 onwards, the successive bailout deals embraced various rounds of cuts in wages/salaries and pensions, increasing flexibility of employment and dismantling of labour rights, a drastic reduction in public spending, and increases in direct and indirect taxes (including special levies). Pension and healthcare reforms have been prominent and have included a mix of structural changes, recalibration measures, and the rolling back of public provision (Petmesidou 2014).

At the onset of the crisis, extreme fragmentation and polarization in social insurance, ballooning administrative costs, and accumulated incentives for early retirement, in combination with rapid demographic ageing and negative economic growth, raised pension expenditure to over 13 per cent of GDP by 2009. In 2010 a path-breaking reform replaced the Bismarckian social insurance system (based primarily on the first pillar) by a unified, multi-tier system that distinguishes between a basic (quasi-universal) non-contributory and a contributory pension and drastically reduced replacement rates for future retirees. The new system merged social insurance funds. These two tiers will need to be complemented by funded pension schemes and private savings.

Inequalities in access to a funded, occupational pension tier (very little developed so far) as well as to private insurance will damage adequacy and collective solidarity. Current pensioners' incomes have also been drastically reduced through successive rounds of cuts (up to 40–50 per cent for certain categories of pensioner) compounded by a tax raid accompanying the successive bailouts, which disproportionately hit middle to lower incomes. The social funds' revenues have been severely strained by steeply falling wages and salaries, galloping unemployment, and the inability of the self-employed and small businesses to continue paying contributions. But above all, the government's decision under the rescue deal to include the social insurance funds in the private sector 'haircut' of March 2012 dealt a devastating blow to social insurance. This led to losses of over 50 per cent in their reserves, undermining the actuarial valuations and forecasts that guided reforms. Thus, in late 2015 the social insurance deficit reached two billion euros, but, according to data by the Panhellenic Federation of Social Policy Organizations Staff, the 'real deficit' is much higher given the fact that a large number of applications for pensions and one-off payments at retirement are pending (and have been so for more than a year), and the National Health Service Organization (EOPYY) also owes money to a large number of providers (Kathimerini 2015a). At the same time, however, the sharp drop in GDP, in parallel with an increasing number of retirements (in the period 2007–14 the number of pensioners rose by a fifth), caused a rapid increase in pension spending from 13.5 to 16 per cent of GDP between 2009 and 2014. This brought the issue of a further deep cut in pensions back on the agenda with the international lenders.

In line with the stipulation of the third bailout, signed in June 2015, requiring Greece to meet a savings target of 3.5 per cent budget surplus before interest payments by 2018,[1] parliament passed a controversial law combining social security reform with additional taxation. On the positive side are further merging of social insurance funds into a single body and uniform (though rising) contributions for the entire economically active population. Large sections of the middle class (civil servants, the liberal professions, and the self-employed) will lose out because contributions for some members of this group will increase to more than four times what they currently pay. Their contributions to primary and supplementary pensions, a retirement lump sum and healthcare will amount to over 35 per cent of their income. The reform is to take effect from January 2017. For farmers contribution increases will be phased in over the coming years. Moreover, the new method of calculation leads to further cuts in pension benefits: on average to a reduction between 10 and 30 per cent, and up to 40 per cent for some categories of pensioners (mainly people with disabilities, widows, low salary workers, and the long-term unemployed). In parallel, further hikes in both direct and indirect taxes (through diminishing tax credits to households without children and with up to two children), the rise of VAT—for a fifth time since 2009—and significant increases to other consumption taxes and excise duties will severely hurt large sections of the population.

In healthcare large-scale public spending cutbacks and a range of policy measures are shifting the cost of care away from the state. Between 2009 and 2015, per capita health spending in real terms dropped by 42 per cent (OECD 2015b) while successive reforms increased user charges, significantly reduced public provision, and imposed rationing through longer waiting times and other blockage mechanisms, such as a cap on the number of patient visits for which doctors under contract with the public healthcare system can be paid, as well in the number of prescriptions and laboratory tests they can issue (Petmesidou et al. 2014: 345–8). There have been positive attempts towards system rationalization, including amalgamation of health insurance funds under a single unity (EOPYY) to improve horizontal equity and a closer monitoring of costs through e-prescribing. However, since its establishment EOPYY has been underfunded. A purchaser–provider split between the fund and clinics followed in 2014.

Controversy permeates reforms in both pensions and healthcare. At the level of rhetoric reforms interlinked with drastic retrenchment are justified on the ground that they will secure the system's long-term viability and promote distributional justice. And indeed some measures do tackle serious functional and financial problems. Yet the imperative of fiscal restraint triggers a kind of 'policy drift' and/or exhaustion, whereby the public systems gradually wither away (Petmesidou et al. 2014: 348). Interestingly, concerns about adequacy are completely absent from the reform agenda of the 'rescue deal', as are any projections of the effects of the ongoing reforms on poverty.[2] Austerity-driven reforms massively weaken the principle of 'universalism' that, however, was not fully realized in Greece even before the crisis. The number of uninsured people rose rapidly. In early 2016, it was estimated by the Ministry of Health that over two million people lacked healthcare coverage. These include a large number of the unemployed and their dependents, illegal immigrants and asylum seekers, and (small) business owners and self-employed workers (including professionals) who became bankrupt or who, even though still active, cannot pay contributions due to severe economic hardship.[3]

The effects on health outcomes may not be highly visible yet, but early indicators are alarming. As Stuckler and Basau (2013) show, 'infant mortality rose by 40 per cent and HIV infections more than doubled, a result of rising intravenous drug use as the budget for needle exchange programmes was cut'. There is mounting evidence of an increase in mental disorders and some infectious diseases, such as malaria, in cardiovascular diseases, unhealthy practices (like alcohol and drugs addiction), HIV incidence, and the suicide rate.[4]

These conditions may exacerbate morbidity problems in the future, seriously diminish healthy life expectancy, and further increase healthcare costs.

As to long-term care, no universal coverage is available. Existing public services are addressed to the neediest groups in absolute poverty. Care for the chronically ill (either in state residential units or in contracted non-profit and for-profit care centres and clinics) hardly covers demand due to inadequate numbers of beds, the low rates paid by social insurance organizations, and a rapidly shrinking public budget. Private insurance for long-term care is negligible and the cost of private residential care, for those who can afford it, is met by out-of-pocket payments.

In relation to the labour market, conditionality under structural adjustment limited the social partners' power to regulate working conditions and weakened workers' rights. Legislation boosted flexible and precarious employment, made dismissals easier, and reformed the collective bargaining system. Reforms facilitated enterprise labour contracts and the individualization of employment conditions, accompanied by reduced remuneration and an increase in uninsured labour.[5] The minimum monthly wage was cut by 22 per cent by law in 2012, a sub-minimum wage was introduced for young people, and unemployment benefits were cut sharply.

Some 90 per cent of unemployed people receive no government support whatsoever. Take-up of a recently introduced extra benefit of 200 euros for the long-term unemployed has been very low at 1.5 per cent due to highly restrictive eligibility criteria. For young workers (age 20–29) entering the labour market, there is only a meagre benefit of 73 euros for up to five months, provided that the new entrants are registered as unemployed for twelve months. According to available data in 2013, only 4,800 young unemployed received this benefit (Petmesidou and Polyzoidis 2015b: 35–6). A minimum income guarantee (GMI) scheme was introduced in November 2014 on a pilot basis, to be expanded to a full national programme in 2015. The SYRIZA–ANEL government discontinued expansion and in early 2015 replaced it by a new programme for addressing the 'humanitarian crisis' in the country. Income thresholds defining eligibility criteria under this scheme are similar to those in the pilot GMI. The scheme includes such measures as free electricity (up to 300 kWh per month), and rent and food allowances, and it is estimated to benefit between 100,000 and 153,000 of the 890,000 households living below the poverty line. The budget was set at 200 million euros for 2015. The government announced the reintroduction of the GMI from spring 2016, once again on a pilot scale (to be fully rolled out in 2017).

New regulations banned strikes and unilateral recourse to arbitration, and also severely limited its scope to minimum wage issues. In response to the trade unions' appeal filed in 2012, the Council of State issued a ruling that found these restrictions unconstitutional, but rejected the appeal against the entire spectrum of reforms that curtailed labour rights. Strikingly, the ND–PASOK coalition government only partly complied with the judgment (unilateral recourse was reinstated but the scope of arbitration remained limited to minimum wages). In its election campaign SYRIZA pledged to restore collective bargaining and increase the minimum wage to its pre-2012 level (that is, to 751 euros). Yet none of these pledges has materialized, as they conflict with the international creditors' demands. Legislation under the bailout deal facilitates the drawing up of employment agreements at the business level, even in very small enterprises and in the absence of enterprise-level unions. This effectively dismantled the collective regulation of working conditions (Petmesidou and Polyzoidis 2015a; Dedoussopoulos et al. 2013).

The proportion of the population at risk of poverty and social exclusion has risen dramatically among the unemployed and also among employed people (particularly among those with no more than secondary education), as well as among families with dependent children (see Figure 8.1). Moreover, the scarring effects of unemployment, poverty, and social exclusion for younger

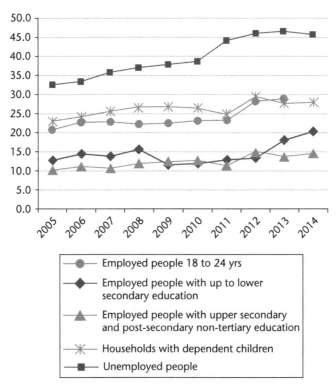

Figure 8.1. In-work poverty and poverty among households with children and among the unemployed in Greece (poverty line: 60% of the median equivalized income).
Source: Eurostat 2016

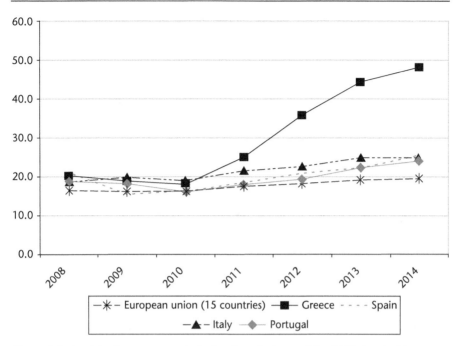

Figure 8.2. At-risk-of-poverty rate (calculated on the basis of the 2008 threshold, poverty line: 60% of the median equivalized income).
Source: Eurostat 2016

cohorts imply a lower lifetime income and trigger higher levels of emigration among the young, skilled labour force. About 200,000 persons aged under 35 have left the country and are currently employed abroad, 70 per cent of them in EU countries. They are skilled and highly educated people pursuing careers and work in sectors such as medicine, finance, engineering, and high-tech (Endeavour-Stavros Niarchos Foundation 2014).

Figure 8.2 shows the rate of poverty, with the poverty threshold fixed at 2008 when the crisis erupted. On the basis of that threshold close to 50 per cent of the population are below the poverty line. This clearly indicates a significant erosion of middle-class incomes. The middle class in Greece (as elsewhere: Petmesidou 2011a) gained ground in previous decades particularly through increasing numbers of self-employed professionals and technical and craft workers. A recent study by the Credit Suisse Research Institute (2015: 34–7) on how the middle class fared since the early 2000s, shows that the Greek middle class expanded between 2000 and 2007 but shrank by about 20 per cent during the crisis. They also found that middle-class people lost over 40 per cent of their wealth between 2007 and 2015. The lower middle class has been most severely hit. Even though income tax data do not fully depict the income distribution because of an extensive informal economy, they provide an indication of

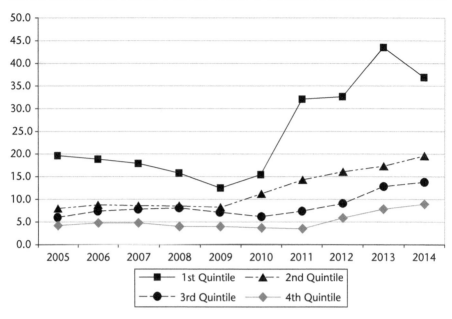

Figure 8.3. People living in households with very low work intensity by income quintile (population aged 0 to 59 years, poverty line).
Source: Eurostat 2016

the deterioration in living standards of large sections of the middle class. The number of persons with an annual household income of between 50,000 and 100,000 euros (upper middle class) dropped by over 50 per cent between 2010 and 2014; those in the income bands directly below (30,000–50,000 euros, and 20,000–30,000) fell by 45 and 26 per cent respectively. At the same time, the number of people with an annual household income below 12,000 euros increased by 14 per cent (Kathimerini 2015b).

Figure 8.3 shows the dramatic increase in the number of people living in households with very low work intensity in the two lowest income quintiles (their number more than doubled during the crisis). However a significant increase is also observed among people in the third income quintile, who constitute the backbone of the middle class. The overall number living in low work intensity households almost tripled, reaching 15 per cent by 2014.

The deteriorating living conditions of many lower- and middle-class people is also evident in the rapid increase in the numbers in hardship, with arrears on utility bills, mortgage and rent payments, and facing great difficulty in making ends meet. Figures 8.4 and 8.5 indicate that hardship is rising among large sections of the population. Among households with an income below 60 per cent of the median (equivalized income), over 60 per cent were in arrears on utility bills and could not make ends meet in 2014. But even among households

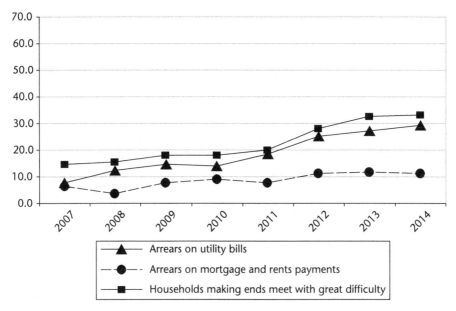

Figure 8.4. Households above the poverty line (60% of the median equivalized income) experiencing hardship.

Source: Eurostat 2016

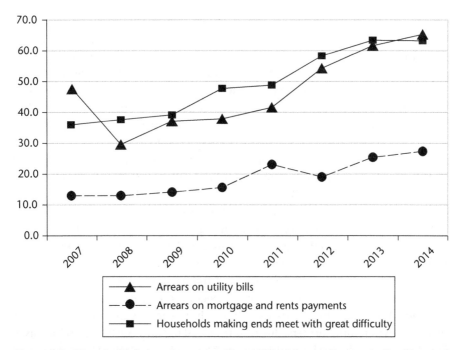

Figure 8.5. Households below the poverty line (60% of the median equivalized income) experiencing hardship.

Source: Eurostat 2016

with higher incomes the percentage of those who are in arrears on utility bills and/or make ends meet with great difficulty more than doubled to about a third between 2007 and 2014.

The direction of Greek welfare state policy after the eruption of the crisis was towards harsher austerity, set squarely in a neo-liberal framework that stressed individual responsibility, privatization, and stringent targeting of the remaining state provision. At the same time, rapid deterioration of living standards among middle- and lower-class strata has greatly strained the family's capacity to perform its role of welfare provider.

Falling living standards for much of the population, widely understood to be caused by protracted deep recession and the demands of the international creditors, have created new social cleavages and opportunities for solidarity. Middle-class voters have traditionally supported either the conservative ND or the centre-left PASOK through clientelistic paths of socio-political integration. As large sections of the middle class are becoming the 'new poor', political radicalization is on the rise. Moreover, the left/right cleavage seems to be overlain by a polarization over the demands placed on Greece by the external lenders. This is reflected in the emergence of extremist and populist right-wing parties, such as Golden Dawn, and in the rise to power of SYRIZA. Extreme left- and right-wing parties tapped into the anti-bailout sentiment of large sections of the crisis-hit urban and rural population. In the run-up to the January 2015 elections SYRIZA's radical leftist rhetoric pledged to pursue a programme combining neo-Keynesian investment and social benefits with a determined fightback repealing virtually all of the austerity reforms. In the event, SYRIZA failed to deliver this and was forced into a humiliating U-turn. The SYRIZA–ANEL coalition government signed a fresh rescue package with the international lenders, which demanded painful reforms accompanied by steep cost-cutting measures and further increases in taxes and extraordinary levies. Before starting to implement the stipulations of the new rescue deal, the government called a snap election in September 2015. As the effects of further harsh austerity measures on household incomes were not yet felt, SYRIZA won the election. But again it had to rely on the ANEL party seats in parliament in order to form an overall majority.

The Janus face of SYRIZA's electoral campaign rhetoric (being anti-austerity in principle but committed to implementing the demands of the creditors) contributed to its success. Since late autumn 2015 social unrest has been on the increase, however, as a drastic overhaul of the pension system and increases in taxation are again on the agenda of the negotiations with the European creditors and the IMF. The reforms will most hurt the liberal professions, small business owners, and farmers, due to substantial tax and contribution increases. Future retirees will also be hurt because of a significant decline in replacement rates, while current retirees face further cuts in their pension income. Road blocks at central junctions around the country by farmers, escalating protest by professionals, and a national strike that paralysed the country on 4 February 2016 (in which several shopkeepers also participated, closing their shops) indicate that large sections of the urban lower and middle classes and of farmers, who rallied behind SYRIZA's anti-austerity pledges, are now alienated from the party. The intensification of refugee (and immigrant) flows in the country in the last year adds to the social and economic strains.

For much of the post-war period Greece was a country of emigration to richer parts of Europe. Following the collapse of Soviet communism in the late 1980s, the country experienced a heavy inflow of mostly undocumented economic migrants from the neighbouring ex-communist Balkan countries. Desperate living conditions and social upheavals in Asia and Africa further exacerbated immigration flows, while Greece's EU membership and growing economy acted as pull factors. In the short span of a decade, immigrants came to represent a little less than ten per cent of Greece's population (in 2001 the National Statistical Service of Greece set the total number of foreigners in the country, including illegal immigrants, at about 800,000: Petmesidou 2006: 44). In 2014 immigrants constituted 11.4 per cent of the population, two thirds of them from non-EU countries (compare Italy: Chapter 7). Nevertheless, the crisis has markedly changed migration trends. It led to the return of a significant number of economic migrants (mostly Albanians) to their country of origin (INSTAT and IOM 2013). Emigration also rose, roughly tripling between 2008 and 2013 to 120,000 a year, with the result that the country returned to the status of a net emigration state (Eurostat 2016). In addition the rapid growth of migration from Afghanistan, Iraq, Syria, Somalia, and Eritrea as a result of war and disruption has resulted in large numbers of refugees seeking to enter Europe. Greece receives by far the largest waterborne migration flow of any EU country, exceeding 120,000 out of a total of about 130,000 in January and February 2016 (UNHCR 2016). In 2014 and 2015 the vast majority of these arrivals moved on to Germany, the UK, France, and Nordic countries. The increased reluctance of other EU countries to take immigrants and refugees and the failure of the EU to agree and implement a relocation and resettlement scheme have led to major problems. By early 2016 border closures in Austria, Hungary, and the Balkans had resulted in large numbers being confined to transit camps under poor conditions in mainland Greece.

Immigration is becoming a major issue in public debate in Greece, with the obvious injustice of one of the poorest and hardest-hit countries in the EU being forced to bear the brunt of a migration crisis. This further strengthens opinion against the EU and reinforces right-wing chauvinist sentiment. How long the situation will last is at present unclear.

Evidently, social cleavages and solidarities have become very fluid under the crisis. Anti-austerity feeling has led to a large wave of social protest. The Greek 'indignados' and 'piazza movements' gathered momentum at the outbreak of crisis, but were soon defused and partly absorbed by SYRIZA during the 2011–12 period. A platform of solidarity nurtured by SYRIZA when in opposition for a return to neo-Keynesian state investment and spending rallied the groups who feared the Memorandum of Understanding with the troika: civil servants concerned about dismissal, pensioners who had suffered income losses, the less well-off self-employed and farmers, the unemployed, the 'new poor', and other disadvantaged social strata. The harsh reforms of the new rescue-deal of July 2015 and the refugee crisis are now causing disillusionment.

Another facet of new expressions of social solidarity concerns the increased third sector involvement in the provision of food, shelter, medicine, and services (the 'Social Clinics', 'Social Groceries', and 'Homeless Shelters' run by NGOs, the Church of Greece, and other agencies), and the proliferation of informal solidarity networks (local networks of direct and moneyless exchange of services, local solidarity clubs running soup kitchens, and time-sharing groups), as a response to heightened need (Clarke et al. 2015). Whether these can evolve into a significant welfare pillar requiring support and regulation in order to fill the social welfare gap under neo-liberal austerity is an open question. Divisive philanthropy (for example Golden Dawn soup kitchens that exclude immigrants) has also emerged and may expand in the future. In the medium to long term it is the social cleavages that will emerge in the context of a reorientation of the economy under the liberalization reforms, and how these will be framed politically, which will dominate the future of social welfare in Greece.

8.4 The Future: The Greek Welfare State at a Critical Juncture

Developments in Greece will take place in the context of the continuing pressures from globalization and Europeanization operating through the structural adjustment programme. Most important are the reforms required by the three bailout deals. These deregulated the labour market, increased flexibility in contracts, and deepened insecurity in employment and income. Underlying these reforms is the redirection of the economy towards greater openness.

Such a reorientation of the economy will cause significant changes in social structure and new social divisions will emerge. The small business sector catering for the internal market will contract. The middle and working classes will become increasingly divided between the winners, those who have high skills and can compete successfully in a new export sector, and the losers, who face persistently high unemployment and insecurity. Of crucial importance is how these emerging social cleavages and solidarities will be linked to socio-political value orientations (the individualization of risk versus a more socially embedded flexibilization; populist and nationalistic values versus a reinvigoration of 'Social Europe') and how these will shape politics. Recent concerns about the rapid increase in immigration from the Middle East provoked by struggles in Syria may also create opportunities for the extreme right and populist movements, adding to instability.

The structural reforms under the bailout deals aim largely at liberalization and an internal devaluation within the constraints of the Eurozone regulations, together with rationalizing administration and shrinking the public sector, in order to increase competitiveness. Liberalization targets are often set by international lenders to match wages and incomes in neighbouring competitor countries, in this case, the other Balkan countries. This approach highlights the gloomy neo-liberal scenario of a race to the very bottom.

As has been stressed, so far the Greek economy has been characterized by a comparatively small tradeable sector that has failed to become a catalyst for growth. Undoubtedly, the way in which the shift towards an outward-facing economy takes place is highly important for understanding the social cleavages that will emerge and the future of welfare. The scenario of a race to the very bottom (with wages in Greece falling to the lowest international levels) coupled with adverse demographics may lead to a contraction of state welfare to the most meagre means-tested social assistance. This is linked to the emergence of social cleavages, such that large sections of the middle class will fall into the ranks of unemployed and new poor, particularly if the destruction of small businesses continues with no opportunities for reintegrating these strata into a vibrant labour market. A labour market that provides real opportunities for jobs and training is essential for a recovery in which a more robust industrial structure is based on a well-functioning innovation system instead of following the well-trodden path of a 'tourism-based economy supplemented by food manufacturing' (Herrmann and Kritikos 2013: 1).

Combating well-entrenched statist practices and redrawing the boundaries between the public and private sector, both major objectives of reform, will trigger considerable reshuffling of the various layers of the middle class, given the fact that large sections of it have so far relied heavily on the revenue-yielding state mechanisms (either through direct access to public sector jobs or, indirectly, through the appropriation of resources by political means and criteria). It is highly likely, though, that structural change will take place under protracted fiscal austerity and drastic hardship for many years ahead, in parallel with severely squeezed social spending and the progressive dismantling of social and labour rights. During this time considerable numbers of traditional middle-class jobs for self-employed, small entrepreneurs and public sector employees will disappear. The most likely outcome is a restructuring of the occupational, employment, and earnings distribution within the middle class. This could trigger a strong division between the upper ranks of the remaining middle sector who comfortably raise their earnings, and the lower income groups who suffer real and substantial losses in income and life chances.

The crisis has led to greater political fluidity and unpredictability in social alliances. Disillusionment is mounting among the social groups which suffered most as a result of the crisis and rallied behind SYRIZA. The government faces insurmountable difficulties, in meeting the requirements of the rescue deal, and countering austerity through neo-Keynesian policies, supporting a consumption-led model. Populist rhetoric without any vision of viable economic recovery hardly facilitates this balancing act. Among the main opposition parties with a strong pro-Europe and pro-bailout stance political debate on how to reform the economy and improve competitiveness in the global market is very limited and tilted towards rhetoric and political expediency.

An alternative scenario, a 'social investment' approach that places a great emphasis on the prevention of disadvantage through quality childcare, family support, education, training, and the balancing of flexibility to security, seems unlikely because austerity-driven reforms are prioritizing drastic cuts in the social budget in these areas. Moreover, in a scenario of increasing social polarization and sharp contraction of the middle class it is highly likely that the individualization of risk will prevail, under conditions in which great strains will also be exerted on the traditional family model of care provision.

Coined as opposite to flexicurity, the term 'flexi-carity', expressing an increasing flexibility leading to precarity (see Hansen 2007), aptly depicts a highly likely scenario of the future of the welfare state in Greece. This is reinforced by the failure of the EU to develop interstate solidarity through deeper consolidation, policy coordination, and redistribution. Strikingly, the ongoing 'refugee crisis' has brought into stark relief the big obstacles towards interstate solidarity and adherence to the values of 'Social Europe'. Greece has come under intense pressure from European institutions as a consequence of the country's difficulties in coping with an expanding flow of refugees that tests its broken economy to the limits. The unprecedented refugee crisis adds a further layer of uncertainty to the country's relationship with the EU.

8.5 Conclusion

This chapter has traced the lagged development of welfare state institutions in Greek society in the 1980s and early 1990s, compared to north-western Europe, emphasizing the hybrid form of social welfare that combines Bismarckian elements (in social insurance) with a social democratic arrangement in healthcare (although a transition to a fully fledged national health system was not reached), together with a liberal–residual element in social care with the family playing a central role. It has discussed the main problems arising in this welfare state configuration, and reviewed the stumbling blocks over the past decades to reforms that might advance institutional rationalization and effective redistribution along the lines of the social citizenship values and criteria that have been pivotal to welfare state development in north-western Europe.

Greece has been hit by the financial crisis primarily as the result of high levels of public debt. This led to a deep and protracted economic recession intensified by the harsh austerity measures enforced by the three bailout deals signed by successive governments with the international lenders. The structural adjustment imposed by the bailout pacts embraces the neo-liberal dogma of sweeping reforms that drastically diminish incomes (mostly for the middle and lower social strata), squeeze job opportunities (particularly for the young), heighten insecurity, increase uncertainty about the circumstances of retirement, and foster dependency on an increasingly feeble state. They also create a solidarity between the loser groups, with political consequences. After five years of recession and a far-reaching austerity programme, signs of a weak recovery (and a small primary surplus) emerged in 2014. In fact, the persistently large public sector arrears to various providers (among others, pharmaceutical companies, contracted clinics, and doctors) and the delays in issuing pensions and in tax returns and refunding of VAT meant that the recovery was virtual rather than real. In early to mid 2015 the rise to power of SYRIZA led to further economic chaos and forced the SYRIZA–ANEL coalition government to negotiate and sign a new bailout package to keep the economy financially afloat.

As the above analysis has shown, externally imposed neo-liberalism, drastically diminishing incomes, and steep cost-cutting trends in public expenditure are rapidly shifting responsibility for social provision to the individual. However, of utmost importance for the future of the welfare state is the reshuffling of social divisions under the 'adjustment recipe' of supranational institutions and, particularly, the way in which a shift towards an outward-facing, competitive economy can be achieved. Such a shift will impact significantly upon large sections of the traditional urban middle class in Greece, as well as the rural population (mostly small farmers). Small family businesses catering for the internal market will certainly lose out. The issue is whether competition in the globalized market will be sought through low-wage policies, indicated by the steep internal devaluation enforced by structural adjustment, or whether a boost in competitiveness can be achieved by a move towards a high-skill, high value-added economy. In the former case social polarization, individualization of risk, and further shrinking of public provision are likely, while the latter scenario may support a more socially embedded form of flexibilization. All indications to date make the former scenario more likely.

To sum up, there are few signs in Greece of a possible move towards a positive welfare state future with mass support for successful wide-ranging social provision on the lines of north-western Europe. The hardship for large numbers of people resulting from the crisis and bailout pacts has caused mass social discontent that was framed politically in a neo-Keynesian fightback. However it proved impossible to reconcile such policies with the demands of the ECB, IMF, or major lenders in countries such as Germany. There is considerable scope for divisions to open up between those with the skills and opportunities to succeed in a more globalized and outward-facing economy and the many losers. There are also extreme right political forces and related concerns about immigration from outside Europe that may fuel further political divisions. This suggests that the future of Greece's welfare state will be marked by tumultuous political confrontation, but ultimately by a grudging acceptance of neo-liberal austerity.

Notes

1. A rather unrealistic target according to the IMF, considering that such a high primary surplus must be maintained for many years in the future, as was assumed in last year's debt sustainability analysis under the third bailout. The IMF considers a lower fiscal target (around 1.5 per cent) much more feasible. Yet this needs to be accompanied by sizeable debt relief for securing debt sustainability, an option strongly opposed by Germany together with some other EU countries.
2. In the structural adjustment programme documentation fiscal consolidation, structural reform and privatization are the main themes, mentioned 2.06 times per page. 'Poverty' is referred to 59 times in the entire documentation, and 'inequality' once (Sapir et al. 2014).
3. Over the last year the increasing flows of Syrian refugees have overstretched the healthcare system and NGOs are the main providers. Greeks increasingly turn to NGO clinics according to 'Les médécins du monde'. In late 2013 measures were taken to achieve free access to primary care units by the uninsured; yet serious barriers remained due to very stringent means-testing criteria and the absence of specialist and hospital care coverage. Recent legislation lifted eligibility barriers for various categories of the uninsured (including legal immigrants) but rising cost-sharing hinders access by various vulnerable groups.
4. See http://www.statistics.gr/el/statistics/pop; Kentikelenis et al. 2011; and the Hellenic Centre for Disease Control & Prevention at http://www.keelpno.gr.
5. The number of undeclared workers in enterprises inspected between 2010 and 2012 rose from 25 to 36.2 per cent. In the first quarter of 2012, part-time employment and job-rotation recruitments surpassed full-time ones for the first time, while the conversion of full-time contracts into flexible employment contracts increased significantly (Labour Inspectorate 2013).

References

Athanasiou, E. (2015) 'Economic Activity of Small and Medium Enterprises in Greece', *Greek Economy* 19: 21–8.

Barslund, M. and Andersen, T. B. (2015) 'Greece's Poor Growth Prospects', *CEPS Commentary*, 21 August 2015, Brussels: Centre for European Policy Studies (CEPS), http://www.ceps.eu/publications/all?page=38, accessed 15 Nov. 2016.

Clarke, J., Houliarias, A., and Sotiropoulos, D. (eds.) (2015) *Austerity and the Third Sector in Greece*, Farnham: Ashgate.

Credit Suisse Research Institute (2015) *Global Wealth Report 2015*, Zurich: Credit Suisse Research Institute, https://www.credit-suisse.com/ch/en/about-us/research/research-institute/publications.html, accessed 15 Nov. 2016.

Dedoussopoulos, A., Aranitou, V., Koutenakis, F., and Maropoulou, M. (2013) *Assessing the Impact of the Memoranda on Greek Labour market and Labour Relations*, working paper no. 53, Geneva: International Labour Office.

Endeavour-Stavros Niarchos Foundation (2014) *Creating Jobs for Youth in Greece—Report*, Athens: Endeavour-Stavros Niarchos Foundation, http://www.snf.org/en/news room/news/2014/06/endeavor-greece-report-creating-jobs-for-youth-in-greece/, accessed 20 Oct. 2015.

Esping-Andersen, G. (1990) *The Three Worlds of Welfare Capitalism*, Cambridge: Polity Press.

Eurostat (2016) *Statistics Database*, http://ec.europa.eu/eurostat/data/database, accessed 15 Nov. 2016.

Ferrera, M. (1996) 'The "Southern Model" of Welfare in Social Europe', *Journal of European Social Policy* 6(1): 17–37.

INE-GSEE (2017) *Annual Report 2017. The Greek Economy and Employment*, Athens: Institute of Labour—Greek General Confederation of Labour, http://www.inegsee.gr/ekdosi/etisia-ekthesi-2017-ine-gsee-i-elliniki-ikonomia-ke-i-apascholisi/, accessed 25 March 2017.

Gros, D., Andersen, T. B., and Barslund, M. (2011) 'Can Greece "Grow Solvent"?', *CEPS Commentary*, 8 September 2011, Brussels: Centre for European Policy Studies (CEPS), http://www.ceps.eu/publications/all?page=1, accessed 15 Nov. 2016.

Guillén, A. and Petmesidou, M. (2008) 'The Private-Public Mix in Southern Europe', in M. Seeleib-Kaiser (ed.) *Welfare State Transformations*, Basingstoke: Palgrave.

Hall, P. and Soskice, D. (2001) *Varieties of Capitalism*, Oxford: Oxford University Press.

Hansen, L. L. (2007) 'From Flexicurity to Flexicarity?' *Journal of Social Sciences* 3(2): 88–93.

Herrmann, B. and Kritikos, A. S. (2013) *Growing out of the Crisis*, IZA Discussion Paper No. 7806, Bonn: Institute for the Study of Labour (IZA), http://ftp.iza.org/dp7806.pdf, accessed 15 Nov. 2016.

INSTAT and IOM (2013) *Return Migration and Reintegration in Albania*, International Organization for Migration Report, Tirana: Institute of Statistics (INSTAT) & International Organization for Migration (IOM), http://www.instat.gov.al/en/themes/population.aspx?tab=tabs-4, accessed 15 Nov. 2016.

Kathimerini [Newspaper] (2015a) Greek Economy, 9 October 2015, http://www.kathimerini.gr/834096/article/oikonomia/ellhnikh-oikonomia/sta-8-dis-to-kryfo-elleimma-twn-tameiwn, accessed 15 Nov. 2016.

Kathimerini [Newspaper] (2015b) Greek Economy, 4 October 2015, http://www.kathimerini.gr/833430/article/oikonomia/ellhnikh-oikonomia/panw-apo-5-ekat-ellhnes-dhlwnoyn-ethsio-atomiko-eisodhma-katw-twn-12000, accessed 15 Nov. 2016.

Kentikelenis, A., Karanikolos, M., Papanicolas, I., Basu, S., McKee, M., and Stuckler, D. (2011) 'Health Effects of Financial Crisis: Omens of a Greek Tragedy', *The Lancet* 378 (9801): 1457–8.

Kovras, I. and Loizides, N. (2014) 'The Greek Debt Crisis and Southern Europe', *Comparative Politics* 47(1): 1–20.

Labour Inspectorate (2013) *Annual Activity Report, 2013* [in Greek], Athens: SEPE.

Matsaganis, M. (2011) 'The Welfare State and the Crisis', *Journal of European Social Policy* 21(5): 501–12.

Monastiriotis, V. and Antoniades, A. (2009) *Reform That! Greece's Failing Reform Technology*, Hellenic Observatory Papers, GreeSE Paper No. 28, London: LSE, http://www.lse.ac.uk/europeanInstitute/research/hellenicObservatory/pubs/GreeSE.aspx, accessed 25 Nov. 2014.

OECD (2015a) *How Does Health Spending in Greece Compare?*, OECD Health statistics 2015, Paris: OECD, http://www.oecd.org/els/health-systems/Country-Note-GREECE-OECD-Health-Statistics-2015.pdf, accessed 15 Nov. 2016.

OECD (2015b) Health Statistics, http://stats.oecd.org/Index.aspx?DataSetCode=SHA, accessed 25 March 2017.

Petmesidou, M. (1991) 'Statism, Social Policy and the Middle-Classes in Greece', *Journal of European Social Policy* 1(1): 31–48.

Petmesidou, M. (2006) 'Tracking Social Protection', in M. Petmesidou and E. Mossialos (eds.) *Social Policy Developments in Greece*, Aldershot: Ashgate.

Petmesidou, M. (2011a) *The Crisis, the Middle-Classes and Social Welfare in Greece*, paper presented at the SEESOX International Conference on Greece, St Antony's College, Oxford, 27–28 May 2011.

Petmesidou, M. (2011b) 'What Future for the Middle-Classes and "Inclusive Solidarity" in South Europe? (A Note)', *Global Social Policy* 11(2–3): 225–7.

Petmesidou, M. (2013) 'Is Social Protection in Greece at a Crossroads?', *European Societies* 15(4): 597–616.

Petmesidou, M. (2014) *Update of the 2013 Annual Report on Pensions, Health and Long-term Care*, ASISP Network, Cologne: GVG.

Petmesidou, M. (2015) 'Greece: Welfare State', in D. Bearfield and M. Dubnick (eds.) *Encyclopaedia of Public Administration and Public Policy*, vol. iii, 3rd edn, New York: Taylor & Francis.

Petmesidou, M. and Guillén, A. (2015) *Economic Crisis and Austerity in Southern Europe*, OSE Research Paper No. 19, January 2015, http://www.ose.be/EN/publications/ose_paper_series.htm, accessed 15 Nov. 2016.

Petmesidou, M., Pavolini, E., and Guillén, A. (2014) 'South European Healthcare Systems under Harsh Austerity', *South European Society and Politics* 19(3): 331–52.

Petmesidou, M. and Polyzoidis, P. (2015a) *What Policy Innovation for Youth in the Era of Prolonged Austerity?*, OSE Research Paper No. 20, July 2015, http://www.ose.be/EN/publications/ose_paper_series.htm, accessed 15 Nov. 2016.

Petmesidou, M. and Polyzoidis, P. (2015b) *Barriers to and Triggers for Innovation and Knowledge Transfer in Greece*, STYLE Project Report, http://www.style-research.eu/publications/working-papers/, accessed 15 Nov. 2016.

Sapir, A., Wolff, G. B., de Sousa, C., and Terzi, A. (2014) *The Troika and Financial Assistance in the Euro Area: Successes and Failures*, Economic Governance Support Unit, DG Internal Policies, Brussels: The European Parliament & Bruegel Organization, http://bruegel.org/2014/02/the-troika-and-financial-assistance-in-the-euro-area-successes-and-failures/, accessed 17 June 2015.

Stuckler, D. and Basau, S. (2013) 'How Austerity Kills?', *New York Times* 12 May 2013, http://www.nytimes.com/2013/05/13/opinion/how-austerity-kills.html?_r=0, accessed 15 Nov. 2016.

UNHCR (2016) *Refugee/Migrants: Emergency Response*, Geneva: UNHCR, http://data.unhcr.org/mediterranean/country.php?id=83, accessed 15 Nov. 2016.

Zartaloudis, S. (2013) 'Wielding Soft Power in a World of Neglect: The Impact of the European Employment Policy in Greece and Portugal', PhD thesis, London School of Economics, London.

9

The Europeanization of the Welfare State

The Case for a 'Differentiated European Social Model'

Benjamin Leruth

9.1 Introduction: Social Policy and the EU

Since the ratification of the Treaty of Rome in 1957, the European Union (EU) has been committed to reducing socio-economic inequalities between member states as part of its integration project. Article 3 of the Treaty on European Union states that the Union 'shall combat social exclusion and discrimination, and shall promote social justice and protection, equality between women and men, solidarity between generations and protection of the rights of the child'. Today, the EU provides cooperation between member states in a wide range of policy areas, from a Common Security and Defence Policy to common agricultural and fisheries policies. The harmonization of social policy has been promoted throughout the history of the EU, to reduce socio-economic disparities between member states. Nowadays the scope of the European Social Model is largely restricted to issues related to the construction of an open labour market, such as employment rights, equal employment opportunities, free movement of labour, health and safety at work, working conditions, and social dialogue (Larsen and Taylor-Gooby 2004). Little progress has been made over the past five decades, despite the introduction of Social Action Programmes in the 1970s and the use of common social strategies in order to reduce disparities within the EU.

Despite these attempts to harmonize social policy at the European level, social inequalities remain high within the EU, and public attitudes towards the welfare state vary considerably from one member state to another. As previous chapters in this volume show, the recent crisis brought the various political and societal challenges to European welfare state to a head. Prominent scholars have suggested the creation of a true Common European Social Policy as a response (for example Allespach and Machnig 2013; Habermas 2013). While such proposals are not new in the field of European studies (see Leibfried 1993; Scharpf 2002), the reaction to the Great Recession at the EU level has been broadly neo-liberal and a common interventionist social policy now appears controversial or even utopian (Crespy and Menz 2015).

This chapter offers an analysis of changes and future prospects at the EU level. It first describes the main steps towards EU social policy harmonization, from Guy Mollet's initial attempt in the 1950s to the most recent 'Europe 2020' strategy. It then focuses on the role of the EU during the Great Recession and the range of policy responses advocated by Brussels in order to combat the multi-faceted crisis, and its implications for the harmonization of social policy. This second section also includes an analysis of public support for a common European welfare state in a range of policy areas based on recent studies and Eurobarometer surveys. The third section reflects on the future of European integration, and the potential for further welfare harmonization between member states. The status quo no longer seems viable, especially after the United Kingdom's vote to leave the EU, but the use of differentiated mechanisms of European integration, such as enhanced cooperation in specific areas, may offer opportunities to relaunch the European social model and reduce inequalities between member states.

9.2 Social Policy Developments at the EU Level

The potential for a true common European social policy, or European Social Union, has been extensively discussed in the existing literature (see for example Leibfried 1993; Leibfried and Pierson 1995; Streeck 1996; Larsen and Taylor-Gooby 2004; Blanke and Hoffmann 2008). The extensive range of the literature on European social policy may lead to confusion since the terms used are often not defined. In a valuable attempt to clarify the debate, Jepsen and Pascual (2005: 232) explain that the notion of the European Social Model, often used to 'describe the European experience of simultaneously promoting sustainable economic growth and social cohesion', can be conceptualized in four ways. The first, stemming from Scharpf's much-cited analysis (2002), studies the European Social Model as an *entity*, a common European objective to achieve full employment, social protection, and equality, used as the motor for harmonization of policy regulation, especially in the field of workers' rights and labour law. The second perceives the European Social Model as an *ideal type*, as advocated by Esping-Andersen (1999) and Ferrera et al. (2001). This approach highlights specific national models, offering basic social protection to all citizens, relatively low levels of income inequality, and a high degree of collective bargaining. The third perceives the European Social Model as a *European project and instrument for cohesion*. This approach emphasizes the need for a transnational and multi-level system of social policy in response to globalization, as economic integration (most importantly through the creation of the Economic and Monetary Union) reduces the capacity of EU member states to use traditional economic policy instruments to achieve their own social policy objectives (see Vaughan-Whitehead 2003). The fourth and final one, added by Jepsen and Pascual in their analysis, studies the European Social Model as a *political project*, used to legitimize European institutions and their actions, in order to foster a European identity based on policy paradigms. This last conceptualization helps in understanding some of the most recent actions from the European institutions, highlighted below.

Throughout the development of the European Community (and now Union), attempts have been made to bring together the very different social welfare systems of member states described in Chapter 1. The first dates back to the creation of the European Economic Community, when French socialist Prime Minister Guy Mollet tried to harmonize social regulations as a key element of the integration of the industrial markets (Scharpf 2002). As policies in the original six member states had been shaped by the Bismarck model of welfare, diversity was not an obstacle to such harmonization. However, more pressing economic and worker-related matters were addressed, and the proposed commitment to harmonization was abandoned despite the creation of the European Social Fund (intended to finance vocational training programmes and to promote occupational mobility) as the first social policy instrument (Laffan 1983). One might argue that the founding member states missed a once in a lifetime opportunity, as further attempts to create a common European social policy failed in the following decades. These attempts could be grouped into three periods: the 1970s, with the emergence of the first Social Action Programme; the 'Delors years' in the mid-1980s and early 1990s, with the promotion of the 'Social Dimension project'; and the Lisbon period, which immediately preceded the Great Recession (Daly 2007).

Following Guy Mollet's initial attempt to harmonize social policy across the six founding member states and a period of political instability throughout the 1960s, the issue only returned to the European Community's agenda in the early 1970s. The 'Report on the Development of the Social Situation in the Community in 1973' published by the European Commission in 1974 effectively revived ideas of harmonization, by stating the objective of 'setting out in a purposeful way the initial practical steps on the road towards the ultimate goal of European Social Union' (quoted in Atkinson 2002: 627). The first Social Action Programme, adopted in 1974 by the European Council of Ministers and driven by social democratic national governments, was the first major attempt to expand the scope of the European Community's social policy

(Streeck 1994). This programme set three main objectives: achieving full and better employment; improving living and working conditions; and improving social dialogue by increasing the involvement of social partners in the economic and social decisions of the Community (European Council 1974). One of the underlying goals of the Programme was for countries with high levels of social protection to protect their own social policy regimes (which entailed higher labour costs) by spreading them to the rest of the member states (Streeck 1996). After running for a period of six to seven years until the early 1980s, the output of this first Social Action Programme was rather modest, with minor improvements made in the areas of gender equality and health and safety at work. As Daly summarizes (2007: 3), '[o]ne of the lessons learned from this first period is that it is hard for social policy to "stick" at the EU level'.

Despite the limited results of the 1974 Social Action Programme, further efforts to promote social policy harmonization were advocated by Jacques Delors, during his two terms as President of the European Commission between 1985 and 1995, once again with the support of a broad social democratic coalition of governments. During this period which saw the ratification of the Maastricht Treaty and the creation of the Economic and Monetary Union, three major developments in terms of European social policy took place. Firstly, economic and social cohesion became a competence of the European Community with the ratification of the Single European Act in 1986. This principle aims at reducing socio-economic disparities between member states through the implementation of European policies and through the use of structural funds such as the European Social Fund, the European Regional Development Fund, and the Cohesion Fund. Secondly, the Community Charter of Fundamental Social Rights of Workers (or 'Social Charter') was adopted in Strasbourg in 1989. The Social Charter was later included within the Maastricht Treaty as the 'Protocol on Social Policy'. This protocol, from which the UK was exempted through a formal opt-out until 1997, set out social objectives for European member states, including 'the promotion of employment, improved living and working conditions, proper social protection, dialogue between management and labour, the development of human resources with a view to lasting high employment, and the combatting of exclusion' (Article 1). Thirdly, a second Social Action Programme including 47 proposals based on the Social Charter was drafted by the European Commission in 1989.

Taken together, these texts led to the adoption of further directives concerning health and safety at work, working conditions, and social dialogue at the European level. There is no consensus on whether the 'Delors years' could be considered as a cornerstone in shaping EU social policy: while some authors describe it as a period of underachievement and political failure (for example Streeck 1995; Keller 2003), others argue that it delivered the necessary institutional innovation which opened up further opportunities to harmonize social policy (Daly 2007). By the end of this period, Streeck (1996: 83) described European social policy as relying on neo-voluntarist practices, which represents 'a break with the practice of the European national welfare state to create "hard", legally enforceable status rights and obligations for individual citizens and organized collectives acting in, taking advantage of, and being disadvantaged by, market relations' (see also Dukes 2014: 144).

The third stage of social policy at the European level is the Lisbon strategy, which ran from 2000 to 2010 and was strongly influenced by the social investment paradigm (Hemerijck 2013). The extraordinary European Council held in Lisbon in March 2000 set up a decade-long strategic goal 'to become the most competitive and dynamic knowledge-based economy in the world, capable of sustainable economic growth with more and better jobs and greater social cohesion' (European Council 2000). Two of the key objectives of the Lisbon strategy were to tackle social exclusion, and to increase the employment rate across all member states. Two new policy instruments were introduced in order to implement this strategy: first, the use of the Open Method of Coordination (OMC) rather than the construction of new Europe-wide agencies for issues relating to 'social protection' and 'social inclusion'; and secondly, a strengthened role for the European Council in terms of coordinating employment, macroeconomic, and social policies (Ferrera et al. 2002). As the objective was to reform national welfare states rather than create an unwanted European welfare union, the OMC was initially perceived as a tool to negotiate common objectives and to propose common policies while comparing national policy performance (Scharpf, 2002; Larsen and Taylor-Gooby, 2004). However, the report on the Lisbon strategy from the High Level Group chaired by Wim Kok (2004) heavily criticized the OMC for failing to mobilize member state commitment to the implementation of the Lisbon strategy. In 2005, following the 'big bang enlargement' which saw the European Union joined by twelve new member states, the Lisbon strategy was relaunched by the European Commission (2005) and the European Council. On the one hand, this Lisbon II plan involved a shift in policy priorities: economic and job growth prevail over social cohesion (Copeland and Daly 2012). On the other hand, the European Commission started to emphasize social investment and flexicurity from 2006 onwards. Guideline 21 of the European Employment Strategy 2007 called for EU member states to 'promote flexibility combined with employment security', to prioritize policies aimed at achieving full employment, to improve productivity, and to strengthen social and territorial cohesion (European Commission 2013a). These goals were later re-emphasized in the Europe 2020 agenda (see sections 9.3.2 and 9.3.3).

Overall, the assessment of the Lisbon strategy is mixed, much like that of the 1974 Social Action programme and the Delors years. Hemerijck (2013: 76) acknowledges that it 'played an important role in raising the importance of

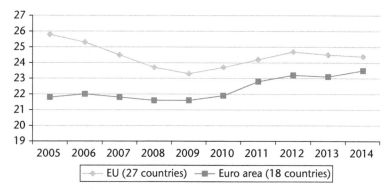

Figure 9.1. Percentage of the population at risk of poverty or social exclusion in the European Union.
Source: Eurostat

the EU's social dimension' and that employment rates have increased considerably across Europe, but also that many of its objectives have not been met, especially with regards to social inclusion. It has failed to address social inequalities, especially after the Great Recession and within Eurozone countries where the percentage of the population at risk of poverty or social exclusion increased from 21.8 per cent in 2005 to 23.2 per cent by 2012 (see Figure 9.1).

The development of welfare provisions at the European level, combined with difficulties in harmonizing policies and creating a truly common European social policy, demonstrates that European welfare provision must operate at several levels involving policies, regulations, and competencies if it is to succeed (Burgoon 2009).

The Great Recession, and the subsequent multi-faceted European crisis, required responses both at the national and the European levels. Hemerijck's assessment (2013: 76) argues that the multi-level dynamics between member states and the European institutions reached a point of no return:

> It does seem that the old division of labour between EU institutions and domestic political arenas, with the former concentrating on market liberalization and the latter seemingly retaining near monopoly over domestic social policy and labour market governance has reached a cul-de-sac in the aftermath of the global financial crisis.

The following section focuses on some of the most recent developments across Europe as well as the policy responses promoted by Brussels.

9.3 The Great Recession and the Role of the European Union

The Great Recession hit the members of the Economic and Monetary Union in late 2009.[1] The level of the gross public debt reached 90 per cent of GDP, and the GDP growth rate for 2009 was negative (−4.5 per cent for the whole EMU area; see Chapter 1). Southern European countries such as Cyprus, Greece, Spain, and Portugal were particularly hit. The impact of the crisis on the European Union is not limited to the period of recession. In her excellent book *Crisis*, Sylvia Walby summarizes the effects, cascading through societies across Europe: 'first, a crisis in finance; next, a crisis in the real economy of production and employment; then a fiscal crisis over government budget deficits; and a political crisis, which is on the edge of becoming a democratic crisis' (Walby 2015: 1). This chapter argues that, from the perspective of the EU, the crisis is composed of six key elements that all had (and will have) an impact on the future of the European welfare state: financial, economic, social, political, migration, and security. These six facets of the crisis are interconnected and cannot be isolated from one another when considering future scenarios for the European Union, especially with regards to the harmonization of social policy. This section focuses on these six elements and highlights the range of policy responses advocated by Brussels.

9.3.1 *Financial Aspects*

As illustrated throughout this volume, policy responses to the *financial* aspect of the crisis vary from one European country to another. In general, however, neo-liberal and austerity programmes prevailed. National governments which opposed this trend (in particular France, Chapter 4, and Greece, Chapter 8) either lost public support or were brought into line by the ECB and EU. Eurozone member states are no longer equipped to face financial shocks at the national level and the European Union established a series of common policy guidelines to cope with the crisis. The Stability and Growth Pact, which came into force in 1999 with the aim of ensuring budgetary balance and low public debt (limiting annual budget deficits to three per cent of GDP), has been revised in two further sets of reforms created on the initiative of the European Commission: the 'Six-Pack', which came into force in 2011 and aimed to correct future economic instabilities and fiscal imbalances, and the 'Two-Pack' agreement between member states, which entails further coordination and surveillance (Buti and Carnot 2012). Taken together, both reform packages have strengthened the role of the European institutions, particularly the ECB, by establishing more detailed monitoring of national financial plans.

'Bailout' deals to safeguard the banking systems of countries threatened with bankruptcy involved stringent austerity measures, including welfare cuts, tax increases, the privatization of state assets, reduced employment protection, and weaker collective bargaining. The most severe was the agreement between Greece and the 'troika' (the European Commission, the International Monetary Fund, and the European Central Bank) which led to the collapse of the government, public protests, and political instability (Chapter 8). Deals were also implemented in Spain (2012), Ireland (2010), Portugal (2011), and Cyprus (2013).

9.3.2 Economic Aspects

As a response to the *economic* aspect of the crisis, the European Union has offered three main strategies in order to stimulate growth. Firstly, the EU launched the European Economic Recovery Plan in December 2008, which included a fiscal stimulus of 1.5 per cent of the EU's GDP (around 200 billion euros), mostly funded by member states (1.2 per cent, with the remaining 0.3 per cent coming from the EU budget). This plan, building on the *acquis* of the Lisbon strategy, further recommended structural policies to member states in order to support employment and household income in the short term. Such policies, funded by national budgets, started to be implemented by EU member states in early 2009. The most frequently pursued of these measures was in line with social investment and flexicurity policy strategies, since it aimed at improving job placement and invested in retraining (implemented in 21 member states). Other neo-Keynesian measures in the European Economic Recovery Plan (European Commission 2009) included a reinforcement of activation policies (implemented in 19 member states); supporting household purchasing power (in 18); cutting labour costs (17); encouraging flexible working time (16); mitigating the impact of the financial crisis on individuals (13); reinforcing social protection (12); enhancing education and lifelong learning (7); and revising employment protection legislation in line with flexicurity (4). However, the impact of the European Economic Recovery Plan as a whole was mixed. Cameron (2012) suggests that by leaving most of the response to the Great Recession to member states, the EU has accentuated a regional divide between members, while Euzéby (2010) suggests that the European Union should look for other ways to reinforce solidarity among EU citizens, for instance, the creation of a European Solidarity Fund.

Secondly, the European Commission (2010) drafted the 2020 Strategy for Smart, Sustainable and Inclusive growth, which followed the Lisbon strategy and focused on three objectives: developing an economy based on knowledge and innovation; promoting a greener and more competitive economy; and fostering a high-employment economy delivering social and territorial cohesion (see Marlier and Natali, 2010).

Thirdly, the European institutions started negotiations with the United States on a massive free trade agreement: the Transatlantic Trade and Investment Partnership (TTIP). This move was heavily criticized by civic movements and left-wing parties, who perceived it as extending neo-liberalism. One of the main criticisms is that TTIP would transfer powers from governments to corporations, threaten existing European food and environmental regulations, and open up public services to commercial providers (Walby 2015; see also De Ville and Siles-Brügge 2015). However, TTIP negotiations have failed to reach any agreement and are likely to be indefinitely deferred, following the more isolationist US Trump presidency and the UK Brexit vote.

9.3.3 *Social Aspects*

National and European responses to the economic and financial facets of the crisis have also fuelled *social* unrest and increased social inequalities within European societies. As illustrated in Figure 9.1, the percentage of people at risk of poverty in the Eurozone increased from 21.6 per cent in 2008 to 23.5 per cent in 2014. Unemployment figures also increased from 7.6 per cent to 11.6 per cent between 2008 and 2014 for Eurozone countries, and from 7 per cent to 10.2 per cent for the same period within the European Union as a whole. Youth unemployment (between the ages of 15 and 24) is even more problematic across the European Union, as it increased from 17.5 per cent in 2008 to 21 per cent in 2014. This rate skyrocketed in Southern European countries, especially Croatia (45.8 per cent by the end of 2014), Italy (40.9 per cent), Greece (51.2 per cent), and Spain (51.8 per cent). Furthermore, civic protest movements across Europe have coordinated their actions to raise awareness about the austerity and neo-liberal policies advocated by the elites, leading to the emergence of transnational Eurosceptic movements (see FitzGibbon et al. 2016).

The European Union attempted to address social concerns by focusing on the shortcomings of the Lisbon strategy in the Europe 2020 strategy published in 2010. Three of the seven flagship policies deal with the issues of employment, social affairs, and inclusion. Firstly, 'youth on the move' aims at tackling youth unemployment by advocating social investment measures such as prioritizing training opportunities for young workers. Secondly, Europe 2020's Agenda for New Skills and Jobs focuses on improving flexicurity, job quality, and the conditions for job creation. Thirdly, the European platform against poverty and social exclusion includes the objective of lifting 'at least 20 million people out of the risk of poverty and exclusion' by 2020. This was the first quantitative social target in the history of the European integration, 'an unlikely and unexpected outcome, which, at first glance anyway, suggests a deepening Europeanization of social policy' (Copeland and Daly 2012: 274). In order to meet this target, the European Union strengthened its monitoring mechanisms through the creation of the European Semester.[2]

The social component of the Europe 2020 agenda was criticized for failing to address work/family life balance and gender equality issues, despite an emphasis on social investment and the introduction of directives such as the 2010 Parental Leave Directive. A report published by the European

Commission (2013a) suggests that in countries where flexicurity policies were in place, flexibility seems to have increased, and that 'the effects of the crisis (in terms of unemployment and GDP growth) have been less severe than in other countries characterized by high labour market rigidities,' though it 'is still unclear whether the increased flexibility will produce the economic advantages to reach enhanced security levels in the long run or if rising social inequality, worsened by flexibility, will rather damage the social fabric and will ultimately be detrimental to the entire economy'.

In addition to these measures, the European Commission launched in 2013 the Social Investment Package for Growth and Cohesion, urging EU member states to put more emphasis on social investment. In this package the European Commission (2013b) determined that social investment 'helps to "prepare" people to confront life's risks, rather than simply "repairing" the consequences' (see also Nolan 2013). Finally, in order to cope with rising concerns from citizens over TTIP, the European Union attempted to outline the social benefits of the proposed treaty, especially on the labour market.

9.3.4 Political Aspects

The European Union has also been facing a series of *political* crises since 2008, both domestic and international in origin. The public lost confidence in the well-established political parties, leading to the rise of Euroscepticism and the emergence of populist parties across the European political spectrum. Right-wing populist Eurosceptic parties have considerably increased their influence in the European Parliament, following the EP elections of 2009 and 2014. Most of these parties either advocate radical reforms for a more flexible and differentiated European Union (such as parties from the European Conservatives and Reformists pan-European group; Leruth 2017), or have rebelled against austerity and neo-liberal measures advocated by the European Commission (such as parties from the pan-European Confederal Group of the United European Left; Holmes 2016). Despite the rise in popularity of these Eurosceptic political parties, the European institutions are still dominated by a Christian democratic and conservative coalition.

The politics of the European crisis reached a tipping point on 24 June 2016, after the UK voted to leave the European Union with 51.9 per cent of the votes and a relatively high turnout of 72.2 per cent. This unexpected result was a huge victory for Eurosceptics across Europe, who called for further referendums to be held in other countries including France, the Netherlands, and Finland. This added to the instability surrounding the European integration project. Such a vote for a member state to leave the European Union is unprecedented in the history of European integration, and may trigger a process of differentiated *dis*integration. While the impact of Brexit on the future of the European Union remains hard to determine at the time of writing, the response of European leaders will be crucial. Brexit could be perceived as an opportunity for European actors to renew and strengthen the European Union, as the UK has always been an 'awkward partner', supporting national sovereignty over the process of deepening European integration. For European leaders, the status quo is no longer an option because a Brexit effectively changes the very nature of European integration.

9.3.5 *Migration*

In recent years, as the result of war and disruption in the Middle East and Afghanistan and poverty elsewhere, the European Union also had to face a *migratory* aspect of the crisis. Throughout 2015 millions of refugees crossed the Aegean Sea between Turkey and Greece to seek asylum in the European Union. Asylum applicants mushroomed in 2015: 1,321,600 as against 225,150 in 2008. Most applications were made in Germany (476,510), Hungary (177,135), and Sweden (162,450). Responses to this facet of the crisis varied greatly from one country to another: while Germany welcomed more than a million refugees between 2015 and 2016, other countries such as Austria, Slovakia, and Macedonia decided to close their borders on a temporary basis or even to build a fence (as in Hungary; see also Chapter 6 on Slovenia). Attempts were made at EU level to find a consensus between member states in order to establish quotas regarding the resettlement of these refugees. However, opposition from many countries (especially from Eastern Europe, led by the Eurosceptic Hungarian Prime Minister Viktor Orbán) led to yet another political failure for the European Union.

Linked to this aspect of the European crisis is the rise of welfare chauvinism across Europe. Some countries, particularly the UK, faced strong public scrutiny over their migration policy. As part of the 2015 renegotiation package between the UK and the European Union, a so-called 'emergency brake' was proposed. This policy proposal would prevent new EU migrants from gaining access to in-work benefits for a specific period of time in countries experiencing an inflow of workers of 'exceptional magnitude' over 'an extended period of time'. While this proposal was not implemented following Britain's 2016 vote to leave the European Union, such an emergency-brake mechanism could be used by other member states in the future, or be part of the new relationship between the UK and the EU.

9.3.6 *Security*

Finally, between 2014 and 2016 the European Union faced a series of *security* threats. Russia's military intervention in Ukraine and the subsequent annexation of Crimea, combined with increasing tensions between the European Union and Turkey, led to geopolitical tensions. In addition, several European cities such as Brussels, Paris, and Nice have been the target of terrorist attacks orchestrated by Daesh. Border controls were also temporarily reintroduced within the European Union in order to cope with these security threats. The attacks fuelled anti-immigration movements across Europe, most particularly in France (see Chapter 4) and Germany (see Chapter 2), and may be used to legitimize the introduction of immigration quotas at the national level in some countries.

So far as social policy goes, even though the financial response to the crisis at EU level strengthened austerity and neo-liberalism in some countries, the economic and social responses included a major emphasis on social investment. Political responses were generally anti-EU and were reinforced by concerns over migration but allowed for the possibility of national initiatives, and the security concerns also strengthened national decision-making. The shift towards neo-liberalism and financial discipline weakened the capacity of EU members to deliver traditional tax and spend policies, but there were some new developments in investment in human capital mainly relevant to the labour market. The impact of austerity in curbing social spending was in general most powerful in the weakest countries.

The multi-faceted European crisis analysed in section 9.3 is thus far from being over. Even though European economies have started to recover, the most recent political and migration shocks have further intensified pressures on the EU and raised questions over the future of European integration. The range of policy guidelines advocated by the European Union are summarized in Table 9.1. The following section highlights the future scenarios for the future of European integration and the European Social Model.

9.4 Future Scenarios and their Impact on the European Welfare State

Even though the potential for deepening the European Social Model has declined considerably over time, the extent of Europeanization of social policy should not be underestimated. As highlighted above, the European Union advocated social investment as one of the main policy responses to the crisis, mostly through targets and recommendations to member states. However, it also imposed austerity measures through the 'Six Pack' reforms and bailout programmes, especially for Greece. This contributed to fuelling Euroscepticism across the continent, and to the emergence of anti-establishment parties on both sides of the political spectrum.

Table 9.1. Aspects of the European crisis, the EU's response, and future scenarios

Aspect of the crisis	The challenge	The EU's response	Future scenarios
Financial	• Sovereign debt crisis	• Strengthening the role of the ECB • 'Six Pack' and 'Two Pack' reforms • Imposing austerity programmes in Greece • Bailout loans to Spain (2012), Ireland (2010), Portugal (2011), and Cyprus (2013)	• Further austerity • 'Grexit': Greece leaving the Economic and Monetary Union
Economic	• Recession • High unemployment rates, especially among young people	• European Economic Recovery Programme (2009) • 2020 Strategy for Smart, Sustainable and Inclusive Growth (Europe 2020) • TTIP negotiations	• New Europe-wide strategy to cope with socio-economic challenges
Social	• Increase in numbers at risk of poverty, especially within the Eurozone • Emergence of transnational Eurosceptic movements (e.g. Stop TTIP)	• Europe 2020 flagships: 'Youth on the move', 'agenda for new skills and jobs', and the 'European platform against poverty and social exclusion' • Promoting flexicurity and social investment policies at the EU and member states levels • 2013 social investment package • Attempts to increase transparency; publication of documents explaining the social advantages of TTIP	• Further social policy harmonization at the EU level: a deepened European Social Model • Positive EU-wide response with social investment and stronger citizen and worker rights • Wider gap between countries committed most strongly to austerity and others
Political	• Rise of Eurosceptic parties nationally and in the European Parliament • UK vote to leave the EU	• Pending projects to relaunch European integration after Brexit	• European disintegration ('soft' or 'hard') • More integrated Union • 'Ever more differentiated Union'
Migratory	• Refugee 'crisis': the increasing flows of refugees into Greece and Italy • Welfare chauvinist responses to migration flows at the national level	• Failed attempts to establish refugee 'quotas' • Temporary reintroduction of border controls between Austria and Croatia • Proposed emergency brake • Support for Turkey to hold back refugees	• End of Schengen • 'Fortress Europe' • 'Fortress member states' • Increased and generalized welfare chauvinism
Security	• Terrorist attacks linked to Daesh in Belgium, France, and Germany • Ukrainian crisis • Cooling-off in EU–Turkey relations	• Temporary reintroduction of border controls for security reasons • Mostly dealt with at the national level	• Use of security threats to legitimize welfare chauvinism • Strengthening the Common Security and Defence Policy

With Brexit, the European Union is now at a crossroads. There is no status quo option. Brexit is unprecedented. All political elites, analysts, and scholars agree that change is needed within the European Union in order to cope with the most recent elements of the European crisis. Increased levels of Euroscepticism, at both the public and elite levels, create further uncertainties over the future of integration. In addition to the structural elements of the crisis described in this chapter, the EU will also have to respond to the long-term economic, social, and demographic changes analysed in this book. These include an ageing population, an increased proportion of the European population at risk of poverty (despite Europe 2020's target of reducing the numbers), and higher unemployment (see Chapter 1). Table 9.1 also summarizes some of the future scenarios based on the six aspects of the crisis discussed earlier. The future of the European Social Model requires us to pay particular attention to future developments regarding European integration and the responses to the political aspect of the European crisis. Three overarching scenarios can be foreseen: the disintegration of the European Union; a more integrated Europe; and an 'ever more differentiated Union'. This section analyses these scenarios and their implications for the future of European social policy.

9.4.1 *Disintegration of the European Union*

This scenario marks the end of the European project as it has developed since the ratification of the Treaty of Rome in 1957. Disintegration of the EU would not necessarily mean the end of cooperation at the European level, or the end of social policy harmonization. Two 'versions' of European disintegration are possible. First, a 'soft' disintegration, meaning that the European Union is drastically reformed and its competence confined to a few policy areas. European integration would take a step back without disappearing. The principle of subsidiarity (established in Article 5 of the Treaty on European Union, whereby the EU can only intervene if it is able to act more effectively than member states at national, regional, or local levels) would be strengthened in order to emphasize national sovereignty over European cooperation. 'Soft' Eurosceptic parties such as Alternative for Germany (which calls for the breakup of the Economic and Monetary Union) advocate this option. Former French President Nicolas Sarkozy also supported this option after the Brexit vote and argued that EU policy should be limited to a maximum of ten priorities, including energy, agriculture, scientific research, and market policy. Soft disintegration is likely to limit EU social policy strictly to the areas directly relevant to competition in an open market in which it is already strongest, including employment protection, working hours, and health and safety at work.

The second option of 'hard' disintegration would return Europe to a collection of nation states. This is the scenario advocated by some of the 'hard' Eurosceptic parties on the populist right across Europe, such as the UK Independence Party, the Dutch Party for Freedom, and, to some extent, the French Front National. The implications for the European Social Model would be catastrophic. One of the immediate consequences of the disintegration of the European Union in either its 'soft' or 'hard' version would be a generalization of welfare chauvinism and the emergence of 'fortress member states', in which European migrants would not have any access to specific benefits and services.

While some analysts fear that the recent Brexit vote will trigger a 'domino effect', with further referendums called in different countries with a similar outcome, the 'hard' disintegration scenario is not favoured by the existing political leadership. However, a generalized 'soft' disintegration, implying the retraction of European authority and an empowerment of nation states, could happen if political divisions between member states continue to deepen.

9.4.2 *A More Integrated Union*

This second scenario implies a positive response by European leaders to the most recent developments in the crisis. Instead of leading to a contraction of European competences as advocated by some, member states would consolidate their relationship by strengthening the competences of the EU. Most particularly, proposals have been made recently to reinforce the powers of the Economic and Monetary Union by constructing mechanisms of economic governance and building a true fiscal union (Natali 2015). This could also lead to the emergence of a deepened European Social Model, where more social regulations are formulated and adopted at the EU level, breaking with the traditional division of labour in terms of policy-making between European institutions and member states.

This option has often been advocated by prominent scholars as a response to the Great Recession (for example Habermas, 2013; Offe, 2013). However, the political obstacles to this scenario are numerous, as it means that all remaining 27 member states would have to agree on a common direction. The recent conflict over refugee quotas demonstrates the EU's incapacity to reach an agreement over sensitive political issues. Yet common solutions to the existing challenges are possible. The scenario of a 'fortress Europe' is one of them, strengthening the European Union border through the creation of a proposed European Border and Coast Guard. While all European citizens would be treated equally, no matter in which member state they lived, 'outsiders' would have limited access to benefits and services. In other words, this would lead to the emergence of a welfare chauvinistic policy at the EU level.

Public opinion is another factor that makes this scenario unrealistic, at least in the short-term future. Increased levels of Euroscepticism means that the European Union is facing a crisis of legitimacy. Using data from the Eurobarometer 2000, Mau (2005) demonstrated that public support for a true common European social policy is linked to the emergence of a European identity, and that the democratization of the European Union does not necessarily lead to increased demand for supranational arrangements. His study suggested that citizens from the most advanced welfare states tend to oppose the Europeanization of social policies, unlike citizens from Southern European countries. Data from the most recent Eurobarometer survey on the future of Europe, conducted in 2014, tend to show similar results: overall, 50 per cent of respondents across Europe believe that more decision-making on health and social security issues should take place at the European level, but support drastically varies from one country to another (ranging from 78 per cent in Cyprus to 21 per cent in Finland). Accordingly, there is no consistent and overwhelming support for a common European social policy within all European member states.

9.4.3 *An Ever More Differentiated Union*

In contrast to the motto of 'ever closer Union' or the disintegration of Europe, this scenario offers a pragmatic 'third way' by suggesting an increased differentiation between member states. Over the past two decades there has been an increase in the use of differentiated integration to cope with the fundamental political and societal divergences between European countries (Leruth and Lord 2015). The literature often mentions a 'two-speed Europe', consisting of the Eurozone on the one hand and other EU member states on the other (see Piris 2012; Majone 2016). Member states and non-member states might cooperate in policy areas where there is a common interest, such as the European Free Trade Association or Schengen. Yet differentiation can go both ways. Some countries might be tempted to advocate differentiated *dis*-integration, by trying to renegotiate the terms of their membership to the European Union, in order to be granted new exemptions or opt-outs from existing European policies, as appeared to be the case in pre-Brexit referendum negotiations. On the other hand, the procedure of enhanced cooperation allows a minimum of nine member states to establish advanced integration within EU structures, without the involvement of other member states. This mechanism, introduced by the Treaty of Amsterdam, has so far only been used in the fields of divorce law, unitary patent regulation, and property regimes for international couples. However, a proposal on a European Union financial transaction tax involving ten member states has been approved and may soon come into force.

The two mechanisms described above can be used to solve any political deadlock not only within the European Union, but also within the Eurozone. As far as the future of the European Social Model is concerned, some member states might use the procedure of enhanced cooperation in order to carry on harmonizing their policies. However, it does not seem to be part of the agenda at the time of writing. Still, an increased differentiation could offer the possibility of 'saving' the European integration project. As public support for more health and social security policy coordination at the EU level is strongly supported in countries such as Cyprus (87 per cent), Italy (76 per cent), and Greece (73 per cent; see European Parliament 2016), a differentiated European Social Model in this area, with further political commitment between member states, could emerge in the near future.

9.5 Concluding Thoughts

The crisis that the European Union has been facing since 2008 is unprecedented. The financial and economic shocks of the Great Recession still affect national economies and the EU still faces high levels of social inequality, political instability, strong migration flows, and security threats. EU policy responses to the economic, social, and financial aspects of the European crisis have focused on social investment and also on enforcing drastic neoliberal and austerity measures for some of its member states (particularly Greece). The future of European integration is now at stake following the UK's vote to leave the Union, and the option of the political status quo is simply not viable.

As this chapter demonstrates, welfare state policies in some areas have gone through a process of Europeanization, from the first Social Action Programme of 1974 to the Europe 2020 strategy emphasizing social investment. Even though the scope and the evolution of the European Social Model over the past decades have been rather limited for some, policy developments at the EU level need to be taken into consideration in order to understand the future of the welfare state across Europe. While the scenarios of European disintegration or increased integration are not currently favoured by political realities or by public opinion, it does not mean that the European Social Model is unlikely to change in the near future. Section 9.4 made the case for the use of differentiated models of integration to bring an unsustainable status quo to an end and escape the crisis. Political willingness to overcome existing challenges is, however, needed in order to achieve this objective.

Notes

1. For a detailed account of the Economic and Monetary Union Sovereign Debt crisis, see Buti and Carnot (2012).
2. The European Semester is a mechanism that 'brings together within a single annual policy coordination cycle a wide range of EU governance instruments with different legal bases and sanctioning authority, from the Stability and Growth Pact, the Macroeconomic Imbalances Procedure, and the Fiscal Treaty to the Europe 2020 Strategy and the Integrated Economic and Employment Policy Guidelines' (Zeitlin and Vanhercke 2014: 11).

References

Allespach, M. and Machnig, J. (2013) 'A Change in Course towards a Social Europe', in A.-M. Grozelier, B. Hacker, W. Kowalsky, J. Machnig H. Meyer, and B. Unger (eds.) *Roadmap to a Social Europe*, London: Social Europe Journal, https://www.socialeurope.eu/wp-content/uploads/2013/10/eBook.pdf, accessed 12 June 2016.

Atkinson, T. (2002) 'Social Inclusion and the European Union', *Journal of Common Market Studies* 40(4): 625–43.

Blanke, T. and Hoffmann, J. (2008) 'Towards a European Social Model: Preconditions, Difficulties and Prospects of a European Social Policy', *International Journal of Public Policy* 3(1–2): 20–38.

Burgoon, B. (2009) 'Social Nation and Social Europe: Support for National and Supranational Welfare Compensation in Europe', *European Union Politics* 10(4): 427–55.

Buti, M. and Carnot, N. (2012) 'The EMU Debt Crisis: Early Lessons and Reforms', *Journal of Common Market Studies* 50(6): 899–911.

Cameron, D. R. (2012) 'European Fiscal Responses to the Great Recession', in N. Bermeo and J. Pontusson (eds.) *Coping with Crisis: Government Reactions to the Great Recession*, New York: Russell Sage, 91–129.

Copeland, P. and Daly, M. (2012) 'Varieties of Poverty Reduction: Inserting the Poverty and Social Exclusion Target into Europe 2020', *Journal of European Social Policy* 22(3): 273–87.

Crespy, A. and Menz, G. (2015) *Social Policy and the Euro Crisis*, Basingstoke: Palgrave Macmillan.

Daly, M. (2007) 'Whither EU Social Policy? An Account and Assessment of Developments in the Lisbon Social Inclusion Process', *Journal of Social Policy* 37(1): 1–19.

De Ville, F. and Siles-Brügge, G. (2015) *TTIP: The Truth about the Transatlantic Trade and Investment Partnership*, Cambridge: Polity Press.

Dukes, R. (2014) *The Labour Constitution: The Enduring Idea of Labour Law*, Oxford: Oxford University Press.

Esping-Andersen, G. (1999) *Social Foundations of Post-Industrial Economies*, Oxford: Oxford University Press.

European Commission (2005) *Communication to the Spring European Council—Working Together for Growth and Jobs—A New Start for the Lisbon Strategy—Communication from President Barroso in Agreement with Vice-President Verheugen*, Brussels: European Commission, http://eur-lex.europa.eu/legal-content/EN/TXT/HTML/?uri=CELEX:-52005DC0024&from=EN, accessed 12 June 2016.

European Commission (2009) 'Economic Crisis in Europe: Causes, Consequences and Responses', *European Economy* 7/2009, Luxembourg: European Communities, http://ec.europa.eu/economy_finance/publications/pages/publication15887_en.pdf, accessed 15 June 2016.

European Commission (2010) *Europe 2020: A strategy for smart, sustainable and inclusive growth*, Brussels: European Commission, http://eur-lex.europa.eu/LexUriServ/LexUriServ.do?uri=CELEX:52010DC2020:EN:HTML, accessed 15 June 2016.

European Commission (2013a) *Flexicurity in Europe*, Brussels: European Commission, http://ec.europa.eu/social/BlobServlet?docId=10227&langId=en, accessed 15 June 2016.

European Commission (2013b) *Towards Social Investment for Growth and Cohesion—including implementing the European Social Fund 2014–2020*, Brussels: European Commission, http://eur-lex.europa.eu/legal-content/EN/TXT/?uri=COM:2013:0083:FIN, accessed 15 June 2016.

European Council (1974) *Council Resolution of 21 January 1974 Concerning a Social Action Programme*, OJ C013, 12 Feb. 1974, 1–4, http://eur-lex.europa.eu/legal-content/EN/TXT/?uri=CELEX%3A31974Y0212(01), accessed 15 June 2016.

European Council (2000) *Presidency Conclusions: Lisbon European Council 23 and 24 March 2000*, http://www.consilium.europa.eu/en/workarea/downloadAsset.aspx?id=40802198157, accessed 15 June 2016.

European Parliament (2016) *Eurobarometer of the European Parliament 85.1*, Brussels: European Parliament, http://www.europarl.europa.eu/external/html/eurobarometer-062016/default_en.htm, accessed 13 Oct. 2016.

Euzéby, A. (2010) 'Economic Crisis and Social Protection in the European Union: Moving beyond Immediate Responses', *International Social Security Review* 63(2): 71–86.

Ferrera, M., Hemerijck, A., and Rhodes, M. (2001) 'The Future of the European "Social Model" in the Global Economy', *Journal of Comparative Analysis: Research and Practice* 3: 163–90.

Ferrera, M., Matsaganis, M., and Sacchi, S. (2002) 'Open Coordination against Poverty: The New EU "Social Inclusion Process"', *Journal of European Social Policy* 12(3): 227–39.

FitzGibbon, J., Leruth, B., and Startin, N. (2016) 'Introduction', in J. FitzGibbon, B. Leruth and N. Startin (eds.) *Euroscepticism as a Transnational and Pan-European Phenomenon: The Emergence of a New Sphere of Opposition*, Abingdon: Routledge, 1–13.

Habermas, J. (2013) *The Crisis of the European Union: A Response*, Cambridge: Polity Press.

Hemerijck, A. (2013) *Changing Welfare States*, Oxford: Oxford University Press.

Holmes, M. (2016) 'Contesting Integration: The Radical Left and Euroscepticism', in J. FitzGibbon, B. Leruth, and N. Startin (eds.) *Euroscepticism as a Transnational and Pan-European Phenomenon: The Emergence of a New Sphere of Opposition*, Abingdon: Routledge, 63–79.

Jepsen, M. and Serrano Pascual, A. (2005) 'The European Social Model: An Exercise in Deconstruction', *Journal of European Social Policy* 15(3): 231–45.

Keller, B. (2003) 'Social Dialogues—The State of the Art a Decade after Maastricht', *Industrial Relations Journal* 34(5): 411–29.

Kok, W. (2004) *Facing the Challenge: The Lisbon Strategy for Growth and Employment. Report from the High Level Group Chaired by Wim Kok*, Brussels: European Commission, https://ec.europa.eu/research/evaluations/pdf/archive/fp6-evidence-base/evaluation_studies_and_reports/evaluation_studies_and_reports_2004/the_lisbon_strategy_for_growth_and_employment__report_from_the_high_level_group.pdf, accessed 15 June 2016.

Laffan, B. (1983) 'Policy Implementation in the European Community: The European Social Fund as a Case Study', *Journal of Common Market Studies* 21(4): 389–408.

Larsen, T. P. and Taylor-Gooby, P. (2004) 'New Risks at the EU Level: A Spillover from Open Market Policies?', in Taylor-Gooby (ed.) *New Risks, New Welfare: The Transformation of the European Welfare State*, Oxford: Oxford University Press, 181–208.

Leibfried, S. (1993) 'Towards a European Welfare State? On Integrating Poverty Regimes into the European Community', in C. Jones (ed.) *New Perspectives on the Welfare State in Europe*, London: Routledge, 120–43.

Leibfried, S. and Pierson, P. (eds.) (1995) *European Social Policy: Between Fragmentation and Integration*, Washington DC: Brookings.

Leruth, B. (2016) 'Is "Eurorealism" the New "Euroscepticism"? Modern Conservatism, the European Conservatives and Reformists and European Integration', in J. FitzGibbon, B. Leruth, and N. Startin (eds.) *Euroscepticism as a Transnational and Pan-European Phenomenon: The Emergence of a New Sphere of Opposition*, Abingdon: Routledge, 46–62.

Leruth, B. and Lord, C. (2015) 'Differentiated Integration in the European Union: A Concept, a Process, a System or a Theory?' *Journal of European Public Policy* 22(6): 754–63.

Majone, G. (2016) 'Patterns of Post-National Europe: The Future of Integration after the Crisis of Monetary Union', in M. Fichera and S. Hänninen (eds.) *Polity and Crisis: Reflections on the European Odyssey*, Abingdon: Routledge, 261–86.

Marlier, E. and Natali, D. (eds.) (2010) *Europe 2020: Towards a More Social EU?* Brussels: Peter Lang.

Mau, S. (2005) 'Democratic Demand for a Social Europe? Preferences of the European Citizenry', *International Journal of Social Welfare* 14: 76–85.

Natali, D. (2015) 'Future Prospects: The EU Political Dilemma, Europe's Democratic Challenge and the Role of Trade Unions in Solving These', in D. Natali and B. Vanhercke (eds.) *Social Policy in the European Union: State of Play 2015*, Brussels: ETUI, 247–63.

Nolan, B. (2013) 'What Use Is "Social Investment"?', *Journal of European Social Policy* 23(5): 459–68.

Offe, C. (2013) 'Europe Entrapped: Does the EU Have the Political Capacity to Overcome its Current Crisis?', *European Law Journal* 19(5): 595–611.

Piris, J.-C. (2012) *The Future of Europe: Towards a Two-Speed EU?* Cambridge: Cambridge University Press.

Scharpf, F. W. (2002) 'The European Social Model: Coping with the Challenges of Diversity', *Journal of Common Market Studies* 40(4): 645–70.

Streeck, W. (1994) 'European Social Policy after Maastricht: The "Social Dialogue" and "Subsidiarity"', *Economic and Industrial Democracy* 15(2): 151–77.

Streeck, W. (1995) 'Neo-Voluntarism: A New European Social Policy Regime?' *European Law Journal* 1(1): 31–59.

Streeck, W. (1996) 'Neo-Voluntarism: A New European Social Policy Regime?', in G. Marks, F. W. Scharpf, P. C. Schmitter, and W. Streeck (eds.) *Governance in the European Union*, London: SAGE, 64–94.

Vaughan-Whitehead, D. (2003) *EU Enlargement versus Social Europe? The Uncertain Future of the European Social Model*, Cheltenham: Edward Elgar.

Walby, S. (2015) *Crisis*, Cambridge: Polity Press.

Zeitlin, J. and Vanhercke, B. (2014) 'Socializing the European Semester? Economic Governance and Social Policy Coordination in Europe 2020', *SIEPS Report* 2014:7, Stockholm: Swedish Institute for European Policy Studies, http://www.sieps.se/en/publications/reports/socializing-the-european-semester-economic-governance-and-social-policy, accessed 15 June 2016.

10

Liberalism, Social Investment, Protectionism, and Chauvinism

New Directions for the European Welfare State

Peter Taylor-Gooby, Benjamin Leruth, and Heejung Chung

10.1 Introduction

We argued in the first chapter that although European welfare states face multiple challenges that are in most cases broadly similar, they have responded differently to these pressures. This concluding chapter summarizes the country chapters, examining pressures on state welfare and the new directions which policy has taken. We then analyse differences and similarities in national policies and discuss the implications for theories of the welfare state. We also consider the likely future outcomes of the national policy directions and the new cleavages and tensions which will surround policy-making.

Our approach follows a most-similar and most-different design. By grouping the countries that are most similar in their institutional legacies by regime type, we can observe whether there is some sort of path-dependency in the directions taken. By comparing countries within regime clusters, we can see how national approaches differ, even when institutional structures are similar and countries face similar challenges. By comparing the countries across regimes (the most-different countries approach) we can see the influence of national institutional legacies and at the same time detect convergence across regimes in relation to the emergence of new political paradigms.

The typology of regimes is developed from the original work of Esping-Andersen (1990). We take France and Germany to typify the continental European regime, the Scandinavian countries for the social democratic regime, Italy, Spain, and Greece for the Southern European regime, the UK for the liberal regime, and Slovenia for the Central and Eastern European (CEE)/post-socialist regime.

We examine convergence and divergence within the framework introduced in our first chapter, which identifies seven types of policy development: austerity; individualization; state interventionism; social investment; predistribution; fightback; and welfare chauvinism. We distinguish between approaches that are directly implemented in policies, for example social investment, neo-liberalism/individualism, and emerging paradigms that shape political debate and demand a response from the mainstream, for example the welfare chauvinist and fightback movements on right and left which both reject the neo-liberal response to globalization and labour market change.

10.2 The Shared Challenges and Pressures on Policy

European welfare states have been influenced by a number of pressures during the past quarter century: population ageing which demands higher spending and creates tensions over the balance of retired people and people of working age; globalization with its insistence on greater national competitiveness; demands for more equal rights, particularly an end to gender discrimination in civil society and in work and education; and changes in work patterns with the decline of the manufacturing and growth of the service sectors, leading to more dualized and unequal labour markets. These changes tend to erode former solidarities and stimulate new directions in politics. More recently all these pressures have been compounded by two exogenous factors: first, the Great Recession, which increased the pressures on budgets and employment, and led to political realignments; and second, the rapid rise in immigration which exacerbated moves towards welfare chauvinism. The largest immigrant flows are into Europe, mostly from the Middle East and Northern African countries, moving initially into Southern and Eastern Europe and then into the richer countries. Movement within the EU, especially from Eastern to Western European countries, has also increased tensions. These pressures affect the different countries in different ways, as the following summary shows.

10.2.1 *Population Ageing, Competitiveness, Gender Rights, and Solidarity*

Welfare systems across Europe have responded to a rise in the proportion of older people with reforms that mitigate pension pressures, improve the cost-efficiency of health and social care systems, and increase the proportion of the population in paid work. Pension ages are rising, and entitlements are being drawn more strictly (Hinrichs and Jessoula 2012). Relevant labour market measures include increased activation, harsher conditionality for the unemployed of working age, but also increases in childcare provision and parental leave to mobilize more women into paid work.

A shift towards a more employment-based society may be seen to enhance competitiveness. Some countries have also invested in education and training (notably Germany and the Scandinavian countries). Better access to employment for women may contribute to economic goals but is also one aspect of equal gender rights.

Moves away from high levels of employment in manufacturing to a more service-oriented society have shifted power away from the labour movement and have led to a more fragmented 'new politics' of welfare in which a range of interests combine to press for change and political groupings are less stable and secure (Bonoli and Natali 2012).

10.2.2 *The Great Recession and its Aftermath*

The recession impacted most severely on the economies of Southern Europe and Ireland, resulting in substantial deficits, precipitate spending cuts, and bailouts by the European Central Bank, the European Union, and the stronger economies, notably Germany. Everywhere a neo-liberal logic of austerity and balanced budgets has dominated policy-making, and been accepted by electorates in most European countries, with the notable exceptions of France in 2012 (Chapter 4) and Greece in 2015 (Chapter 8), where left-wing governments with a popular mandate sought to reverse austerity. This reinforced a liberal turn at the national level, but also led to political dissent and fightback, demanding that the government takes a stronger interventionist and protective role. This is particularly strong among those who feel they have lost out as governments everywhere open their economies to international competition and their borders to immigration. Populist left-wing Eurosceptic political movements have emerged or become more prominent from 2009 onwards, initially in Southern European countries (for example Podemos in Spain and SYRIZA in Greece). Populist right-wing chauvinist responses among those who blame liberalism, immigration, and the austerity policies pursued by the EU and ECB for the failure of their own living standards to rise have also become important (FitzGibbon et al. 2016). These are discussed in 10.2.3.

Several mainstream left-wing parties have adopted fightback policies (for example Labour in the UK under Corbyn in 2015). In countries where left-wing governments were elected (most notably France and Greece) austerity or neo-liberal measures were implemented despite public resistance. More broadly, the Great Recession has strengthened a neo-Keynesian social investment movement, pressing for government to broaden opportunities and promote growth, alongside the dominant neo-liberalism. Social investment in education and training and in childcare has been promoted by the EU in its Europe 2020 programme and also in national policies.

10.2.3 *Immigration and Welfare Chauvinism*

Immigration has been a major issue for the majority of European countries. Two types of immigration can be distinguished across Europe, each with a different impact. First, non-EU migration, mostly consisting of asylum seekers and refugees from countries affected by military conflicts such as Afghanistan, Iraq, Libya, Somalia, and Syria. These immigrants travel across the Mediterranean and into Greece, Italy, and Spain, and overland from Turkey through Romania, Greece, and Eastern Europe. Secondly, EU migration, as some EU citizens, particularly from the CEE 2004 and 2007 accession states, used their mobility rights to seek better socio-economic opportunities. Concerns over security and welfare abuse have strengthened demand for anti-immigration policies across Europe, although some governments (especially in Germany) supported the most recent wave of migration. The net outcome has been to reinforce chauvinism, particularly among those who see themselves as losing out in competition with immigrant workers (Teney et al. 2014). West European anti-immigrant political parties, such as the UK Independence Party, the French Front National, the Danish People's Party, the Swedish Democrats, and Alternative for Germany, have exerted real political influence despite not sitting in government. The like-minded Fidesz in Hungary, the Finns Party in Finland, and the Progress Party in Norway have been coalition partners.

The EU is identified with free trade and open borders and as a result the new national protectionist parties of left and right view the EU and particularly the ECB with scepticism and in some cases hostility. One outcome is the UK decision to leave the EU after a bitterly fought referendum in 2016 (Hobolt 2016). While the impact of this decision is still unclear, the future of European integration is now at stake (Chapter 3). EU membership is high on the agenda of the Front National in the French 2017 national election and for challenger parties in Germany and the Netherlands. A shift in power has the potential to destabilize the union.

10.3 New Directions in Policy

The main response to the pressures outlined above has been a neo-liberal commitment to balanced budgets across most of Europe, leading to austerity and spending constraint. The EU's commitment to budgetary balance is contained in the Growth and Stability Pact, strengthened by the 'Six Pack' and 'Two Pack' (see Chapter 9). Interventionist state spending has not contracted but the rate of growth has declined sharply. The expanding needs of older people as populations age, backed up by the political clout of this group, result in a tendency to favour spending on older generations against younger ones.

Figure 10.1 shows that during the period from 2005 to the most recent available data for 2012, spending on old age, healthcare, and sick and disabled people's and survivors welfare increased from about 5,400 euros per inhabitant in EU27 to about 6,200, a rise of 15 per cent. Spending on working-age families (benefits for families and children and for low-waged or unemployed people, housing benefits, and social exclusion) increased at less than half that rate, from 1,100 to 1,180 euros or about seven per cent. For the Eurozone 18 the percentage increases were about 16 and about eight per cent. The latter comparison may be clearer since it is not affected by the wave of reform in accession states to bring national systems in line with EU standards.

The needs (and demands) of an increasing number of old people squeeze the needs of younger generations, and the benefit regime for those of working age designed to mobilize people into paid work has got tougher. There have also been policies to support women in paid work (most notably childcare;

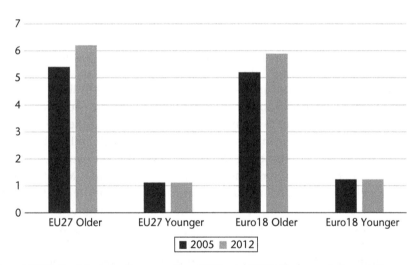

Figure 10.1. Social protection spending 2005 and 2012 (Esspros via Eurostat).

1. *Notes: social protection spending for older people is total spending per head on provision that goes entirely or mainly to older people: pensions, healthcare, sick, disabled, and survivors benefits; spending for younger people is the total spending per head on provision for working-age people: family and children, unemployment, housing, and social protection benefits.*

2. *The statistics are given in thousands of euros per inhabitant, aggregated using a purchasing power standard.*

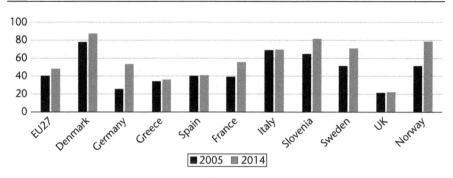

Figure 10.2. Percentage of children aged three to compulsory school age in formal childcare for 30 or more hours each week (Eurostat).

Note: Childcare includes pre-schooling within schools and daycare centres.

see Figure 10.2). The chart shows the proportion of children aged three to compulsory school age who are in childcare for more than 30 hours a week, enabling parents to work for something approaching a full week. In all the countries covered, childcare in this age group for less than 30 hours complements this to cover between 85 and 95 per cent of children, with the exception of the UK, where the proportion covered in total is only 70 per cent. The Scandinavian countries, Italy, and post-socialist Slovenia have high levels of care. Particularly striking is the shift in Germany, a country where gender divisions were once seen as deeply entrenched and where women's employment has grown rapidly.

The provision of childcare services can contribute to a social investment strategy: the state intervenes to promote national interests in a more globalized and competitive world, and at the same time enhances individual opportunities. In most countries social investment in education and training has been pursued. This stance is reinforced by industrial strategies to generate higher-quality jobs (European Commission 2010). Research and development spending is one aspect of these. Figure 10.3 shows that Scandinavian countries score highly here, as in other areas of social investment, and Mediterranean countries relatively low. Corporatist countries come in the middle with Germany close towards Danish levels and Sweden converging downwards. The UK spends rather less. Slovenia has high levels of spending with a recent downturn. The pattern broadly follows that of education spending.

At the individual level these changes promote a stronger and more moralistic work ethic, with greater personal responsibility for outcomes. They have also fed demands for state protectionism and fightback against the neo-liberal programme of open markets and limited state power, and welfare chauvinism. The upshot at the political level has been a decline of trust in established parties and in elites in most countries, particularly since the recession. Trust in

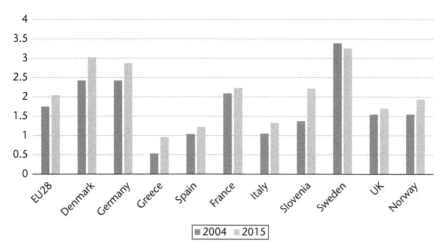

Figure 10.3. Research and Development spending, public and private (% of GDP, Eurostat).

government, as measured by assent to a Eurobarometer question about whether one tends to trust the national government, fell somewhat on average across all 28 EU countries from 32 to 27 per cent (European Commission 2016). The average masks sharper falls in Southern and CEE Europe and France. The decline was particularly marked in Spain and Greece (from about 50 to about 15 per cent between 2004 and 2015), followed by Slovenia, France, and Italy (from about 30 to 15 per cent). Elsewhere political trust remained more stable, highest in the Scandinavian countries (45 per cent), then corporatist Germany (40 per cent) and the UK (35 per cent).

Within this overall framework the different countries discussed in this volume have pursued policy directions that differed to some extent, despite their overall similarities. Table 10.1 summarizes the various national policy trajectories.

Germany, the dominant European power, was fortunate to have virtually completed major reforms in pensions and health social care to contain its future spending commitments before the recession (see Chapter 2). It had also introduced legislation which facilitated the creation of less-regulated jobs and imposed stricter constraints on the unemployed. There are also signs of social investment strategies in Germany, with childcare and family-friendly working arrangements developing rapidly. Elsewhere in the corporatist 'world' of welfare, changes are in train, with France, led by a socialist government, none-theless moving towards a more flexible labour market, although retaining strong childcare and redistributive policies. In both countries, inequality is on the rise with a stronger polarization between labour market insiders and outsiders. Public distrust towards political elites is growing, aggravated by high

Table 10.1. Policy developments after the Great Recession: European, national, and EU levels

	Overall trajectory	Retreat from interventionism	New forms of interventionism	Challenges	Cleavages
Germany	From corporatism/conservative to dualized and female worker; greater individual responsibility; levels of provision remain high; balanced budget already embedded	Pension reform and social security cuts pre-Great Recession and Hartz IV reforms	Emphasis on education and childcare; new minimum wage	Rising inequality; high immigration (refugees)	Insider/outsider; immigration
France	Moving away from corporatism towards social liberalism; level of provision remains high	Pension cuts; neo-liberal anti-union measures; more means-testing; pressures on the 35-hour working week	Strengthening established childcare and education; minimum wage	Deficit; immigration; inequality; declining trust	Rich/poor; Immigration
United Kingdom	From a moderate spending welfare state to acceptance of austerity; cutbacks especially for those of working age, and lower taxes	Sharp cuts for local government; social housing; working-age benefits; protection for pensions	Childcare/National Living Wage	Brexit; budget deficit; immigration; rising inequality; growing mistrust of political system	Immigration; rich/poor
Slovenia	Egalitarian society with developed provision—now shifting towards more austerity; some cutbacks	Spending constraint; more means-testing	Increasing the minimum wage	Deficit; rising inequality; growing mistrust of political system; transit immigration	Rich/poor
Spain	Social investment; initial neo-Keynesianism followed by austerity and cutbacks	Severe cuts; EU loan; austerity and flexibilization	Increasing minimum wage; emphasis on education and childcare	Rising inequality; growing mistrust of political system	Rich/poor; insider/outsider
Italy	Long-lasting austerity and cutbacks with some moves towards social investment since 2012	Severe cuts; no EU loan; austerity and flexibilization	More limited; move to decentralized collective bargaining	Rising inequality; growing mistrust of political system	Rich/poor; insider/outsider
Greece	Clientelist developing welfare state hit very hard by crisis and bailout conditions; levels of provision declining sharply	Crisis; bailout; major cutbacks—attempt at neo-Keynesianism defeated by ECB; flexibilization of labour market	Some attempts to improve access to training	Deficit and bailout; immigration; mistrust of political system and EU	Rich/poor; immigration; poverty

Denmark	Social democracy under pressure; provision remains strong but greater individual responsibility	Retrenchment of benefits and new taxes; means-testing and 'flexicurity'	Limited spending constraints for established strong social investment and services	Immigration; pressures on spending	Immigration
Sweden	Social democracy under pressure; strong provision, but with more individual responsibility; means-testing, labour flexibility, and privatization	Retrenchment of benefits and new taxes; some means-testing	Strong social investment and services—some restrictions and targeting now; also privatized service delivery	Immigration; pressures on spending and implementation of reforms	Immigration
Norway	Pressures on social democracy less marked due to oil wealth; limited shifts towards greater labour flexibility	Use of pension and oil funds	Strong social investment; services remain strong overall	Immigration; pressures on spending; longer-term decline in oil income	Divisions tend to be weaker than elsewhere; tensions over immigration
European Union	From more interventionist/harmonization via OMC to more labour market policies via aspiration	Major role of ECB in driving austerity in bailout states	Various attempts to promote and coordinate this—some success in accession states?	Brexit; failure to coordinate responses to immigration or commitments to social investment; uncertainties over political integration	Immigration tensions; ECB (austerity) vs EU (social investment); inner core vs outer core
Overall	Dominant theme of a shift towards austerity and neo-liberalism, more rapid in some countries than others	Major bailouts for national banks; defeat of attempts to shift in a neo-Keynesian direction in Greece and France	Expansion of childcare and family-friendly work; other aspects of social investment less widely progressed	Managing deficits; immigration; problems of political trust	Immigration; insider/outsider and rich/poor in many countries

rates of immigration and terrorist attacks blamed on radical Islamic groups. This benefits far-right populist groups. Other corporatist countries (such as Austria, Belgium, and the Netherlands) are also moving in this direction. The striking feature of corporatism is the success in shifting away from systems based mainly on the needs of the typical male worker with secure well-paid industrial employment, and the development of new policies for women in paid employment and for less secure lower-paid workers.

Across Europe the direction of change has been broadly speaking towards more neo-liberal approaches. The traditionally liberal-leaning United Kingdom has perhaps moved furthest among the richer countries, with high and growing levels of inequality, severe cuts in spending, and a deepening division between provision for those in paid work and outsiders. On top of these issues, the country is now facing major socio-economic challenges following the uncertainty caused by the Brexit vote. Immigration, as a highly politicized issue (the most important factor in the Brexit vote: Kaufmann 2016), is likely to be the main point of discussion in determining the future relationship between the UK and the EU. The Labour party elected Jeremy Corbyn as leader in 2015 and has moved away from social investment to promote fightback policies. The Sure Start nursery programme targeted particularly at disadvantaged families has been cut back, but state-subsidized day care in private nurseries is expanding. Neo-liberalism is the dominant direction across Europe, but neo-liberal policies are causing severe tensions between winners and losers in the most liberal European country.

Post-socialist countries have liberalized their economies and to some extent their substantial welfare systems, but in most cases retain relatively high levels of social investment. The more developed CEE countries (especially Poland, Hungary, and the Czech Republic) have been less affected by the recession than elsewhere in Europe. The less developed countries have high levels of poverty and unemployment. In Hungary, Poland, and Slovakia extreme right-wing and anti-immigrant movements have become prominent. In Slovenia an austerity package has been implemented and inequality is rising, but the minimum wage for those in work has also increased. Here concerns about migration are as much about the loss of better educated Slovenes to richer parts of Europe as about the burden of managing large numbers of Middle-Eastern immigrants passing through the country.

Mediterranean countries have all pursued policies to make the labour market more flexible. In the case of Spain (Chapter 7) there have also been a number of measures to enhance opportunities, promote childcare, and advance equality through tax reform. In all these countries and most notably in Greece, fightback movements have emerged alongside established parties. The left-wing SYRIZA government attempted to resist the demands of the troika (the EC, IMF, and ECB) to make stringent, across-the-board cuts in benefits and services but was forced to back down: failed fightback. Faced with exceptionally high levels of debt, it has had little leeway to invest.

The Scandinavian countries (Chapter 5) are all seeking to retain their traditional commitment to high levels of welfare spending and particularly of service provision, reflected in social investment, despite real pressures on their budgets. Yet there is also a move towards the privatization of service delivery to improve choice and efficiency, especially in Sweden. This is paralleled by a shift away from universalism towards greater use of means-testing, leading to stronger divisions between labour market insiders and outsiders. In recent years, the three Scandinavian countries have experienced high immigration both from asylum seekers and EU citizens (mostly coming from Eastern Europe). Welfare chauvinist parties gained support and there are demands for immigration quotas, especially in Sweden. The social rights of immigrants as equivalent to those of citizens have been maintained in Norway and in Sweden.

Finally the European Union has established effective regulation of cross-border welfare and issued directives on working time, discrimination in the workplace, and working conditions, the most directly work-related aspects of welfare, but achieved little in the greater harmonization of policies. This contrasts with its success in establishing market freedoms between members. The union always retained elements of the original commitment to Social Europe and these have emerged in the social investment aspects of the current Europe 2020 programme, intended to improve international competitiveness and also expand opportunities and promote social equality. At present the programme appears to have limited success in driving towards a common social investment approach. Similarly the EU has found great difficulty in brokering agreement on the sharing out of immigrants among countries (Robert et al. 2015). The European Central Bank on the other hand remains firmly committed to the goal of controlling inflation and ensuring that European countries restrict borrowing, and its policies do not give priority to employment rates or to the position of vulnerable groups (Stiglitz 2016). At the EU level and particularly for the Eurozone this leads to conflicts, in which it is the economic concerns that predominate, as in the case of Greece. Social policy remains firmly at the national level and appears likely to remain so.

The EU remains committed to open borders and an open economy. The UK decision to leave the EU brings to a head the dissatisfaction with and distrust of the EU in many member countries, particularly among the less-skilled groups and those who believe they have lost out from globalization and the competition from immigrants. Trust in the European Union as an institution has decreased over time, falling from 41 per cent in 2003 to 33 per cent in 2016 according to Eurobarometer surveys. Whether the UK withdrawal will have implications for further referenda or for an increasingly differentiated

Europe, where some members refuse to implement policies that open their markets and their borders more widely, is at present unclear (see Chapter 9).

A number of common themes emerge across European welfare policy: a commitment to spending restraint and to prioritizing deficit reduction; a tendency to favour spending on older people against younger age groups; restrictions on entitlement, benefit cuts, and expansion of childcare to enhance labour market flexibility; and concern about immigration and the emergence of anti-immigrant parties. This means that, in the categorization of Table 1.2 in Chapter 1, neo-liberalism, spending constraint, and individual responsibility are dominant themes; protectionism and welfare chauvinism have become increasingly influential and have shaped policies in countries such as the United Kingdom and Germany; and there is some neo-Keynesianism, and rather more social investment, concerned with enhancing competitiveness rather than with individual opportunities. Predistribution is limited, while fightback is a common theme at the political level (marked by the emergence of a range of new parties with populist anti-cuts platforms) but does not appear so far to have had a strong policy effect.

10.4 Differences and Similarities in National Policies

Following the most-similar/most-different design we first examine policies by regime type in order to see how far regime differences determine policy directions.

While obvious contrasts between corporatist, liberal, Mediterranean, post-socialist, and social democratic Europe remain, there are also real differences in the pathways taken by the various countries within these groups. Germany and France, the most developed corporatist nations, are diverging, with Germany taking much stronger and more effective measures to restrain spending commitments on pensions and healthcare and to promote flexibility and adapt to the expansion of the lower-wage sector of the economy. Among Mediterranean countries, Spain and Italy are moving in different directions with childcare and social investment emerging as important policy directions in the former and to a more limited extent in the latter. Sweden is moving fastest in modifying the Scandinavian social citizenship model with the development of a rather different regime for unemployed people, in response to a growing dualization of the economy and in the extent of its privatization of services. The regime approach still captures real policy differences across Europe, but regimes are less clear-cut than previously, with new directions (liberalism, individual responsibility, social investment in childcare) cross-cutting and progressing at different speeds in different countries. The influence of institutional inertia seems to be limited compared to that of political discourse in determining policy directions in European countries.

Our second stage of analysis compares countries within regime clusters. Following from the above we can see that real national differences emerge. Perhaps the dominant directions are three. First, some countries are adapting to change more effectively than others. This is particularly true in the response to population ageing and in the development of policies to mobilize workforces, improve skills, and ensure more flexible working, with the aim of enhancing productivity as economies are exposed to more intense international competition and as manufacturing industry ceases to dominate. Secondly, while neo-liberal budgetary management dominates economic policies, some countries have moved much further than others in implementing the logic of austerity; everywhere there has been real resistance, and in some cases fightback has had a real effect on policy. Thirdly, there are real differences in the level of social investment. Examples of countries pursuing different policies within these overall directions can be found within each of the regimes. The contrast between Germany and France (Chapters 2 and 4), or between Sweden and Denmark (Chapter 5) applies to the first, between Spain and Greece (Chapters 7 and 8) to the second, and between the UK (Chapter 3) and Ireland or between Spain and Italy (Chapter 7) or between Germany and Austria to the third.

These points take us to the third stage of the most-similar/most-different analysis: comparing country differences across regimes. The discussion above shows that strong differences in policy between different members of the same regime also reflect similarities across different regime types. Patterns here are complex, but it does seem that we can identify countries that respond to structural changes—population ageing, labour market dualization, and demands for greater gender equality (or to look at it another way, the mobilization of women workers)—by accepting greater income inequality and the insecurity that goes with increased individual responsibility and finding ways to manage it, such as Germany (Chapter 2), Sweden and Denmark (Chapter 5), and Spain (Chapter 7). In contrast, there are countries that resist change, at least initially, such as France (Chapter 4), Greece (Chapter 8), and Italy. Slovenia (Chapter 8) and the UK pursue rather different directions. In the former case the more universalist and egalitarian legacy of socialism still has an influence on institutions and policy despite the demands for a shift towards austerity. The latter has always pursued a distinctively liberal direction and continues to do so, but is noticeably weak in providing services to support the losers in more competitive and individualist markets.

Rather than a clustering of countries within regimes, what we find is a convergence in certain policy areas. In general, across different regimes we find signs of cuts and austerity measures designed to reduce generosity towards unemployed and disabled people, the latter group increasingly subject to tests to separate the deserving and the undeserving. We also see relatively greater protection for transfers to older people, as well as more *social investment*, most notably in family policies and childcare provision. Another more general trend, not observed in all countries but found across regimes, is the *privatization and individualization* of policies as a response to but not simply caused by the financial crisis and the austerity measures/budgetary constraints that followed. A third finding is a movement across a number of countries towards *predistributive* policies, as in the introduction or strengthening of a national minimum wage, especially where wage bargaining is decentralized and weak.

We also find examples of institutional 'stickiness' within the general paradigms of policy change. In the Scandinavian countries there is still a relatively high support for the universalist welfare state, despite the cuts in benefit levels in some areas of policies, and particularly strong support for *activation* and *social investment* strategies. The conservative welfare states, despite shifting towards a more liberalized system, still maintain their *interventionist* statist approach, directing most support to the insiders in the labour market and to that extent reinforcing status differences. The Southern European countries have also collectively moved towards retrenchment in their less developed welfare states with major cuts and *austerity* programmes to a great extent imposed from without, by IMF and ECB, alongside flexibilization of the labour market. This has led to the emergence of substantial institutionalized *fightback* movements, so far with limited success. The similarities here result more from their shared economic positions after the recession rather than their institutional legacies. Finally, the UK, as our only liberal case, has accelerated along the path towards a stronger *liberalization* and dismantling of its welfare state. The experience of the crisis has fuelled support for cutbacks and led to the acceptance of harsh spending constraints. More recently a *fightback* movement has emerged among the Labour party but this seems unlikely to achieve much. The Scottish National Party, pursuing independence for Scotland, has recently adopted fightback policies and opposes Brexit.

In terms of Streeck and Thelen's framework of convergence, structured diversity, and 'beyond continuity' in policy directions, discussed in Chapter 1, a case can be made for each approach. There is clear *convergence* in the adaptation of the main spending areas of the welfare state to the pressures experienced in different countries, the division emerging between the resilience of provision for the needs of older age groups and the greater vulnerability of spending on working age welfare, the development of dualization and flexibilization, the part played by social investment in childcare, and the overall move to neo-liberalism and individualism. Another direction that appears in many but not all of the national chapters is welfare chauvinism.

There is also an element of *structured diversity* in the extent to which different countries enable an expansion of employment through subsidized childcare and better education and training, in predistribution through labour market regulation and minimum wage legislation, and in the overall extent to which welfare state restructuring has taken place.

In addition, it is possible to make a case in this context for the *beyond continuity* argument: national policies change in a common direction but in ways that vary from country to country, mediated by national politics, and the variations may be more important than the commonalities. This fits with the 'new politics' approach, which stresses the fragmentation of the traditional class alliances that supported state welfare and the emergence of a broader range of possible coalitions and groupings leading to a more unstable politics of welfare.

10.5 Overview

From the 1980s onwards the European welfare state has faced severe and increasingly insistent challenges from globalization, population ageing, the transformation of work, and demands for greater gender equality. More recently, the Great Recession and very high levels of immigration have reinforced the pressures on governments. This book reviews and seeks to interpret developments in a range of countries. It points to a number of policy themes, most notably the shift to a neo-liberal approach with greater individual responsibility and with a more marked division between the welfare state for those designated dependent and for those of working age. It also shows that while neo-liberalism and austerity dominate, they are not the sole direction of change. There is also a less emphatic move to support economic growth through social investment in childcare and in education and training. Fightback and welfare chauvinist movements, resisting the liberal response to globalization and labour market transformation (free trade and open borders) and demanding a more protectionist stance by government, have emerged on left and right. These movements also benefit from the increasing public distrust in mainstream political parties and institutions.

Within this general envelope the differences between countries specified by regime theories persist, but the gaps between countries within regime types are growing wider and we find many examples of similar lines of development in countries from within different regimes.

From this perspective, all three of Streeck and Thelen's approaches seem to be true at the same time—a departure from traditional regime theory which implies that patterned difference will be the keynote of welfare state development. There are common directions in welfare, though not necessarily a simple convergence on neo-liberalism. Major national differences, large enough to enable us to talk in terms of a real but weakening structured diversity, persist. National politics appears to have become more powerful in shifting the positions of individual countries, beyond continuity.

10.6 Future Developments

New directions in national political discourse and in the factors that are likely to influence it seem important. The substantial continuity in welfare states enables us to suggest that social provision is likely to be supported by substantial majorities into the future as a major component in the programme of any national government. It is also clear that it is welfare for the traditional deserving groups (old, sick, disabled, survivors) that is most favoured. This implies that the gap between largely old age and largely working-age welfare states will widen. This gap is already increasing as a result of technical and organizational changes in work and tougher global competition. Poverty will continue to rise, especially among working-age populations.

Other current trends, such as the growth of welfare chauvinism, are powerful but seem less universal. The impact of chauvinism varies, with considerable effects in some countries (and among groups who believe themselves left behind in a changing world) and less elsewhere. Public distrust in political elites also varies from one country to another. Distrust offers a window of opportunity for new, populist political parties, but is not the only factor explaining their emergence. If these parties are sufficiently influential they may have major effects on the future development of political institutions (as illustrated by the impact of the UK Independence Party in forcing the UK Brexit vote: Chapter 3). Increasingly, protectionism is linked to demands to sustain spending against austerity, at least for nationals, which suggest an attempt to defend social provision.

All this leads to the overall conclusion that state welfare will continue to be a feature of European democracies, but will have a stronger emphasis on individual responsibility and higher levels of mobilization into paid work and will direct a greater proportion of constrained resources than at present to benefits and services for older people. At the same time, the new directions of policy to support women in paid work and in many cases to invest in the quality of national labour forces through education and training will continue.

One way of analysing the overall pattern of development is to start from the demands of globalization and the profound changes in the labour market. These pressures permit three kinds of response: governments can open up their economy and their borders and put their faith in market forces as the primary allocator of resources, or they can direct their efforts much more to investment that will enhance their ability to compete effectively in a globalized world, or they can resist globalization, imposing strict controls on immigration and regulating international trade. The first approach implies a liberal programme with the emphasis on individual responsibility in welfare, a high priority for a balanced budget and limited interventionism. The second approach, social investment, redirects government interventions to support welfare and national success in a more globalized and competitive world. It endorses a much stronger role for government in improving human capital and broadening opportunities, mostly through better access to education, training, and childcare. It also requires individuals to take more responsibility for outcomes. The third, protectionism, stands against globalization and associated changes and requires government to defend its citizens against the world market and the incursions of immigrants into the national welfare state. It goes hand in hand with a rejection of institutions such as the EU identified with globalization and open borders. From the perspective of the left protectionism emerges as fightback, from the right as chauvinism.

These different approaches emerge in all the countries reviewed, but with differing strengths. Among the leading corporatist countries, Germany has so far succeeded in combining a more open liberalism with social investment and a greater role of individual responsibility. France has become less stable in the years following the Great Recession and has been torn between liberalism and neo-Keynesian social investment while protectionism has been increasingly prominent among opposition parties. The liberal UK has pursued open policies, with strong social investment before the 2010 election, since then much weakened, and now with a lurch towards chauvinist anti-immigrant, anti-EU protectionism. This shift generates severe social tensions. Postsocialist Slovenia retains much of the high social investment of the previous era but pursues market freedoms and experiences greater inequalities. Mediterranean countries differ in their responses. Spain has pursued a mixture of neo-Keynesianism and austerity with some social investment. Fightback is most vigorous in Greece and evident elsewhere. Scandinavian countries maintain an open stance and have the highest levels of social investment. At the European level, the EU stands for open markets and open borders. It is also strongly committed to social investment. Protectionism at the EU level does not seem to be a current priority, though recent developments following Brexit and the election of Donald Trump as United States President could lead to a change in policy directions.

From this perspective it seems that real contradictions are emerging in responses to globalization, the transformation of work, and the opening up of markets, both within and between European countries. The patterns of welfare state development in the future will be driven by how far national governments follow the liberal programme of greater openness to international markets, how far they pursue social investments to enhance opportunities and share them more broadly (or simply shift responsibility for outcomes to individuals), and how far they retreat from openness to protectionism and limit their concerns to defined national populations within strong borders. While Scandinavian countries still combine openness with strong social provision and only a limited shift of responsibility to individuals, national trajectories appear to be growing stronger than regime type elsewhere. Germany is moving beyond corporatism in order to enhance social investment and promote greater individual responsibility, France has resisted this shift but there are now signs of movement, Mediterranean countries seek different accommodations with liberal openness from fightback to social investment, post-socialist Slovenia vigorously pursues greater openness, but seeks to protect lower-income groups, and the UK appears divided between an aggressive market-centred liberalism and a protectionist retreat from open borders.

European countries have entered a period of greater political instability. Future policy directions will be decided, as always, at the national level, but the forces in play vary greatly between countries. Neo-liberal austerity, often tinged with social investment (most notably in childcare), predominates, but fightback and protectionist policies are gaining support. The balance of tensions and pressures between these different approaches will determine the shape of European welfare states as they address the longer-term challenges of globalization and population ageing that now confront us after austerity.

References

Bonoli, G. and Natali, D. (2012) *The Politics of the New Welfare State*, Oxford: Oxford University Press.

Esping-Andersen, G. (1990) *The Three Worlds of Welfare Capitalism*, Princeton, NJ: Princeton University Press.

European Commission (2010) *A Strategy for Smart, Sustainable and Inclusive Growth: Europe 2020*, EC Brussels, http://eur-lex.europa.eu/LexUriServ/LexUriServ.do?uri=COM:2010:2020:FIN:EN:PDF, accessed 23 Nov. 2016.

European Commission (2016) *Eurobarometer Interactive*, http://ec.europa.eu/COMMFrontOffice/publicopinion/index.cfm/Chart/index, accessed 23 Nov. 2016.

FitzGibbon, J., Leruth, B., and Startin, N. (eds.) (2016) *Euroscepticism as a Transnational and Pan-European Phenomenon: The Emergence of a New Sphere of Opposition*, London: Routledge.

Hinrichs, K. and Jessoula, M. (eds.) (2012) *Labour Market Flexibility and Pension Reforms: Flexible Today, Secure Tomorrow?*, Basingstoke: Palgrave Macmillan.

Hobolt, S. (2016) 'The Brexit Vote: A Divided Nation, a Divided Continent', *Journal of European Public Policy* 23(9): 1259–77.

Kaufmann, E. (2016) 'Trump and Brexit: Why It's Again NOT the Economy, Stupid', LSE EUROPP blog, http://blogs.lse.ac.uk/politicsandpolicy/trump-and-brexit-why-its-again-not-the-economy-stupid/, accessed 13 Nov. 2016.

Robert, A. et al. (2015) *Many EU Countries Say 'No' to Immigration Quotas*, Euractiv.com, 8 June 2015, http://www.euractiv.com/section/justice-home-affairs/news/many-eu-countries-say-no-to-immigration-quotas/, accessed 23 Nov. 2016.

Stiglitz, J. (2016) *The Euro: and Its Threat to the Future of Europe*, London: Allen Lane.

Teney, C., Lacewell, O., and De Wilde, P. (2014) 'Winners and Losers of Globalization in Europe: Attitudes and Ideologies', *European Political Science Review* 6(4): 575–95.

Index

Note: Figures are mentioned by '*f*' and tables '*t*'

ageing population 3, 8*t*
  dependency ratios 93*f*
  France 70, 71, 72, 73, 82
  Germany 30
  Greece 160, 161, 162
  and immigration 9, 62
  Scandinavia 89, 92, 96, 103
  shared challenge of 202, 203, 213
  UK 50, 54, 58, 60, 62
ALLBUS *see* German General Social Survey
ALMP (Active Labour Market Policy) 91*f*,
    99, 102
Armingeon, K. 36, 122
asylum seekers 204
  Germany 41, 190
  Greece 164
  Hungary 190
  Italy 140
  Scandinavia 101, 103, 109, 190, 211
  Slovenia 129–30
  Spain 140
Aubry, Martine 76
Ayrault, Jean-Marc 78, 79

Balladur, Édouard 67
'beyond continuity' approach 14, 17, 18,
    214, 215
Bismarckian social insurance system 159, 162,
    174, 182
Blair, Tony 50, 79
Brexit 52
  and exit movements 3, 23, 193–4
  'hard' 49
  and immigration 57, 58, 62, 204, 210
  impact on UK economy 3, 13
  as opportunity for EU 190
  and protectionism 217
  and Scottish National Party 214
  and Transatlantic Trade and Investment
    Partnership 188
  and UK Independence Party 216
British Social Attitudes survey 58, 59
Brown, Gordon 53
budget deficit reduction 10, 19, 22, 186,
    203, 212

France 68, 69, 72, 73, 74, 77, 79, 80, 82, 84
Germany 27, 37
Greece 157, 159, 161, 163
Italy 137, 139, 140
Scandinavia 90
Spain 137, 139, 140
UK 49, 54, 59, 60, 63

Cahuzac, Jérôme 78
capitalism, varieties of 16–18, 19, 20, 156
Caritas 143
CEE (Central and Eastern European)
    countries 202, 204, 207, 210
childcare 204, 214, 215, 218
  and female employment 3, 9, 15, 19, 203,
    205, 206–7
  France 70, 85
  Germany 33, 34, 37, 38, 206
  Greece 174
  Italy 138, 143, 206, 212
  Scandinavia 91, 100, 109, 206
  Slovenia 119, 122, 123
  Spain 138, 143, 210, 212
  UK 51, 53, 55, 58, 60, 206
China 2
Chirac, Jacques 70, 74
Christian Democrats 14, 17, 28, 31, 33, 189
class alliances 7, 11, 14, 15, 17, 174, 205
collective provision 11, 15
common European social policy 22, 23, 181,
    182, 185, 195
competitiveness 16, 202, 203, 211, 212
  France 73, 79
  Germany 30, 31
  Greece 173, 174, 175
  Scandinavia 90
  UK 64
consensus democracies 6, 16, 17, 18, 19,
    28, 144
conservative-corporatist model 138
consumption, public 36, 90, 103, 104, 105,
    107, 174
convergence theories 14, 15, 213, 214
coordinated market economies 17, 136
Corbyn, Jeremy 60, 61, 210

corporatism 18, 19, 20, 210
  France 17, 80, 82, 85, 212
  Germany 17, 206, 207, 212, 217, 218
corruption 129, 146, 147–50, 160
Credit Suisse Research Institute 167
CSA Research (2015) survey, France 81, 82
currency stability 10
'curse of abundant natural resources' 90, 91
Cyprus 186, 187, 195, 196

decommodification 16, 98
Delors, Jacques 183
Denmark
  Active Labour Market Policy 99
  credit liberalization 95
  currency linked to euro 89
  Danish People's Party 102
  disability and sickness absence 96–7
  earnings 4f
  economy before Great Recession 90
  exit movement 3
  GDP 92
  and Great Recession 95, 209t
  immigration 5f, 101–2, 103, 104
  labour market 97–8
  Liberal government 95
  New Public Management 100–1
  pensions 95–6
  People's Party 14, 109
  privatization 107
  Progress Party 102
  social protection 105
  Social Democratic government 95
  state expenditure 92
  targeting 108
  taxation 99–100
  traditional welfare state 6f
  welfare chauvinism 12, 108
  welfare model 103, 104
  '2025 plan' 106, 107
developing and newly developed countries 2
D'Hondt electoral method 140
'differentiated integration' 180–96
  Great Recession and role of EU 185,
    186–91, 192t

earned income tax credit see EITC
earnings 4
ECB see European Central Bank
Economic and Monetary Union 52, 182, 183,
    185, 186, 193, 194
EITC (earned income tax credit) 99, 103
employment
  European Employment Strategy 184
  and childcare 3, 9, 15, 19, 203, 205,
    206–7
  European Social Model 181

female 30, 42, 94f, 119, 120, 160, 203,
    206, 210
industrial 2, 7
and Lisbon Treaty 184, 185, 187
precarious 12, 32, 33, 35, 40, 71, 82, 165
protection of 16, 28, 39, 40, 56, 75, 96, 123,
    142, 186
public 142
rates 55–64; years 94f
and recession 4
refugee employment 102
Social Action Programme 183
Social Charter 183
'standard employment' 29, 30, 40
Esping-Andersen, G. 8, 16, 17, 18, 39, 136, 159,
    181, 201
EU (European Union)
  anti-establishment parties 191
  approach in social and labour policies 144
  Area of Freedom, Security, and Justice 52
  bailout programmes 162, 163, 173, 186,
    187, 191
  Charter on Fundamental Rights 52, 183
  and cohesion 182
  core convergence criteria 161
  Directive on Parental Leave 123
  enlargement and immigration 52
  Europe 2020 programme 187, 188, 204
  European Economic Recovery Plan 187
  European Social Union 180–5
  exit movements 3
  financial conditionality of fiscal
    stimulus 187
  GDP 9, 186
  gender equality 188
  greater possible integration 194–5
  greater possible differentiation 195, 196
  gross public debt 185
  national policies 18–23, 212–15
  possible disintegration of 193–4
  public support for coordination 196
  reduction of inequalities 180
  'Six Pack' reforms 191
  Social Action Programmes 180, 182, 183
  Stability and Growth Pact 90, 186
  Structural Funds 161
  supranational governance 144
  theoretical approaches 14–17, 18
  trust in 211
Eurobarometer 195
European Central Bank (ECB) 10, 53,
    155, 211
European Commission 80, 155, 182, 183, 184,
    186, 187, 189
European Economic Community, creation
    of 182
European Fiscal Compact 76

European Social Fund 182
European Social Model 180, 181–2, 191, 193, 194, 196
Euroscepticism 4, 188, 189, 193–5, 203
Eurozone
  exports 10
  fixed exchange rate 35
  growth rate 53
  poverty 188
  productivity levels 57
  regulation 173, 211
  unemployment 188
exchange rates 3, 10, 35, 89

fightback programmes 12, 13t, 21, 203, 206, 210–15, 217–18
  France 78t, 79, 82, 83
  Germany 33
  Greece 158, 170, 176
  Italy 147, 151
  Slovenia 117, 127
  Spain 147, 151
  UK 48, 49
France 67–85
  ageing population 70, 71, 72, 73, 82
  anti-immigration movements 191
  associational liberalism 69
  'beyond continuity' approaches 17
  budget deficit reduction 68, 69, 72, 73, 74, 77, 79, 80, 82, 84
  centrism 70
  childcare 70, 85
  competitiveness 73, 79
  contrats de génération 76
  Contribution pour le Remboursement de la Dette Sociale (CRDS) 72
  Contribution Sociale Généralisée (CSG) 72
  corporatism 17, 80, 82, 85, 212
  deregulation 68, 79, 80
  dirigisme 68, 69
  earnings 4
  economic Gaullism 75
  economic growth rate 83
  Euroscepticism 3, 14, 83
  expansion of RMI 10
  family policies 70
  fertility rate 70
  fightback 78t, 79, 82, 83
  Fillon government 75
  Front de Gauch 83
  Front National (FN) 12, 14, 67, 68, 70, 79, 83
  GDP growth rate 75
  General Review of Public Policies 74
  government deficits and gross debt 1978–2009 74f
  and Great Recession 67, 75, 76, 77, 208t
  healthcare 72

immigration 5f, 67, 70, 77, 80, 81, 82
institutional trust 148
labour market 73, 74, 82
'law in favour of labour, employment and purchasing power' (loi en faveur du travail, de l'emploi et du pouvoir d'achat) 74
Les Républicains (formerly Union pour un Mouvement Populaire, UMP) 68, 70, 83
major reform projects 79, 80
neo-dirigiste response 75, 77
neo-Keynesian social measures 18, 73, 75
neo-liberalism 69, 73, 74
Nuit Debout 80, 83
pensions 69, 70, 72, 75, 77
poverty 84f
predistribution 78t
Prime pour l'Emploi 77
redistribution 70
same-sex marriage 78
sécurité sociale 68
semi-presidential system 67
social expenditure 6f, 67, 69f
Socialist Party 70, 76, 79
spending freeze 79
Stability and Growth Pact 80
tax evasion 77, 78
taxation 72, 74, 76, 77
tensions 81f
terrorist attacks 80
trade unions 75, 80, 149
trust in mainstream parties 82
unemployment 11, 67, 70, 71, 75, 76, 77, 83
welfare chauvinism 12, 67, 70, 77, 78t, 82, 83, 84
welfare state before Great Recession 68–73
French National Institute of Statistics and Economic Studies see INSEE

gender
  and equality 3, 91, 188, 203
  German social security system 30, 38
  and modernization 139
  public attitude 43n8
  and unemployment 42n4
German Democratic Republic (GDR), collapse of 30, 31
German General Social Survey (ALLBUS) 43n8
Germany 27–42
  ageing population 30
  'Agenda 2010' 42
  Alternative for Germany (AfD) 12, 41, 193
  asylum seekers 41, 190
  Alternative for Germany 193
  authoritarianism and paternalism 29
  'automatic stabilizers' 35
  benefit cuts 33, 34

Germany (*cont.*)
  'beyond continuity' approaches 17
  budget deficit reduction 27, 37
  childcare 33, 34, 37, 38, 206
  Christian Democrats (CDU/CSU) 28, 30,
    31, 33
  Christian–Liberal government 37
  'compensatory' measures 38
  competitiveness 30, 31
  'consensus democracy' 19, 28, 33
  'conservative' welfare state 28, 29
  'coordinated market economy' 28
  corporatism 17, 206, 207, 212, 217, 218
  'debt brake' (*Schuldenbremse*) 37
  demand management 35
  earnings 4
  earnings-related social insurance system 38
  and Eurozone 35, 53
  exchange rate 10
  exports 27, 28, 35
  'express laws' 35
  female unemployment 42n4
  fightback 33
  Free Democratic Party (FDP) 31
  gender 30, 38
  GDP 35
  'Grand Coalition' government 33
  and Great Recession 28, 29, 35–7, 38, 208*t*
  Green Party 31
  Hartz reforms 10, 32, 34, 39
  healthcare 32, 34
  immigration 5*f*, 12, 27, 37, 38, 40, 41,
    190, 191
  individual responsibility 34
  inequality 39
  'Labour and Social Justice: The Electoral
    Alternative' (*Arbeit und Soziale Gerechtigkeit*:
    Die Wahlalternative) 32
  labour market 31, 32, 36, 39, 40
  Die Linke 14, 32
  long-term care insurance 31
  neo-corporatism 28
  neo-Keynesianism 37
  'one euro-jobs' 32
  Party of Democratic Socialism (*Partei des
    demokratischen Sozialismus*) 32
  pensions 31, 32, 33, 34
  privatization 37
  redistribution 38, 39, 42
  refugee crisis 41
  right-wing populist movements 41
  short-term work scheme
    (*Kurzarbeitergeld*) 35, 36
  'Skilled Workers Initiative'
    ('*Fachkräftekonzept*') 37
  Social Democrats (SPD) 28, 31, 33, 38
  social investment policies 37
  'social market economy' (*Soziale
    Marktwirtschaft*) 31
  'solidarity surcharge' (*Solidaritätszuschlag*) 31
  status fear 29, 30, 40, 41
  taxation 36, 39
  traditional welfare state 6*f*
  trade unions 149
  trust 148, 207
  unemployment 30, 31, 35
  unification 30
  welfare chauvinism 41
  'wrecking premium' cars 36
Ghent system 103
Giscard d'Estaing, Valéry 70
globalization
  and convergence 15
  and economic change 2, 30
  and loss of trust 211
  responses to 89, 103, 182, 202, 215, 216, 217
Great Recession 2007–8 1, 3, 13*t*, 14
  economic response 187, 188
  exchange rates 3
  Eurozone 186
  financial response 186, 187
  impact on young people 6
  impact Southern European countries 186
  interventionist responses 11
  migration and response 190
  neo-liberal and austerity programmes 186
  political response 9–14, 189, 190
  and role of EU 185, 186–91
  shared challenge of 202–3, 204
  social response 188–9
  and Southern Europe 1
  welfare chauvinism 12, 13
Greece 21, 22, 155–76
  ageing population 160, 161, 162
  anti-austerity feeling 171, 172
  asylum seekers 164
  authoritarian rule 158
  'bailout' deals 162, 163, 173, 186, 187, 191
  Bismarckian system 162
  budget deficit reduction 157, 159, 161, 163
  childcare 174
  clientelistic–particularistic exchanges 159
  competitiveness 173, 174, 175
  debt crisis 162–72
  democracy restored 158, 159
  earnings 4
  economic crisis 53, 161
  emigration 167, 171
  EOPYY (National Health Service
    Organization) 163, 164
  exports 155
  female employment 160
  fightback 158, 170, 176
  'flexi-carity' 174

GDP 155, 163
Golden Dawn 12, 170, 172
and Great Recession 208t
health and social care 159, 160, 163, 164–5
hybrid social protection system 159
immigration 5f, 12, 171, 173
Independent Greeks (ANEL) 157, 165,
170, 175
internal devaluation 156
labour market 165–6
Memorandum of Understanding 172
minimum income guarantee 165
ND–PASOK coalition 166
New Democracy (ND) 157, 161
'non-tradeable' sector 156
Panhellenic Federation of Social Policy
Organizations 163
Panhellenic Socialist Party (PASOK) 157, 159
pensions 162–3
political fluidity 174
populism 159
poverty 166–70
privatization 161
public expenditure 6f, 156, 159, 160
redistribution 158, 159, 162, 175
refugee crisis 172
'rescue-deal' 155
social insurance deficit 163
'social investment' approach 174
statist–clientelistic practices 156, 157, 160
'structural adjustment' 158
SYRIZA 14, 157, 158, 165, 166, 170, 171,
172, 174, 175
taxation 160, 163, 164
third sector 172
trade unions 156
unemployment 155, 164, 165, 166
welfare chauvinism 171
Green parties 12
G7 countries, productivity levels 57

Hollande, François 68, 76–81
Horizon 2020 programme 15
Hungary 190

IMF (International Monetary Fund) 155,
176n1
immigration 5f
and political alliances 7
quotas 101, 190, 191, 194, 211
refugees 27, 37, 38, 41, 62, 84, 89, 101–2,
129, 137, 140, 171–2, 174, 190, 194, 204
and welfare chauvinism 9, 12–13, 202, 204
income inequality 3, 4, 5f
Indignados 12
individualism 7, 11, 15, 49–50, 54, 57–64
industrial employment, decline in 7

INSEE (French National Institute of Statistics
and Economic Studies) 82
International Monetary Fund see IMF
International Social Survey Programme 43n8
interventionism 11, 13t, 77, 137, 181, 203,
205, 214
Ireland 9, 11, 187
Italy 136–51
asylum seekers 140
'beyond continuity' approaches 17
budget deficit reduction 137, 139, 140
childcare 138, 143, 206, 212
'consensus democracy' and 'two-coalitions'
system 144, 145
conservative-corporatist model 138–40
Constitutional Reform 144
consultation in policy making 145
corruption 147
decentralization 138, 144
elderly care policies 139
European Monetary Union 137
exit movements 3
fightback 147, 151
fiscal consolidation and market
liberalization 141
Five Star Movement 146
Fratelli di Italia 149
gender 139
generational divide 151
and Great Recession 208t
homelessness 143
immigration 5f, 140, 147
institutional crisis 147–9
labour market 136, 141, 142
Lega Nord 149
Pact on Productivity 142
pensions 138, 141
political stability 146
poverty 142, 143
private and public debt 139, 140
proportional electoral system 140
public sector employment 142
re-centralization of government 145, 146
redistribution 137
reforms of health and education 138
refugee crisis 137
regulation of industrial relations 142
second recession 21
social policy reform 138, 140, 141–3
trade unions 145, 149
traditional welfare state 6f
transformation of policy-making 145
unemployment 141
welfare chauvinism 147

Janša, Janez 119
Jospin, Lionel 73

Juppé, Alain 67, 72
'Juppé Plan' 72

knowledge-based economy 15
Kohl, Helmut 31
Kok, Wim 184

labour market
  regulation of 7
  dualization of 2, 3, 15, 29, 32, 40, 82, 123,
    159, 165, 213
  undermining of 7
Lagrade, Christine 18
Le Pen, Jean-Marie 70
Le Pen, Marine 70, 77
Lisbon Treaty 15, 182, 184, 187, 188
London 49

Maastricht Treaty 52, 161, 183
Macron, Emmanuel 79
majoritarian democracies 16, 17, 18
manufacturing, decline in 2
May, Theresa 52
Médiapart (journal) 77
Mediterranean states 12, 21, 22, 136, 206, 210,
  217–18 *see also* Greece; Italy; Spain
Merkel, Angela 33
Mitterand, François 69
Mollet, Guy 182

neo-corporatism 28, 115
neo-Keynesianism 203
neo-liberalism
  France 69, 70, 73, 74
  Germany 40
  Greece 157, 158, 170, 172, 173, 175
  impact of 2, 11–12, 14, 15, 17–23, 181,
    186–9, 191, 202–4, 206, 210, 212–15, 218
  Italy 147, 151
  Scandinavia 96, 104, 106, 107
  Slovenia 115, 117, 119, 122–4, 130
  Spain 147, 151
  Transatlantic Trade and Investment
    Partnership 187
  UK 48, 49, 50–3, 60, 61, 63
  New Public Management (NPM) 89,
    100–1, 103
'new risk' welfare state 5, 6–7
Nordic countries, strong left politics 17
'Nordic dual income tax' 99
Nordic welfare model 103, 104
Norway
  disability and sickness absence 96–7
  economy 90
  exchange rate 89
  gender equality 91
  and Great Recession 95, 209t

immigration 5f, 101–2, 103
labour market reforms 97
New Public Management (NPM) 89,
  100–1, 103
oil revenue 90, 92, 106, 109
pensions 95–6
Progress Party 14, 102, 108
state expenditure 91, 92
taxation 99–100
traditional welfare state 6f
welfare chauvinism 108
nuclear family 30

'old risk' welfare state 6
Open Method of Coordination (OMC) 184
Orbán, Viktor 190

parental rights 7, 9
path dependency 16
Pirate parties 12
Poland 4, 14
Portugal 9, 187
post-socialist countries 1, 210 *see also* Slovenia
predistribution 12, 13t, 214
  France 78t
  Slovenia 123
  UK 49, 50, 53, 58, 59, 60
privatization 11, 22, 211, 214
  Germany 37
  Greece 161
  Scandinavia 100–7, 211
  Slovenia 117, 129, 130
  UK 48, 49, 50, 53, 55
protectionism 69, 115, 130, 204, 206, 215,
  216–18

redistribution 7, 8, 12, 19
  France 70
  Germany 38, 39, 42
  Greece 158, 159, 162, 175
  Italy 137
  Scandinavia 92, 93, 99
  Spain 137
'Report on the Development of the Social
  Situation in the Community in 1973'
  (EC) 182
research and development spending 207f
Russia 190

Sarkozy, Nicolas 68, 70, 73, 74–8, 193
Scandinavian countries (Denmark, Norway,
  and Sweden) 20, 21, 89–109
  ageing population 89, 92, 97, 103
  Active Labour Market Policy 102
  asylum seekers 101, 103, 108, 109,
    190, 211
  budget deficit reduction 90

childcare 91, 100, 109, 206
competitiveness 90
disability and sickness absence 96–7
GDP 90, 93f
and Great Recession 90–4
'guest worker' 101
healthcare 100, 101
high fertility rates 92
immigration 101–2, 103, 109
inequality 96
labour market 97–8, 99
New Public Management 89, 100–1, 106
pensions 95–6
privatization 100–7, 211
prolonged austerity 105, 106
public consumption 103, 104
public service reform 105
redistribution 92, 93, 99
social democratic welfare model 89
social expenditure 91f, 92t
social investment strategy 91
targeting 108
taxation 99–100, 103
unemployment 92, 93, 97–8, 99, 103
welfare chauvinism 108, 109
Schengen Agreement 52
Schröder, Gerhard 31, 79
Scotland, nationalism 48
self-employment 56, 156
service sector employment 2
Single European Act 183
single-parent households 3
Slovenia 21, 115–31
    ageing population 127, 128
    asylum seekers 129–30
    austerity measures 121–4
    childcare 119, 122, 123
    Democratic Party of Slovenian
        Pensioners 128
    Employment Relationship Act 123
    Exercise of Rights to Public Funds Act 121
    female employment 119, 120
    fightback 117, 127
    Financial Social Assistance Act 121
    flexicurity 123
    GDP 116f, 126
    and Great Recession 121–5, 129, 208t
    immigration 5f, 120, 121, 129
    income inequality 127, 128f
    individual responsibility 129
    labour market 119, 121, 123
    Labour Market Regulation Act 123
    Liberal Democratic Party (Liberalna
        demokracija Slovenije) 117
    membership of EU 115
    membership of Eurozone 116
    Minimum Wage Act 123, 124
    Modern Centre Party (Stranka modernega
        centra) 122, 127
    national debt 116f
    neo-corporatism 115
    neo- Keynesianism 121
    neo-liberalism 122, 124
    Parental Protection and Family Benefits
        Act 122, 123
    Pension and Disability Insurance Act 124
    pensions 121, 124
    political discontent 126, 127
    poverty 125
    predistribution 123
    privatization 117, 129, 130
    recession 116
    Slovenian Democratic Party (Slovenska
        demokratska stranka) 119, 122, 127
    social investment strategy 126
    social protection 120f
    state socialist welfare system 115
    taxation 118, 126
    trade unions 118
    traditional welfare state 6f
    unemployment 119, 123
    Unified Left party (Združena levica) 127
    welfare chauvinism 121
    welfare state reforms 117, 118–20, 121
social cleavage, definition 1, 2
social protection spending 205f
solidarity, shared challenge of 203
'South European welfare regime' 159
Soviet Union, break-up of 2
Spain 21, 136–51
    asylum seekers 140
    austerity measures 11, 137
    'bailout' deal 187
    budget deficit reduction 137, 139, 140
    Catalonia 151n2
    childcare 138, 143, 210, 212
    conservative-corporatist model 138–40
    corruption 147
    decentralization 138, 144
    Dependence Law 139
    devolution 144
    economic growth rate 139
    elderly care policies 139
    European Monetary Union 137
    fightback 147, 151
    fiscal consolidation and market
        liberalization 141
    food banks 143
    GDP 140
    generational divide 151
    and Great Recession 9, 208t
    homelessness 143
    immigration 5f, 140
    Indignados movement 80

Spain (*cont.*)
  institutional crisis 147–9
  labour market 136, 141, 142
  'majoritarian democracy' 144, 145
  modernization 139
  pensions 139, 141
  Podemos 12, 14, 146, 149
  policy-making process 143, 144–6, 147
  poverty 10, 142, 143
  proportional electoral system 140
  public sector deficits 139
  public sector employment 142
  real estate bubble 140
  re-centralization 145, 146
  redistribution 137
  reforms in health and education 138
  social assistance 138
  social policy reform 140, 141–3
  trade unions 142, 145, 148, 149
  traditional welfare state 6*f*
  unemployment 141
status maintenance 38
stratification 16
Strauss-Khan, Dominique 76
Streeck, W. and Thelen, K. 14, 17
structured diversity theories 14, 16, 17
Sweden
  Active Labour Market Policy 99
  asylum seekers 190
  cuts 109
  disability and sickness absence 96–7
  earnings 4
  economy 90
  exchange rate 89
  GDP 92
  gender equality 91
  and Great Recession 95, 209*t*
  immigration 5*f*, 101–2, 103
  labour market 97–8
  New Public Management 100–1
  pensions 95–6
  privatization 107
  Sweden Democrats 102, 108
  state expenditure 91, 92
  taxation 99–100
  traditional welfare state 6*f*
  welfare chauvinism 108
  welfare model 103, 104
Syria, civil war 101, 173

terrorism 57, 62, 68, 80, 81, 191, 210
Thatcher, Margaret 50
'Third Way' 50, 79
trade unions 7, 15–16
  France 80, 149
  Germany 149

Greece 156
Italy 145, 149
Slovenia 118
Spain 145, 148
UK 50, 60
Transatlantic Trade and Investment
  Partnership (TTIP) 187, 188
Transparency International index of
  corruption 147
Treaty of Amsterdam 195
Treaty of Rome 180
Tressell Trust 56
Trump, Donald 188
trust 49, 56, 82, 147, 148, 207, 211
TTIP *see* Transatlantic Trade and Investment
  Partnership

UK (United Kingdom) 48–64, 210
  ageing population 50, 54, 58, 60, 62
  bedroom tax 55
  benefit cuts 55, 56, 59
  Brexit 3, 48, 49, 52, 57, 61
  budget deficit reduction 49, 54, 59,
    60, 63
  childcare 51, 53, 55, 58, 60, 206
  competitiveness 64
  Conservative–Liberal Democrat coalition 51,
    53, 54
  Conservative Party 50, 57, 60
  dualized economy 61
  earnings 4
  employment protection 56
  fall real wages 19, 20
  feedback loops 61, 62
  fightback 48, 49
  food banks 56
  general election 2010 53
  general election 2015 57
  government funding of failing banks 53
  and Great Recession 53–8, 208*t*
  homelessness 56
  immigration 5*f*, 12, 49, 52, 54, 57, 59, 61,
    62, 190
  individualism 54, 58
  Jobseeker's Allowance 11
  Labour Party 60, 61
  low-income households 51*f*
  majoritarian democracy 19, 48
  Nationality Act 1981 52
  National Living Wage 60
  National Minimum Wage 51, 53, 57
  neo-liberalism 18, 50–3, 60, 61
  'New Deal' 50
  New Labour 31, 48, 50, 51, 53
  NHS 51, 55, 57, 59
  oil revenue 91

pay rates 56
pensions 51, 54, 56
poverty 10, 51, 52
predistribution 49, 50, 53, 58, 59, 60
privatization 48, 49, 50, 53, 55
productivity levels 57
self-employment 56
social investment 51, 60
structural reform 54, 55
Sure Start 53, 55, 210
taxation 54, 60
'Third Way' programme 50
trade unions 50, 57, 60
traditional welfare state 6*f*
trust 49, 147
unemployment 56, 59
UK Independence Party (UKIP) 12, 14
Universal Credit 56
welfare chauvinism 12, 49, 52, 54,
    59, 61
Working Tax Credit 55
zero-hour contracts 56
unemployment
East Germany 31
Eurozone 188
France 11, 67, 70, 71, 75, 76, 77, 83
Germany 30, 31, 35
Greece 155, 164, 165, 166
Italy 141
Scandinavian countries 92, 93, 97–8,
    99, 103
Slovenia 119, 123

Spain 141
UK 56, 59
US (United States) 4*f*, 187, 188

Valls, Manuel 79

welfare chauvinism 9, 12–13, 194, 216
Denmark 12, 108
France 12, 67, 70, 77, 78*t*, 82, 83, 84
Germany 41
Greece 171
Italy 147
Scandinavia 108, 109
Slovenia 121
UK 12, 49, 52, 54, 59, 61
welfare state 201–18
economic changes 2–3
national policies 212–15
new policy directions 204, 205–12
'new risk' 5, 6–7
'old risk' 6
political changes 5, 6–9
prior to Great recession 68–73
shared challenges 202–4
social changes 3–5
structural change 8*t*
traditional 6*t*
World Bank Control of Corruption
    indicator 147
World Trade Organization (WTO) 2

Yugoslavia 115